LEVEL II PRACTICE EXAMS – VOLUME 2

D1245034

SCHWESER 2013 CFA LEVEL II PRACTICE EXAMS VOLUME 2

©2012 Kaplan, Inc. All rights reserved.

Published in 2012 by Kaplan Schweser.

Printed in the United States of America.

ISBN: 978-1-4277-4228-5 / 1-4277-4228-6

PPN: 3200-2867

HOW TO USE THE LEVEL II PRACTICE EXAMS

Thank you for purchasing the Schweser Practice Exams. We hope that you find this volume effective and user-friendly. The following suggestions are designed to help you get the most out of these practice exams and prepare for the actual Level II Exam.

Save the practice exams for last. Save the practice exams for the last month before the exam. A good strategy would be to take one exam in each of the three weeks leading up to the test. Do your best to mimic actual exam conditions for at least one of the practice exams (e.g., time yourself, have someone turn the heat down and up so that you go from freezing to boiling, hire a construction crew to do some blasting outside your window).

Remember, no matter how challenging we make our practice exams, the actual exam will be different. Also, mainly due to the stress of the day, your perception will be that the actual exam was much more difficult than any practice exam or old exam you have ever seen.

Then, use your results as a diagnostic tool to help you identify areas in which you are weak. One good way to accomplish this is to use your online access to Performance Tracker. This is a tool that will provide you with exam diagnostics to target your study and review effort, and allow you to compare your scores on practice exams to those of other candidates.

Make sure you understand the mistake(s) you made on every question you got wrong. Make a flashcard that illustrates that particular concept, carry it around with you, and read it until you are confident you have mastered the concept. Also, make sure that for every correct answer, you got it right for the right reason. This "feedback" loop (practice exam, diagnosis of results, identification of concepts yet to be mastered, more study of those concepts, and then another practice exam) is a very effective study strategy in the last month before exam day.

Be ready for a new format. The format of the Level II exam is different from Level I. The exam consists of item sets, which are vignettes or short cases followed by six multiple-choice questions (CFA Institute calls these "mini-cases"). There will be 20 item sets (120 questions) on the exam: 10 item sets (60 questions) in the morning and 10 more item sets (60 more questions) in the afternoon. Each question is worth 3 points (and 3 minutes), and there are 360 total points available. Each selected-response question will have three possible choices (A, B, or C).

Any topic can be tested in the morning and/or the afternoon, so you might have an economics item set in the morning and another one in the afternoon. Don't spend a lot of time guessing which topics might appear in which session.

Topic Area	Guideline Topic Area Weight	
Ethical and Professional Standards (total)		10%
Quantitative Methods	5 to 10%	
Economics	5 to 10%	
Financial Reporting and Analysis	15 to 25%	
Corporate Finance	5 to 15%	
Investment Tools (total)		30 to 60%
Equity Investments	20 to 30%	
Fixed Income	5 to 15%	
Derivatives	5 to 15%	
Alternative Investments	5 to 15%	
Asset Classes (total)		35 to 75%
Portfolio Management (total)		5 to 15%
TOTAL		100%

Expect the unexpected. Be prepared for difficult questions on unexpected topics. Only one thing is certain about the exam: you will be surprised by some of the questions.

Guess if you must. It should take you approximately 18 minutes to read the vignette and answer the six questions that make up each item set. Don't fall behind: the successful candidates know when to cut their losses by guessing and moving on. Try to eliminate one of the incorrect answers, and then pick one of the remaining choices. If you eliminate one choice you know is wrong, you have a 50/50 chance of selecting the correct answer. There is no penalty for guessing.

Be ready for more than just number-crunching. Your reading comprehension ability is a very important component of success on the Level II exam. The vignettes will be long and full of information. Your job is to focus on finding the important pieces of information and answer the questions correctly.

There are two approaches to these item sets. You can read the vignette first and then answer the questions, or you can read the questions first. We recommend the second approach because it saves time and helps you to focus on the details you need. When taking the practice exams, experiment with both techniques and do what works best for you!

My thanks to the Schweser team. I would like to thank all of my colleagues at Schweser for their incredible work ethic and commitment to quality. Kaplan Schweser would not be the company it is, nor could it provide the quality products you see, without the help of these content and editing professionals.

You may expect me to end this introduction with a "good luck on the exam." To me that suggests you need to be lucky to pass Level II. With your hard work and our assistance, luck will have nothing to do with it. Instead, I'll simply say, "See you next year at Level III."

Best Regards,

Bijesh Tolia

Dr. Bijesh Tolia, CFA, CA
VP of CFA Education and Level II Manager

Kaplan Schweser

Exam 1
Morning Session

Question	Topic	Minutes (Points)
1 to 6	Ethical and Professional Standards	18
7 to 12	Economics	18
13 to 18	Asset Valuation – Equity	18
19 to 24	Financial Reporting and Analysis	18
25 to 30	Corporate Finance	18
31 to 42	Asset Valuation – Equity	36
43 to 48	Asset Valuation – Fixed Income	18
49 to 54	Asset Valuation – Derivatives	18
55 to 60	Asset Valuation – Alternative Investments	18

1.	(A)	(B)	(C)		41.	(A)	(B)	(C)
2.	(A)	(B)	(C)		42.	(A)	(B)	(C)
3.	(A)	(B)	(C)		43.	(A)	(B)	(C)
4.	(A)	(B)	(C)		44.	(A)	(B)	(C)
5.	(A)	(B)	(C)		45.	(A)	(B)	(C)
6.	(A)	(B)	(C)		46.	(A)	(B)	(C)
7.	(A)	(B)	(C)		47.	(A)	(B)	(C)
8.	(A)	(B)	(C)		48.	(A)	(B)	(C)
9.	(A)	(B)	(C)		49.	(A)	(B)	(C)
10.	(A)	(B)	(C)		50.	(A)	(B)	(C)
11.	(A)	(B)	(C)		51.	(A)	(B)	(C)
12.	(A)	(B)	(C)		52.	(A)	(B)	(C)
13.	(A)	(B)	(C)		53.	(A)	(B)	(C)
14.	(A)	(B)	(C)		54.	(A)	(B)	(C)
15.	(A)	(B)	(C)		55.	(A)	(B)	(C)
16.	(A)	(B)	(C)		56.	(A)	(B)	(C)
17.	(A)	(B)	(C)		57.	(A)	(B)	(C)
18.	(A)	(B)	(C)		58.	(A)	(B)	(C)
19.	(A)	(B)	(C)		59.	(A)	(B)	(C)
20.	(A)	(B)	(C)		60.	(A)	(B)	(C)
21.	(A)	(B)	(C)					
22.	(A)	(B)	(C)					
23.	(A)	(B)	(C)					
24.	(A)	(B)	(C)					
25.	(A)	(B)	(C)					
26.	(A)	(B)	(C)					
27.	(A)	(B)	(C)					
28.	(A)	(B)	(C)					
29.	(A)	(B)	(C)					
30.	(A)	(B)	(C)					
31.	(A)	(B)	(C)					
32.	(A)	(B)	(C)					
33.	(A)	(B)	(C)					
34.	(A)	(B)	(C)					
35.	(A)	(B)	(C)					
36.	(A)	(B)	(C)					
37.	(A)	(B)	(C)					
38.	(A)	(B)	(C)					
39.	(A)	(B)	(C)					
40.	(A)	(B)	(C)					

Exam 1
Morning Session

Use the following information to answer Questions 1 through 6.

Martha Gillis, CFA, trades currencies for Trent, LLC. Trent is one of the largest investment firms in the world, and its foreign currency department trades more currency on a daily basis than any other firm. Gillis specializes in currencies of emerging nations.

Gillis received an invitation from the new finance minister of Binaria, one of the emerging nations included in Gillis's portfolio. The minister has proposed a number of fiscal reforms that he hopes will help support Binaria's weakening currency. He is asking currency specialists from several of the largest foreign exchange banks to visit Binaria for a conference on the planned reforms. Because of its remote location, Binaria will pay all travel expenses of the attendees, as well as lodging in government-owned facilities in the capital city. As a further inducement, attendees will also receive small bags of uncut emeralds (because emeralds are a principal export of Binaria), with an estimated market value of $500.

Gillis has approximately 25 clients that she deals with regularly, most of whom are large financial institutions interested in trading currencies. One of the services Gillis provides to these clients is a weekly summary of important trends in the emerging market currencies she follows. Gillis talks to local government officials and reads research reports prepared by local analysts, which are paid for by Trent. These inputs, along with Gillis's interpretation, form the basis of most of Gillis's weekly reports.

Gillis decided to attend the conference in Binaria. In anticipation of a favorable reception for the proposed reforms, Gillis purchased a long Binaria currency position in her personal account before leaving on the trip. After hearing the finance minister's proposals in person, however, she decides that the reforms are poorly timed and likely to cause the currency to depreciate. She issues a negative recommendation upon her return. Before issuing the recommendation, she liquidates the long position in her personal account but does not take a short position.

Gillis's supervisor, Steve Howlett, CFA, has been reviewing Gillis's personal trading. Howlett has not seen any details of the Binaria currency trade but has found two other instances in the past year where he believes Gillis has violated Trent's written policies regarding trading in personal accounts.

One of the currency trading strategies employed by Trent is based on interest rate parity. Trent monitors spot exchange rates, forward rates, and short-term government interest rates. On the rare occasions when the forward rates do not accurately reflect the interest differential between two countries, Trent places trades to take advantage of the riskless arbitrage opportunity. Because Trent is such a large player in the exchange markets, its transactions costs are very low, and Trent is often able to take advantage of mispricings that are too small for others to capitalize on. In describing these trading opportunities to clients, Trent suggests that "clients willing to participate in this type of arbitrage strategy are guaranteed riskless profits until the market pricing returns to equilibrium."

1. According to CFA Institute Standards of Professional Conduct, Gillis may accept the invitation to attend the conference in Binaria without violating the Standards:
    A. so long as she pays her own travel expenses and refuses the gift of emeralds.
    B. so long as she refuses the gift of emeralds.
    C. because she would be the guest of a sovereign government.

2. Given that Gillis's weekly reports to clients are market summaries rather than specific investment recommendations, what are her record-keeping obligations according to CFA Institute Standards of Professional Conduct? Gillis must:
    A. maintain records of her conversations with local government officials and also keep copies of the research reports prepared by local analysts.
    B. only maintain records of her conversations with local government officials and her own summaries of the research reports prepared by local analysts.
    C. keep her own summaries of the research reports prepared by local analysts, but she has no obligation to maintain records of her conversations with local government officials.

3. Regarding Gillis's transactions in the Binaria currency, she has violated the Standards by:
    A. taking the long position and by selling the position before issuing a recommendation to clients.
    B. selling the position before issuing the recommendation to clients, although taking the long position was not a violation.
    C. not disclosing the trades in her report because the trades are acceptable as long as they are disclosed.

4. According to CFA Institute Standards of Professional Conduct, Howlett's best course of action with regard to the suspected violations by Gillis would be to:
    A. meet with Gillis in person, explain the nature of the violations, and seek assurances that such violations will not recur.
    B. warn Gillis to cease the trading activities and report the violation to Howlett's supervisor immediately.
    C. place limits on Gillis's personal trading and increase monitoring of Gillis's personal trades.

5. Based on the information given, and according to CFA Institute Standards, which of the following statements *best* describes Trent's compliance procedures relating to personal trading in foreign currencies? The compliance procedures:
    A. appear adequate because Howlett was able to identify potential violations.
    B. appear adequate, but Howlett's monitoring of Gillis's trades indicates poor supervisory responsibility.
    C. should include both duplicate confirmations of transactions and preclearance procedures for personal trades.

6. Trent's arbitrage trading based on interest rate parity is successful mostly due to Trent's large size, which provides it with an advantage relative to smaller, competing currency trading firms. Has Trent violated CFA Institute Standards of Professional Conduct with respect to its trading strategy or its guarantee of results?
    A. The trading strategy and guarantee of results are both violations of CFA Institute Standards.
    B. The trading strategy is legitimate and does not violate CFA Institute Standards, but the guarantee of investment return is a violation of Standards.
    C. Both the trading strategy and guarantee statement comply with CFA Institute Standards.

Use the following information to answer Questions 7 through 12.

Jill Surratt, CFA, and Elizabeth Castillo, CFA, are analysts for Summit Consulting. Summit provides investment advice to hedge funds and actively managed investment funds throughout the United States and Canada.

Surratt and Castillo have a client, Tom Carr, who is interested in increasing his returns from foreign currency positions. Carr currently has a position in Japanese yen (¥) that he wishes to convert to Taiwanese dollars (NT$) because he thinks the Taiwanese currency will appreciate in the near term. He does not have a quote for yen in terms of the NT$ but has received quotes for both currencies in terms of the U.S. dollar. The quotes are $0.008852-56 for the yen and $0.02874-6 for the Taiwanese dollar. He would like to purchase NT$10 million.

In discussing these quotes, Surratt notes that the bid-ask spread is affected by many factors. She states that if an economic crisis were expected in the Asian markets, then the bid-ask spread of the currency quotes should widen. Castillo states that if a dealer wished to unload an excess inventory of yen, the typical response would be to lower her ask for the yen, thereby narrowing the bid-ask spread.

In regards to changes in currency values, Surratt states that if the U.S. Federal Reserve restricts the growth of the money supply and foreign interest rates remain constant, then the interest rate differential (U.S. interest rate minus counter currency interest rate) should increase, thereby increasing the value of the dollar.

In addition to using monetary policy, Summit Consulting uses anticipated changes in fiscal policy to forecast exchange rates and the balance of payments for a country. Castillo states that, under the Mundell-Fleming model, if the U.S. Congress were to unexpectedly reduce the budget deficit, then this should have a positive impact on the value of the dollar in the short run because foreigners would have more confidence in the U.S. economy.

Another of Summit's clients is Jack Ponder. Ponder would like to investigate the possibility of using covered interest arbitrage to earn risk-free profits over the next three months, assuming initial capital of $1 million. He asks Surratt to gather information on the inflation rates, interest rates, spot rates, and forward rates for the U.S. dollar and the Swiss franc (SF). Surratt has also used technical analysis to obtain a projection of the future spot rate for the two countries' currencies. The information is presented below:

Spot rate	$0.85 / SF
Three-month forward rate (as of today) for SF	$0.80 / SF
Expected spot rate three months from now	$0.60 / SF
Three-month inflation rate in Switzerland (annualized)	2.0%
Three-month inflation rate in the U.S. (annualized)	6.0%
Three-month interest rate for SF (annualized)	12.0%
Three-month interest rate for U.S. dollars (annualized)	18.0%

∪ 🔟 🔟

Ponder currently has several FX carry trades open and is concerned about unhedged foreign currency risk in his portfolio. Castillo recommends that whenever the funding currency appears to be significantly overvalued according to PPP, the position should be reversed. Surratt states that currency options can be useful indicators of potential risk in carry trades and recommends that if the implied volatility of the investment currency exceeds a predetermined threshold, a carry trade should be reversed.

7. The yen cost to Carr of buying NT$10 million is *closest* to:
    A. ¥3,077,000.
    B. ¥32,453,000.
    C. ¥32,490,000.

8. Are Surratt and Castillo correct with regard to their statements concerning the currency bid-ask spreads?
    A. Only Surratt is correct.
    B. Only Castillo is correct.
    C. Both Surratt and Castillo are correct.

9. Evaluate Surratt's statements concerning the impact of monetary policy on currency values. Surratt is:
    A. correct.
    B. incorrect, because restrictive monetary policy in the United States would lead to a lower value of the dollar.
    C. incorrect, because restrictive U.S. monetary policy would be matched by foreign governments.

10. Regarding Castillo's statements concerning the effect of fiscal policy on currency values, Castillo is:
    A. correct.
    B. incorrect, because under the Mundell-Fleming model, restrictive U.S. fiscal policies lead to a short-run devaluation of the dollar.
    C. incorrect, because under the Mundell-Fleming model, restrictive U.S. fiscal policies lead to an increase in the value of the dollar in the long run.

11. Which of the following *best* describes the covered interest arbitrage that Ponder should execute? Borrow in:
    A. Swiss francs to make an arbitrage profit of $80,313.
    B. U.S. dollars to make an arbitrage profit of $80,313.
    C. Swiss francs to make an arbitrage profit of $75,588.

12. Regarding Castillo's and Surratt's statements about risk management of Ponder's FX carry trades:
    A. only Castillo is correct.
    B. only Surratt is correct.
    C. both Castillo and Surratt are correct.

Use the following information to answer Questions 13 through 18.

Marsha McDonnell and Frank Lutge are analysts for the private equity firm Thorngate Ventures. Their primary responsibility is to value the equity of private firms in developed global economies. Thorngate's clients consist of wealthy individuals and institutional investors. The firm invests in and subsequently actively manages its portfolio of private firms.

During a discussion with junior analysts at the firm, McDonnell compares the characteristics of private firms with those of public firms and makes the following statements:

Statement 1:   Private firms typically have higher risk premiums and required returns than public firms because private firms are usually smaller and thus thought to be riskier. Furthermore, the lack of access to liquid public equity markets can limit a private firm's growth.

Statement 2:   Because of their higher risk, private firms may not be able to attract as many qualified applicants for top positions as public firms. Due to the higher risk, the managers they do attract tend to have a shorter-term view of the firm and their tenure at the firm, compared to public firm managers. As a result, the private firm may neglect profitable long-term projects.

Due to its considerable success, Thorngate has recently attracted a substantial inflow of capital from investors. To deploy that capital, McDonnell and Lutge are considering the purchase of Albion Biotechnology. Albion is using advances in biotechnology for application in the pharmaceutical field. The analysts are primarily interested in Albion because the firm's research team is developing a drug that Thorngate's current pharmaceutical firm is also working on. McDonnell estimates that combining research teams would result in advances that no pharmaceutical competitor could match for at least two years. The firm is currently owned by its founders, who are familiar to Lutge through previous social contacts. Lutge hopes to avoid a competitive bidding process for the firm, because its founders have not publicly advertised the firm's sale.

McDonnell is also examining the prospects of Balanced Metals, a metal fabrication firm. Thorngate currently does not have any manufacturing firms in its portfolio, and Balanced would provide needed exposure. The growth in sales at Balanced has been impressive recently, but it is expected to slow considerably in the years ahead due to increased competition from overseas firms. The firm's most valuable assets are its equipment and factory, located in a prime industrial area.

Balanced was previously considered for possible purchase by a competitor in the metal fabrication industry. Although the sale was not consummated, McDonnell has learned that the firm estimated that costs could be reduced at Balanced by eliminating redundant overhead expenses. McDonnell has obtained the following financial figures from the Balanced Metals CFO, as well as the previously estimated synergistic savings from cost reductions. Capital expenditures will equal depreciation plus approximately 4% of the firm's incremental revenues.

Current revenues	$22,000,000
Revenue growth	7%
Gross profit margin	25%
Depreciation expense as a percent of sales	1%
Working capital as a percent of sales	15%
SG&A expenses	$5,400,000
Synergistic cost savings	$1,200,000
Tax rate	30%

Lutge is valuing a noncontrolling equity interest in Jensen Gear, a small outdoors equipment retailer. Jensen has experienced healthy growth in earnings over the past three years. However, given its size and private status, Lutge does not expect that Jensen can be easily sold. To obtain the appropriate price multiple for the Jensen valuation, he has prepared a database of price multiples from the sale of entire public and private companies over the past ten years, organized by industry classification. Using historical data, Lutge estimates a control premium of 18.7% and discount for lack of marketability of 24%.

To obtain the cost of capital for Jensen, Lutge uses a cost of capital database that includes public company betas, cost of equity, weighted average cost of capital, and other financial statistics by industry. Given Jensen's small size, Lutge obtains a size premium using the smallest-firm-size decile of the database. McDonnell examines Lutge's cost of capital calculations and makes the following statements.

Statement 1: I am concerned about the use of this database. The estimate of the size premium may result in an undervaluation of the Jensen equity interest.

Statement 2: The use of betas and the CAPM from the database may be inappropriate. If so, Lutge should consider using the build-up method whereby an industry risk premium is used instead of beta.

13.   Regarding the statements made by McDonnell on the comparison of
      private firms and public firms, are both statements correct?
      A. Yes.
      B. No, both statements are incorrect.
      C. No, one statement is correct, but the other statement is incorrect.

14.   Which of the following *best* describes the standard of value that
      McDonnell and Lutge will apply to Albion Biotechnology?
      A. Market value.
      B. Intrinsic value.
      C. Investment value.

15.   Which of the following is *closest* to the FCFF that McDonnell should
      estimate for Balanced Metals?
      A. –$117,800.
      B. $344,120.
      C. $722,120.

16.   Which of the following income approaches would be *most* appropriate
      for valuing Balanced Metals?
      A. The free cash flow method.
      B. The excess earnings method.
      C. The capitalized cash flow method.

17.   Which of the following is *closest* to the total adjustment for control
      and marketability that would be applied to the Jensen valuation?
      A. A discount of 5.3% would be applied.
      B. A discount of 36.0% would be applied.
      C. A discount of 42.7% would be applied.

18.   Regarding the statements made by McDonnell on Lutge's cost of
      capital calculations for Jensen, are both statements correct?
      A. Yes.
      B. No, both statements are incorrect.
      C. No, one statement is correct, but the other statement is incorrect.

$$\left[(1-0.16)(1-0.24)\right]$$

$$1 - 0.84 \times 0.75$$

Use the following information to answer Questions 19 through 24.

Lauren Jacobs, CFA, is an equity analyst for DF Investments. She is evaluating Iron Parts Inc. Iron Parts is a manufacturer of interior systems and components for automobiles. The company is the world's second-largest original equipment auto parts supplier, with a market capitalization of $1.8 billion. Based on Iron Parts's low price-to-book value ratio of 0.9× and low price-to-sales ratio of 0.15×, Jacobs believes the stock could be an interesting investment. However, she wants to review the disclosures found in the company's financial statements. In particular, Jacobs is concerned about Iron Parts's defined benefit pension plan. The following information for 20X7 and 20X8 is provided.

In millions, December 31	20X8	20X7
Projected benefit obligation (PBO)	$635	$500
Current service cost	37	33
Actual return on plan assets	37	32
Benefits paid	22	15
Past service cost	80	45
Fair market value of plan assets	395	327
Discount rate	6.0%	5.5%
Expected return on plan assets	8.2%	7.5%
Rate of compensation increase	4.0%	4.0%

Iron Parts reports under U.S. GAAP.

Jacobs wants to fully understand the impact of changing pension assumptions on Iron Parts's balance sheet and income statement. In addition, she would like to compute Iron Parts's true pension expense.

19. As of December 31, 20X8, the pension plan would be reflected on Iron Parts's balance sheet as a:
    A. $175 million liability.
    √B. $240 million liability.
    C. $183 million asset.

20. Which of the following *best* describes the effects of the change in Iron Parts's discount rate for 20X8, all else being equal?
    √A. Service cost decreased and the pension plan appeared more funded.
    B. Pension expense decreased and the PBO increased.
    C. Interest cost increased and retained earnings decreased.

21. How much did Iron Parts contribute to its pension plan during 20X8?
    A. $31 million.
    B. $36 million.
    ✓C. $53 million.

22. Which of the following *best* describes the effect(s) of the change in Iron Parts's expected return on the plan assets, all else being equal?
    A. Pension expense decreased and the PBO increased.
    B. Retained earnings increased and the pension plan appeared more funded.
    C. Net income increased.

23. For this question only, assume that Iron Parts reports under IFRS. The amount of periodic pension cost reported on P&L would be *closest* to:
    A. $48 million.
    B. $69 million.
    C. $127 million.

24. For the year ended December 31, 20X8, Iron Parts's total periodic pension cost is *closest* to:
    A. $67 million.
    B. $120 million.
    C. $157 million.

Use the following information to answer Questions 25 through 30.

Donnie Nelson, CFA, has just taken over as chief financial officer of MavsHD, a high-tech company that delivers high-definition technology to a broad-based group of sports enthusiasts. MavsHD has 40% debt and 60% equity in its capital structure. For the year just ended, net income and dividends for MavsHD were $145 million and $21.75 million, respectively. The consensus estimate for net income at the end of the current year is $153 million. The company's current book value is $550 million. MavsHD's stock is currently trading on the NYSE for a price of $50 per share and has been steadily decreasing for the past 12 months.

MavsHD has gone through its pioneer and growth phases and is now settling in to the early stages of maturity. The business model is starting to shift from relying almost exclusively on new customers to retaining and satisfying existing customers. The previously experienced very high growth rate has slowed considerably. Nelson believes that shareholder composition has changed over time as well, favoring shareholders who have a greater interest in dividend stability than in explosive growth. In the past, however, the firm has favored a low dividend rate due to the availability of attractive internal investment opportunities.

Nelson wants to develop an optimal dividend policy for MavsHD that will create the most value for the shareholders and at the same time protect corporate assets. He is concerned, however, that there is sometimes a disconnect between an optimal dividend policy and how actual dividend rates are perceived in the marketplace.

Nelson is preparing a recommendation to senior management and the board of directors regarding the firm's dividend policy going forward. Nelson is considering recommending that MavsHD engage in a stock repurchase plan and repurchase 1.5 million shares of the 12.75 million shares outstanding. This repurchase would eliminate any need to increase the cash dividend payout. Other managers at the firm, besides Nelson, believe MavsHD should increase its dividend and gravitate toward what they perceive to be the target payout ratio over the next eight years. Thus, at the end of the current year, the firm would increase the dividend payment by $250,000 over the dividend in the prior year.

During the board meeting, two of the directors raised concerns over Nelson's proposed repurchase plan. The directors' comments follow:

Director 1: I support the repurchase plan, especially relative to varying our dividend. Firms should not vary dividends—this lowers investors' confidence and can adversely impact the firm's cost of equity and its share price.

Director 2:   A share repurchase does not take away the uncertainty associated with future stock value. According to the bird-in-the-hand theory, investors prefer higher dividends because capital gains are uncertain. The theory states that if we increase our dividend payout, the value of MavsHD equity will increase. Thus, I propose a dividend increase rather than a repurchase.

One of the board members, Jason Neely, proposed an alternative dividend policy plan one week after the meeting at which Nelson presented his plan. Neely's proposal involves utilizing a residual dividend model. Neely rationalizes his plan by claiming that relative to a stable dividend policy, his proposal would increase the volatility of dollar dividends paid to shareholders but would simultaneously increase the firm's ability to exploit value additive investment projects using internally generated funds. Because of this enhanced access to value additive projects, MavsHD's cost of equity capital will experience a marginal decrease, which will further increase the overall value of the firm.

25.   Using the target payout ratio adjustment model approach to estimate dividend increases, determine which of the following is *closest* to the target payout ratio estimated by MavsHD's managers.
    A. 15%.
    B. 20%.
    C. 25%.

26.   If the board proceeds with Nelson's proposed stock repurchase plan as suggested, which of the following is *least likely* to be true? MavsHD:
    A. would be increasing financial leverage.
    B. is trying to signal the market that despite the declining share price, future prospects for the company are good.
    C. will reduce the wealth of all shareholders, including those who tender their shares for repurchase if the repurchase price is at a premium to the current stock price.

27.   For this question only, assume that MavsHD's marginal investor is in a 39.6% tax bracket for capital gains and a 15% tax bracket for dividends. If MavsHD declares a dividend of $2.25 per share, the change in MavsHD's stock price when the stock goes ex-dividend will be *closest* to:
    A. 1.36.
    B. 1.91.
    C. 3.17.

28. In light of the fact that several different groups of investors hold shares in MavsHD, evaluate the directors' comments regarding Nelson's proposed stock repurchase plan.
   A. Only Director 1 is correct.
   B. Only Director 2 is correct.
   C. Both Director 1 and Director 2 are correct.

29. If MavsHD plans to make $160 million in net investments in the current year, what will be the company's dividend payout ratio using the residual dividend model?
   A. 37.3%. ✓
   B. 58.2%.
   C. 62.8%.

30. Evaluate Neely's comments about his proposed residual dividend plan. Neely's comments are:
   A. correct.
   B. incorrect, because the equity cost of capital would not decrease under the proposed plan.
   C. incorrect, because the firm would not have greater access to internal funds for investment.

Use the following information to answer Questions 31 through 36.

Jared Rojas, CFA, is an analyst at Van Westmoreland Investments, an international equities investment firm. Rojas has been assigned to value three U.S. companies in the paper products industry. The long-term growth rate for this industry is expected to be 3.4%.

Basil Montreux Company (BMC) is the largest company in the paper products industry. BMC is considered to be a stable and mature company. The equity beta of BMC based on a single factor capital asset pricing model is 0.90.

Exhibit 1 shows selected information from BMC's financial statements for the fiscal year ending 20X2.

Exhibit 1: Selected Financial Information for BMC

Income Statement	20X2
Revenue	$20,000.0 million
EBITDA	$3,750.0 million
Operating income	$3,290.0 million
Interest expense	$600.0 million
Income tax rate	30.0%
Payout ratio	72.0%
Total assets	$31,997.0 million

Exhibit 2: Additional Information

Risk-free rate	4.0%
Market risk premium	5.0%
Size premium	2.0%
Value premium	4.0%
Liquidity premium	4.5%

Marcel Schultz Company (MSC) is another company in the paper products industry; MSC focuses on the specialty products niche. MSC is expected to enjoy a growth rate of 25% over the next three years, after which the growth rate is expected to match the overall industry growth rate. Last year's reported dividend was $278.0 million and reported earnings were $505.4 million.

MSC's market model regression beta is 1.12. Due to beta drift, this beta needs to be adjusted.

Sunil Gurpreet Company (SGC) is a small company focusing on new high-density paper, which has found application in the aerospace industry. SGC's earnings and revenues are expected to grow at 30% for eight years, after which time the technology will lose patent protection and SGC's growth rate will revert to the industry's overall growth rate. Last year's reported earnings were $160.3 million but these earnings are believed to be of poor quality. SGC has never paid dividends. SGC's earnings can be volatile, but cash flows have been positive and stable. Rojas obtains inputs to estimate SGC's cost of equity as shown in Exhibit 3.

Exhibit 3: SGC's Cost of Equity Factor Exposures

SGC	β Market	β Size	β Value	β Liquidity
Factor sensitivities	1.20	0.50	−0.20	0.20

Rojas additionally gathers the following market data regarding the three companies:

Exhibit 4: Current Market Price and Shares Outstanding

Company	Market Price	Shares outstanding (millions)
BMC	$26.50	1,000
MSC	$34.25	250
SGC	$28.45	100

31. _ Using an appropriate valuation model, the estimated value per share of BMC is *closest* to:
    A. $16.50.
    B. $26.50.
    C. $27.60.

32. Using an appropriate valuation model, the estimated value per share of MSC is *closest* to:
     $ 33.00.
    $ 33.80.
    $ 34.50.

33.   The *most appropriate* model to use in estimating the value of SCG is
        the:
        A. residual income model.
        B. dividend discount model.
        ✓ C. free cash flow model.

34.   The fraction of SGC's market price that is attributable to the value of
        growth is *closest* to:
        A. 21%.
        ✓ B. 34%.
        ✗ C. 50%.

35.   If the justified leading P/E for BMC stock is 14.1X, then BMC stock is
        best described as:
        A. overvalued.
        ✓ B. undervalued.
        C. fairly valued.

36.   For this question only, assume that SGC's cost of equity is 12% and
        that the firm pays a regular dividend, most recently $0.80. If the initial
        growth rate is expected to decrease linearly over the coming eight
        years to the long-term industry growth rate, the estimated value of
        SGC stock is *closest* to:
        ✓ A. $20.
        B. $26.
        C. $30.

$$V_0 = \frac{E}{r} + PVGO$$

$$\frac{(1-b)(1+g)}{(r-g)}$$

$$28.45 = \frac{160.3}{r} +$$

$$18.83$$

Use the following information to answer Questions 37 through 42.

Arnaud Aims is assisting with the analysis of several firms in the retail department store industry. Because one of the industry members, Flavia Stores, has negative earnings for the current year, Aims wishes to normalize earnings to establish more meaningful P/E ratios. For the current year (2008) and six previous years, selected financial data are given below. All data are in euros.

Exhibit 1: Selected Financial Data for Flavia Stores, 2002–2008

	2008	2007	2006	2005	2004	2003	2002
Earnings per share	(1.05)	1.90	1.65	0.99	1.35	0.77	1.04
Book value per share	9.11	10.66	9.26	8.11	7.62	6.77	6.50
Return on equity	(0.115)	0.178	0.178	0.122	0.177	0.114	0.160

Aims wishes to estimate normalized EPS for 2008 using two different methods, the method of historical average EPS and the method of average rate of return on equity. He will leave 2008 EPS and ROI out of his estimates. Based on his normalized EPS estimates, he will compute a trailing P/E for 2008. The stock price for Flavia Stores is €26.50.

Aims is also looking at price-to-book ratios as an alternative to price-to-earnings ratios. Three of the advantages of P/B ratios that Aims recalls are as follows:

Advantage 1: Because book value is a cumulative balance sheet account encompassing several years, book value is more likely than EPS to be positive.

Advantage 2: For many companies, especially service companies, human capital is more important than physical capital as an operating asset.

Advantage 3: Book value represents the historical purchase cost of assets, as well as accumulated accounting depreciation expenses. Inflation and technological changes can drive a wedge between the book value and market value of assets.

Aims used a constant growth DDM to establish a justified P/E ratio based on forecasted fundamentals. One of his associates asked Aims whether he could easily establish a justified price-to-sales (P/S) ratio and price-to-book (P/B) ratio from his justified P/E ratio. Aims replied, "I could do this fairly easily.

If I multiply the trailing P/E ratio times the net profit margin, the ratio of net income to sales, the result will be the P/S ratio. If I multiply the leading P/E ratio times the return on equity, the ratio of net income to beginning book value of equity, the result will be the P/B ratio."

Aims's associate likes to use the price-earnings-to-growth (PEG) ratio because it appears to address the effect of growth on the P/E ratio. For example, if a firm's P/E ratio is 20 and its forecasted 5-year growth rate is 10%, the PEG ratio is 2.0. The associate likes to invest in firms that have an above-industry-average PEG ratio. The associate also says that he likes to invest in firms whose leading P/E is greater than its trailing P/E. Aims tells the associate that he would like to further investigate these two investment criteria.

Finally, Aims makes two comments to his associate about valuation ratios based on EBITDA and on dividends.

Comment 1: EBITDA is a pre-interest-expense figure, so I prefer a ratio of total equity value to EBITDA over a ratio of enterprise value to EBITDA.

Comment 2: Dividend yields are useful information because they are one component of total return. However, they can be an incomplete measure of return, because investors trade off future earnings growth to receive higher current dividends.

37.   Using the information in Exhibit 1, estimate the 2008 P/E ratio for Flavia Stores using the method of historical average EPS. The P/E ratio is *closest* to:
       A. 18.4.
       B. 20.6.
       C. 27.9.

38.   Using the information in Exhibit 1, estimate the 2008 P/E ratio for Flavia Stores using the method of average return on equity. The P/E ratio is *closest* to:
       A. 16.0.
       B. 18.8.
       C. 25.0.

39.   Which one of the three advantages recalled by Aims *most likely* represents a good reason to consider using a P/B ratio?
       A. Advantage 1.
       B. Advantage 2.
       C. Advantage 3.

40.   Is Aims correct in describing how we could transform a justified P/E ratio into a P/S ratio or a P/B ratio?

   A. Yes.

   B. No. He is correct about the P/S ratio but incorrect about the P/B ratio.

   C. No. He is correct about the P/B ratio but incorrect about the P/S ratio.

41.   When Aims further investigates the two investment criteria (the PEG ratio and the comparison between the trailing and leading P/E ratio), should he find his colleague's use of them to be appropriate?

   A. No.

   B. The PEG ratio criterion is appropriate, but the P/E ratio criterion is not.

   C. The P/E ratio criterion is appropriate, but the PEG ratio criterion is not.

42.   Are Aims's two comments about the dividend yield and EBITDA ratios correct?

   A. Yes.

   B. No. The comment about EBITDA ratios is correct, but the comment about dividend yields is incorrect.

   C. No. The comment about dividend yields is correct, but the comment about EBITDA ratios is incorrect.

Use the following information to answer Questions 43 through 48.

Jonathan Weil, CFA, is the managing director of Weil Capital Management (WCM). Weil has decided to reevaluate the asset-backed security (ABS) positions in his investors' portfolios because a recent, and severe, credit problem in the subprime lending industry has had ripple effects on other fixed-income markets. Weil expects the interest rate term structure to remain flat but shift upward as credit terms tighten. Weil has asked one of his analysts, Vanessa Ordon, to assist him in analyzing potential ABS investments, including some products he is unfamiliar with.

Ordon provides an assessment of ABS backed by auto loans, credit card receivables, and closed-end home equity loans. Ordon has assembled the following information on the collateral, credit enhancements, and prepayment risk associated with each type of ABS.

Exhibit 1: Features of Auto Loan ABS and Credit Card Receivable ABS

	Auto Loan ABS	*Credit Card Receivable ABS*
Collateral	Generally, the collateral structure will change for an auto loan ABS because additional loan collateral will be added to the portfolio using principal payments and prepayments during the lockout period. This information should be detailed in the prospectus.	ABS backed by credit card receivables often contain a cleanup call provision in the collateral structure. If the value of the collateral falls below a specified level, the cleanup call requires that the cash flows be directed at reduction of principal rather than at replenishment of the collateral portfolio.
Credit Enhancement	According to the prospectus, the collateral backing the ABS has a weighted average coupon of 11.5%, with a range of coupons from 8% to 15%. The weighted average coupon on the tranches created by the issuer is 10.8%, with a range of coupons from 7% to 16%.	The prospectus specifies that the ABS issuer has obtained from its primary bank a pledge to absorb defaults of up to 5% of the value of the underlying collateral. Collateral defaults in excess of 5% are not covered by the bank's agreement.
Prepayment Risk	A sudden increase in interest rates, such as the one expected by Weil, is unlikely to significantly affect the prepayment rate of the loan collateral backing the auto loan ABS.	Assuming the cleanup call provision has not been invoked, a credit card receivable backed ABS will experience an increase in the prepayment rate during the lockout period if interest rates change as expected by Weil. This will cause a contraction for investors.

Ordon has also assembled the following information on the structure of a closed-end home equity loan (HEL) asset-backed security. Ordon has presented the security to Weil as a potential investment opportunity, but Weil is concerned about its default and prepayment risks. The HEL ABS does not have a shifting interest mechanism.

Exhibit 2: Home Equity Loan Asset-Backed Security

	Average Life	Coupon Rate	Principal	Initial Collar
Collateral	5.8 yrs	6.00%	$475,000,000	
Senior Tranches				
Tranche A – PAC I	4.5 yrs	5.25%	$180,000,000	90 – 300 PPC
Tranche B – PAC I	5.8 yrs	5.25%	$112,500,000	90 – 300 PPC
Tranche C – PAC II	4.0 yrs	6.50%	$67,500,000	150 – 225 PPC
Tranche D – Non-PAC Support	8.5 yrs	7.25%	$36,000,000	
Subordinated Tranche				
Tranche E	5.0 yrs	8.00%	$54,000,000	

Ordon has also developed an assessment of mortgage-backed securities (MBS). Ordon has assembled the following information related to a mortgage-backed security.

Exhibit 3: Mortgage-Backed Security

	OAS	Nominal Spread	Effective Duration
PAC Tranches			
PT1	8 bp	15 bp	1.5 yrs
PT2	16 bp	22 bp	3.1 yrs
PT3	22 bp	32 bp	4.8 yrs
PT4	38 bp	54 bp	6.7 yrs
PT5	47 bp	62 bp	7.9 yrs
Support Tranches			
ST1	36 bp	60 bp	1.3 yrs
ST2	35 bp	69 bp	1.7 yrs
ST3	65 bp	115 bp	3.5 yrs

43. Has Ordon correctly described the features of auto loan and credit card receivable backed ABS with respect to the securities' collateral?
     A. Ordon is only correct with regard to the auto loan ABS.
     B. Ordon is only correct with regard to the credit card receivable ABS.
     C. Ordon is correct with regard to the auto loan ABS and the credit card receivable ABS.

44. Which of the following statements regarding the types of credit enhancement for the auto loan and credit card receivable ABS described by Ordon is *most likely* correct?
     A. The auto loan ABS credit enhancement is an excess servicing spread.
     B. The credit card receivable ABS credit enhancement is a corporate guarantee.
     C. The credit enhancements for both the auto loan ABS and the credit card receivable ABS are external.

45. Evaluate Ordon's description of the prepayment risk associated with auto loan and credit card receivable backed ABS. Ordon is:
     A. correct.
     B. incorrect, because Weil's expected interest rate increase would cause the prepayment rate on auto loan ABS to decrease.
     C. incorrect, because Weil's expected interest rate increase would not cause a contraction on credit card receivable ABS.

46. Which of the following *best* describes the initial reaction of the home equity loan backed ABS that Ordon presented to Weil if there is a collateral default of $30 million?
     A. The principal value of Tranche E will fall to $49 million.
     B. The principal value of Tranche D will fall to $31 million.
     C. The principal value of Tranche E will fall to $24 million.

47. The prepayment speed on the home equity loan ABS has been constant at 200 PPC. If the prepayment rate suddenly increased to 350 PPC, which of the following tranches would have the largest contraction?
     A. Tranche B.
     B. Tranche C.
     C. Tranche D.

48. Weil has decided to invest in the MBS identified by Ordon but wants to keep the interest rate sensitivity of the investment low while gaining a substantially large option-adjusted spread at a cheap price. Weil is not concerned with credit risk in this case. Which of the MBS tranches is *most likely* to fulfill Weil's objectives?
     A. PT5.
     B. ST1.
     C. ST2.

Use the following information to answer Questions 49 through 54.

Paul Durham, CFA, is a senior manager in the structured bond department within Newton Capital Partners (NCP), an investment banking firm located in the United States. Durham has just returned from an international marketing campaign for NCP's latest structured note offering, a series of equity-linked fixed-income securities or ELFS. The bonds will offer a 4.5% coupon paid annually along with the annual return on the S&P 500 Index and will have a maturity of five years. The total face value of the ELFS series is expected to be $200 million.

Susan Jacobs, a fixed-income portfolio manager and principal with Smith & Associates, has decided to include $10 million worth of ELFS in her fixed-income portfolio. At the end of the first year, however, the S&P 500 Index value is 1,054, significantly lower than the initial value of 1,112 set by NCP at the time of the ELFS offering. Jacobs is concerned that the four remaining years of the ELFS life could have similar results and is considering her alternatives to offset the equity exposure of the ELFS position without selling the bonds. Jacobs decides to offset her portfolio's exposure to the ELFS by entering into an equity-swap contract. The LIBOR term structure is shown below in Exhibit 1.

Exhibit 1: LIBOR Term Structure

	LIBOR	Discount Factor
1-Year	3.2%	0.9690
2-Year	4.1%	0.9242
3-Year	4.9%	0.8718
4-Year	5.3%	0.8251

After hearing of her plan, one of the other partners with Smith & Associates, Jonathan Widby, feels it is necessary to meet with Jacobs regarding her proposed strategy. Widby makes the following comments during the meeting:

"You should also know that I am quite bullish on the stock market for the near future. Therefore, as an alternative strategy, I recommend that you establish a long position in a 1 × 3 payer swaption. This strategy would allow you to wait and see how the market performs next year but will give you the ability to enter into a 2-year swap with terms that can be established today should the market have another down year.

If, however, you choose to proceed with your strategy, know that credit risk for a swap is greatest toward the end of the swap's life. Thus, analysts tracking your portfolio will not be happy with the added credit risk that your portfolio will be exposed to as the swap nears the end of its tenor. You should think about what credit derivatives you can use to manage this risk when the time comes."

To offset any credit risk associated with the equity swap, Widby recommends using an index trade strategy by entering into a credit default swap (CDS) as a protection buyer. Widby's strategy would involve purchasing credit protection on an index comprising largely the same issuers (companies) included in the equity index underlying the swap. Widby suggests the CDS should have a maturity equal to that of the swap to provide maximum credit protection.

49. Which of the following strategies would be *most* appropriate given Jacobs's situation and desire to offset the equity exposure of the ELFS position in her portfolio? Establish an equity swap as the:
    A. floating-rate payer and S&P 500 Index return receiver.
    B. fixed-rate receiver and S&P 500 Index return payer.
    C. fixed-rate payer and S&P 500 Index return receiver.

50. Based on the strategy appropriate for Jacobs's portfolio, determine the contract rate on the swap strategy.
    A. 4.5%.
    B. 3.6%.
    C. 4.9%.

51. If Jacobs enters into a $10 million 4-year annual-pay floating-rate equity swap based on 1-year LIBOR and the total return on the S&P 500 Index, what is the value of the remaining 3-year swap to the floating-rate payer after one year if the index has increased from 1,054 to 1,103 and the LIBOR term structure is as given below?

    LIBOR
    1-year: 4.1%
    2-year: 4.7%
    3-year: 5.3%

    A. 0.
    B. $48,935.
    C. $9,583.

52. Jacobs has observed declining swap spreads on several of the equity swaps that she is considering as potential investments. What do the declining swap spreads indicate?
    A. The term structure of LIBOR has shifted down.
    B. Credit risk for Smith & Associates is declining.
    C. Credit risk in the market as a whole is declining.

53. Evaluate, in light of the appropriate equity swap strategy for Jacobs's portfolio, Widby's comments regarding the credit risk and use of swaptions in Jacobs's portfolio.
   A. Widby is correct only with respect to credit risk.
   B. Widby is correct only with respect to the swaptions.
   C. Widby is incorrect with respect to both credit risk and the swaptions.

54. Which of the following *best* evaluates Widby's suggested use of credit default swaps to offset the credit risk of the equity swap? Widby's recommended strategy is:
   A. correct.
   B. incorrect, because the maturity of the CDS is not properly specified.
   C. incorrect, because the CDS does not reference the proper credit risk.

Use the following information to answer Questions 55 through 60.

Jasmine Williams, a client of private wealth manager Colby Nash, is open to adding alternative assets to her portfolio. Nash suggests that an allocation to hedge funds may allow Williams's portfolio to produce higher return and lower risk. However, Williams is unfamiliar with hedge funds and is concerned that an investment in hedge funds may expose her portfolio to more risk than she is willing to take. Nash believes that Williams's attitude towards hedge funds has been influenced by recent negative press coverage of hedge funds. Nash decides to ease Williams's concerns by explaining to her some of the characteristics of hedge funds.

Nash feels that the Neptune fund, a merger arbitrage hedge fund, may be an appropriate addition to Williams's portfolio. Williams is unfamiliar with the concept of merger arbitrage and asks Nash for an explanation of how merger arbitrage works. Nash explains that Neptune takes highly leveraged positions in securities in advance of a potential merger. Another option that Nash considers for Williams's portfolio is to invest in a fund of funds, rather than investing in a single manager fund such as Neptune.

Williams asks Nash if, rather than investing in hedge funds, the same kind of results can be achieved by investing in more traditional investments like stocks and bonds. Nash explains that this is indeed possible and may be accomplished by using factor models to determine a hedge fund's exposures to traditional risk factors. However, Nash admits that whether a large portion of a fund's return can be explained using this process depends on the hedge fund strategy in question.

Williams is familiar with mean-variance analysis from her undergraduate degree in finance and asks Nash if he is planning to use this method to evaluate how much hedge fund exposure would be optimal for Williams's portfolio. Nash explains that applying such traditional portfolio analysis to hedge funds can be problematic.

Additionally, Nash considers adding an allocation to real estate investments to Williams's portfolio. Nash makes the following statements to Williams:

Statement 1: While analyzing REITs, analysts often compute funds from operations (FFO), which excludes depreciation, deferred tax charges, and straight line rent from accounting income. FFO is a better indicator of future earnings than reported net income.

Statement 2: Some of the risk factors of investing in private real estate deals include demographics, cost of equity and debt capital, and unexpected inflation.

55. From her previous investing experience, Williams is familiar with mutual funds and asks Nash how hedge funds are similar to or different from mutual funds. As Nash explains to Williams the factors that distinguish hedge funds from mutual funds, Nash should explain that compared to mutual funds, a hedge fund is *more likely* to:
    A. have a low minimum investment requirement.
    B. hold multiple asset classes.
    C. feature symmetric fee structures.

56. Nash could *most accurately* describe Neptune's strategy as:
    A. taking a long position in a target's stock and a short position in the acquirer's stock.
    B. attempting to profit from large mispricings.
    C. similar to buying insurance against the failure of a merger.

57. When describing the expected return distribution of the Neptune fund, Nash should explain to Williams that the return distribution of a merger arbitrage fund is *most likely* to exhibit:
    A. negative skewness.
    B. low positive kurtosis.
    C. negative kurtosis.

58. Nash should explain to Williams that the use of factor models to explain returns is *least likely* to be successful for a hedge fund using a strategy classified as:
    A. long/short equity.
    B. fixed-income arbitrage.
    C. distressed debt.

59. In explaining to Williams the advantages and disadvantages of funds of funds relative to single manager funds, Nash should point out that compared to the average single manager hedge fund, a fund of funds is *most likely* to exhibit higher:
    A. liquidity.
    B. return.
    C. volatility.

60. Regarding Nash's Statements 1 and 2 related to real estate investments, are both statements correct?
    A. Yes, both statements are correct.
    B. No, both statements are incorrect.
    C. No, only one statement is correct.

End of Morning Session

Exam 1
Afternoon Session

Question	Topic	Minutes (Points)
61 to 66	Ethical and Professional Standards	18
67 to 72	Quantitative Analysis	18
73 to 78	Portfolio Management	18
79 to 90	Financial Reporting and Analysis	36
91 to 102	Asset Valuation – Equity	36
103 to 114	Asset Valuation – Fixed Income	36
115 to 120	Asset Valuation – Derivatives	18

Reading 19

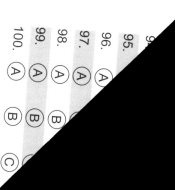

61.	(A)	(B)	(C)
62.	(A)	(B)	(C)
63.	(A)	(B)	(C)
64.	(A)	(B)	(C)
65.	(A)	(B)	(C)
66.	(A)	(B)	(C)
67.	(A)	(B)	(C)
68.	(A)	(B)	(C)
69.	(A)	(B)	(C)
70.	(A)	(B)	(C)

71.	(A)	(B)	(C)
72.	(A)	(B)	(C)
73.	(A)	(B)	(C)
74.	(A)	(B)	(C)
75.	(A)	(B)	(C)
76.	(A)	(B)	(C)
77.	(A)	(B)	(C)
78.	(A)	(B)	(C)
79.	(A)	(B)	(C)
80.	(A)	(B)	(C)

81.	(A)	(B)	(C)
82.	(A)	(B)	(C)
83.	(A)	(B)	(C)
84.	(A)	(B)	(C)
85.	(A)	(B)	(C)
86.	(A)	(B)	(C)
87.	(A)	(B)	(C)
88.	(A)	(B)	(C)
89.	(A)	(B)	(C)
90.	(A)	(B)	(C)

91.	(A)	(B)	(C)
92.	(A)	(B)	(C)
93.	(A)	(B)	(C)
4.	(A)	(B)	(C)
	(A)	(B)	(C)
		(B)	(C)
		(B)	(C)
			(C)
			(C)

101.	(A)	(B)	(C)
102.	(A)	(B)	(C)
103.	(A)	(B)	(C)
104.	(A)	(B)	(C)
105.	(A)	(B)	(C)
106.	(A)	(B)	(C)
107.	(A)	(B)	(C)
108.	(A)	(B)	(C)
109.	(A)	(B)	(C)
110.	(A)	(B)	(C)

111.	(A)	(B)	(C)
112.	(A)	(B)	(C)
113.	(A)	(B)	(C)
114.	(A)	(B)	(C)
115.	(A)	(B)	(C)
116.	(A)	(B)	(C)
117.	(A)	(B)	(C)
118.	(A)	(B)	(C)
119.	(A)	(B)	(C)
120.	(A)	(B)	(C)

Exam 1
Afternoon Session

Use the following information to answer Questions 61 through 66.

Susan Foley, CFA, is chief investment officer of Federated Investment Management Co. (FIMCO), a large investment management firm that includes a family of mutual funds as well as individually managed accounts. The individually managed accounts include individuals, personal trusts, and employee benefit plans. In the past few months, Foley has encountered a couple of problems.

The Tasty IPO

Most portfolio managers of FIMCO have not participated in the initial public offering (IPO) market in recent years. However, recent changes to the compensation calculation at FIMCO have tied manager bonuses to portfolio performance. The changes were outlined in a letter that was sent out to clients and prospects shortly before the new bonus structure took effect. Carl Lee, CFA, is one portfolio manager who believes that investing in IPOs might add to his client's equity performance and, in turn, increase his bonus. While Lee's individual clients have done quite well this year, his employee benefit plans have suffered as a result of limited exposure to the strongest performing sector of the market. Lee has placed an order for all employee benefit plans to receive an allocation of the Tasty Doughnut IPO. Tasty is an oversubscribed IPO that Lee knew would make money for his clients. When he placed the order, Lee's assistant reminded him that one pension plan, Ultra Airlines, was explicitly prohibited from investing in IPOs in its investment policy statement, due to the underfunded status of the pension plan. Lee responded that the Tasty IPO would never actually be owned in Ultra's account, because he would sell the IPO stock before the end of the day and realize a profit before the position ever hit the books.

Another manager, Franz Mason, CFA, who manages accounts for about 150 individuals, is also interested in the Tasty IPO. Mason visits Lee's portfolio assistant and quizzes him about Lee's participation in the Tasty deal. Mason is sure that Lee would not have bought into Tasty unless he had done his homework. Mason places an order for 10,000 shares of the IPO. Mason returns to his desk and begins to allocate the IPO shares among his clients. Mason divides his client base into two groups: clients who are income-oriented and clients who are capital gains-oriented. Mason believes those clients that are income-oriented are fairly risk averse and could not replace lost capital if the Tasty Doughnut deal lost money. Mason believes the capital gains-oriented accounts are better able to withstand the potential loss associated with the Tasty IPO. Accordingly, Mason allocates his 10,000 share order of the Tasty IPO strictly to his capital appreciation clients using a pro rata allocation based on the size of the assets under management in each account.

FIMCO Income Fund (FIF)

Over the past three years, the FIF, with $5 billion in assets, has been the company's best performing mutual fund. Jane Ryan, CFA, managed the FIF for seven years but resigned one year ago to start her own hedge fund. Under Ryan, the FIF invested in large-cap stocks with reliable dividends. The fund's prospectus specifies that FIF will invest only in stocks that have paid a dividend for at least two quarters and have a market capitalization in excess of $2.5 billion. Foley appointed FIMCO's next best manager (based on 5-year performance numbers) Steve Parsons, CFA, to replace Ryan. Parsons had been a very successful manager of the FIMCO Opportunity Fund, which specialized in small capitalization stocks. Six months after Parsons took over the helm at FIF, the portfolio had changed. The average market capitalization of FIF's holdings was $12.8 billion, as opposed to $21 billion a year ago. Over the same period, the average dividend yield on the portfolio had fallen from 3.8% to 3.1%. The performance of the FIF lagged behind its peer group for the first time in three years. In response to the lagging performance, Parsons purchased five stocks six months ago. Parsons bought all five stocks, none of which paid a dividend at the time of purchase, in anticipation that each company was likely to initiate dividends in the near future. So far, four of the stocks have initiated dividend payments, and their performance has benefited as a result. The fifth stock did not initiate a dividend, and Parsons sold the position last week. Largely due to the addition of the five new stocks, the FIF's performance has led its peer group over the past six months.

Before leaving FIMCO, Ryan had told Foley that above-average returns from both the management and the client side could be gained from entering into the risk-arbitrage hedge fund market. Ryan had tried to convince FIMCO management to enter the risk-arbitrage market, but the firm determined that no one had the experience or research capability to run a risk-arbitrage operation. As a result, Ryan started the Plasma Fund LLC one month after leaving FIMCO. Foley remembers seeing Ryan at the annual FIMCO client dinner party (before she left the firm) discussing the profits to be made from risk-arbitrage investing with several large FIF shareholders. Ryan mentioned that she would be opening the Plasma Fund to these FIMCO clients, several of whom made substantial investments in the first months of Plasma Fund's life. After Ryan resigned and left her office, Foley performed an inventory of firm assets signed out to Ryan. One of the copies of the proprietary stock selection software packages, FIMCO-SelectStock, assigned to Ryan was missing along with several of the SelectStock operating manuals. When Foley contacted

Ryan about the missing software and manuals, Ryan stated that the reason she took the SelectStock software was that it was an out-of-date version that FIMCO's information technology staff had urged all managers to discard.

61. Regarding Lee's order for employee benefit plans to receive an allocation of the Tasty Doughnut IPO and his purchase of the Tasty Doughnut IPO for the Ultra Airlines Pension account, which of the following statements is *most* accurate?
    A. Lee's order for all employee benefit plans to receive an allocation of the Tasty Doughnuts IPO is acceptable, but Lee has violated CFA Institute Standards by placing the IPO order in the Ultra Airlines pension account.
    B. Lee's order for all employee benefit plans to receive an allocation of the Tasty Doughnuts IPO is acceptable because it is appropriate for his clients' employee benefit plans, and Lee has followed the CFA Institute Standards by notifying clients about recent compensation calculation changes, but Lee has violated CFA Institute Standards by placing the IPO order in the Ultra Airlines pension account.
    C. By allocating the Tasty Doughnuts IPO to employee benefit accounts only, Lee is discriminating against other accounts that may have also wanted to participate in the Tasty IPO. Purchasing shares in the Tasty Doughnuts IPO for the Ultra Airlines account is a violation of CFA Institute Standards, since it violates the investment policy statement (IPS).

62. Mason used two allocation plans for the Tasty IPO: the first decision was based on the orientation of the account (income versus capital gains), and the second decision was based on the relative size of each account. Did Mason violate CFA Institute Standards of Professional Conduct with respect to either allocation decision?
    A. Both Mason's allocation screens, based on orientation of the account and on relative size of account, violate CFA Institute Standards.
    B. Both of Mason's allocation screens appear to fully conform with CFA Institute Standards.
    C. Mason's pro rata allocation system is acceptable, but he should have allocated some IPO shares to his income-oriented accounts.

63. Which of the following is *most likely* consistent with CFA Institute Standards of Professional Conduct?
    A. Lee assumed that Ultra's Tasty IPO position was acceptable as an intraday transaction.
    B. Improved performance in Lee's employee benefit plan accounts increases his bonus.
    C. Mason relied on Lee's investment decision as adequate rationale to buy into the Tasty IPO.

64. Has there been any violation of CFA Institute Standards of Professional Conduct relating to either the change in the average holdings of the FIF during the first six months of Parsons's leadership or in Parsons's subsequent investment in the non-dividend-paying stocks?
   A. Both actions. The change in average holdings and the purchase of non-dividend-paying stocks are violations of CFA Institute Standards.
   B. The change in average holdings would not have been a violation of CFA Institute Standards if client notification had occurred before the change was initiated.
   C. There is no violation regarding the change in average holdings, but the purchase of non-dividend-paying stocks is a violation.

65. Which of the following statements is *most* accurate with regard to Ryan's discussion of the new Plasma Fund with FIMCO clients?
   A. Ryan is within the CFA Institute Standards because the Plasma Fund was only in the planning stages at the time of her discussion.
   B. Ryan is within the CFA Institute Standards by discussing Plasma with the clients because the product she was discussing did not compete with her present employer (FIMCO) in any way.
   C. Ryan has violated CFA Institute Standard IV(A) – Duties to Employers – Loyalty. In the meeting with potential clients, even though FIMCO had no experience or research capability to enter the risk-arbitrage market, Ryan is offering an asset-management service that is directing funds away from FIMCO.

66. Which of the following statements is *most* accurate with regard to Ryan's taking the out-of-date version of the SelectStock software?
   A. The inappropriate misappropriation of the software and manuals is a violation of CFA Institute Standard IV(A) – Duties to Employers – Loyalty, regardless of the circumstances. Written permission from the employer (FIMCO) should have been requested and received.
   B. Ryan's possession of the out-of-date software is perfectly acceptable because her IT staff had made it clear that is was no longer needed by FIMCO.
   C. Ryan's possession of the out-of-date software is perfectly acceptable because the software is of no use to FIMCO and because it was an outdated version, which indicates that it had no economic value.

Use the following information to answer Questions 67 through 72.

Research associate Kate Sawyer is responsible for identifying the determinants of performance for her firm's Progressive Fund (PF). All tests performed at Sawyer's firm are examined at the 0.05 level of significance. Sawyer examines the following regressions using monthly data observed for a 36 month period:

(1) $R_{PF,t} = b_0 + b_1 R_{M,t} + b_2 VMG_t + e_{PF,t}$

(2) $\hat{e}^2_{PF,t} = a_0 + a_1 R_{M,t} + a_2 VMG_t + u_{PF,t}$

   where:

   $R_{PF,t}$ = the return on the Progressive Fund in month t

   $R_{M,t}$ = the return on the Wilshire 5000 stock market index in month t

   VMG_t = the return on value stocks minus the return on growth stocks in month t

   $\hat{e}^2_{PF,t}$ = the estimated squared regression errors derived from equation (1)

Exhibit 1: Equation (1) Regression Results

Variable	Coefficient	p-values
Constant	−0.005	0.030
R_M	1.250	0.001
VMG	0.200	0.980

The R^2 from equation (1) equals 0.80. A colleague, Jack Lockhart, makes two recommendations to Sawyer:

Recommendation 1: My research indicates that inflation-rate changes are highly correlated with the Wilshire 5000 stock index returns. Therefore, I recommend adding the inflation change variable to your regression.

Recommendation 2: My research indicates that the slope coefficients of your regression changed significantly after the passage of Regulation Fair Disclosure, which took place in the middle of your 3-year sample period. Your regression pools across two distinct sample periods. Therefore, I recommend correcting your current regression equation (1) for model misspecification.

In her conversation with Lockhart, Sawyer explains that she is concerned that her regression equation (1) may ignore other important determinants of performance for the Progressive Fund. Sawyer explains that she is aware that the omission of important independent variables affects the quality of the parameter estimates of the regression. She makes the following claims, assuming the omitted variables are correlated with the included variables:

Claim 1: The parameter estimates of equation (1) are unbiased.

Claim 2: The parameter estimates of equation (1) are inconsistent.

67. Of the slopes for the two independent variables, R_M and VMG, determine which are statistically significant at the 0.05 level?
    A. Both slopes are statistically significant.
    B. Only the slope for R_M is statistically significant.
    C. Only the slope for VMG is statistically significant.

68. The R^2 derived for equation (1) indicates which of the following for equation (1)?
    A. Regression sum of squares exceeds the error sum of squares.
    B. Regression sum of squares exceeds the total sum of squares.
    C. Mean regression sum of squares is less than the mean total sum of squares.

69. Sawyer decides to test regression equation (1) for the existence of conditional heteroskedasticity. Sawyer is likely to conclude that her regression does not exhibit conditional heteroskedasticity if the R^2 from equation (2) is:
    A. close to 0.
    B. close to 1.
    C. close to 0.80.

70. Regarding Lockhart's Recommendation 1, the econometric problem that is *most likely* to be introduced by including the inflation change variable in regression equation (1) is:
    A. model misspecification.
    B. serial correlation.
    C. multicollinearity.

71. Regarding Lockhart's Recommendation 2, the *most likely* form of model misspecification to which he refers is:
    A. stationarity model misspecification.
    B. time-series model misspecification.
    C. functional form model misspecification.

72. Regarding Claim 1 and Claim 2 made by Sawyer about the effects of omitted variables, which claims are correct?
    A. Claim 1 only.
    B. Claim 2 only.
    C. Both Claim 1 and Claim 2.

Use the following information to answer Questions 73 through 78.

Anders Nissen, Bertil Jespersen, and Bjarne Svendsen are portfolio managers at Dantopse, a private wealth management firm. Each portfolio manager is assigned 35–40 clients, and each portfolio manager is responsible for all aspects of those clients' portfolios. Typical Dantopse clients have over 3 million DKK (Danish Krone) in assets. Dantopse is also in the process of introducing asset management services for small- to medium-sized private pension plans.

Nissen, Jespersen, and Svendsen attend a CFA Institute continuing education seminar in Zurich, Switzerland. Towards the end of the seminar, the three meet to discuss how they are going to apply what they learned at the seminar.

Nissen makes the following statements:

Statement 1: We should focus on security selection when constructing a client investment strategy.

Statement 2: We should use employee age and turnover rate as inputs to determine the liquidity and time horizon constraints for defined benefit plans.

Nissen then mentions his frustrations with mean-variance optimization. He states that the optimization results tend to be highly unstable.

Jespersen asks his colleagues for clarification of several points that the seminar raised about the information ratio. He then makes the following statements about the implications of the CAPM:

Statement 1: Because all investors hold the same risky portfolio, the weight on each asset must be equal to the ratio of its market value to the market value of all risky assets.

Statement 2: All investors can satisfy their investment needs by combining the tangency portfolio with the risk-free asset.

Svendsen states that the seminar has inspired him to employ an arbitrage strategy to profit from mispriced securities. He uses an example to illustrate his point. Exhibit 1 shows three hypothetical stocks and their expected returns and factor sensitivities based on a single factor model.

$$\beta \quad \frac{SST-SSE}{SST} \quad \frac{0.8}{1}$$

Exhibit 1: Expected Returns and Factor Sensitivities

Stock	Expected Return	Factor Sensitivity
A	0.12	1.00
B	0.08	0.50
C	0.09	0.55

Nissen asks Svendson about macroeconomic factor models. Svendson describes a two-factor model describing returns for stocks X and Y, where the two factors are surprises in interest rates and oil prices.

$$R_X = 0.15 + 0.8 \, F_{Int} + 1.2 \, F_{Oil}$$

$$R_Y = 0.12 + 1.1 \, F_{Int} + 0.9 \, F_{Oil}$$

73. Regarding Statements 1 and 2 made by Nissen:
    A. only Statement 1 is correct.
    B. only Statement 2 is correct.
    C. neither Statement 1 nor Statement 2 are correct.

74. Which of the following is *least likely* to be a problem related to the instability of the minimum variance frontier?
    A. Infrequent rebalancing.
    B. Time instability.
    C. Overfitting.

75. Which of the following statements about the information ratio is *most accurate*?
    A. The information ratio is a relative form of the Sharpe ratio.
    B. The information ratio is almost always higher for active managers than it is for passive managers.
    C. Risk-adjusted return is defined as expected return divided by expected information ratio.

76. Regarding the statements made by Jespersen:
    A. neither statement is accurate.
    B. only one of the statements is accurate.
    C. both statements are accurate.

77. Using the information in Exhibit 1, the expected profits of an arbitrage portfolio consisting of a 1 million DKK long position in stock C funded by short positions in stocks A and B is *closest* to:
     A. DKK (1,000).
     B. DKK 4,800.
     ✓C. DKK 6,000.

78. For an investor that wishes to hedge oil price risk, the *most appropriate* allocation to stock X in a portfolio consisting of stocks X and Y as a percentage of investable assets is:
     A. −300%.
     B. 40%.
     C. 60%.

$$E(R_P) = R_F + \beta_1 (\lambda_1) + \beta_2 (\lambda_2) + \beta_3 (\lambda_3) \cdots$$

$$0 + 1(0.12) + 0.5(0.08) + 0.55(0.09)$$

$$1.2(\omega) + 0.9(1-\omega) = 0$$

$$1.2\omega + 0.9 - 0.9\omega = 0$$

$$0.3\omega = -0.9$$

$$\omega = -3$$

$$1(x) + 2(1-x) = 1.5$$

$$x + 2 - 2x = 1.5$$

$$-x = x + 0.5$$

$$x = 50$$

$$\frac{\overline{R_P} - \overline{R_B}}{S(R_P - R_B)} = \sqrt{\frac{E(R_P - R_B)^2}{n-1}}$$

Active Return = $R_P - R_B$

Use the following information to answer Questions 79 through 84.

Voyager Inc., a primarily Internet-based media company, is buying The Daily, a media company with exposure to newspapers, television, and the Internet.

Company Descriptions
Voyager Inc. is organized into two segments: Internet and newspaper publishing. The Internet segment operates Web sites that offer news, entertainment, and advertising content in text and video format. The Internet segment represents 75% of the company's total revenues. The newspaper publishing segment publishes 10 daily newspapers. The newspaper publishing segment represents 25% of the company's total revenues.
The Daily is organized into three segments: newspaper publishing (60% of revenues), broadcasting (35% of revenues), and Internet (5% of revenues). The newspaper publishing segment publishes 101 daily newspapers. The broadcasting segment owns and operates 25 television stations. The Internet segment consists of an Internet advertising service. The Daily's newspaper publishing and broadcasting segments cover the 20 largest markets in the United States.

Voyager's acquisition of The Daily is the company's second major acquisition in its history. The previous acquisition was at the height of the merger boom in the year 2000. Voyager purchased the Dragon Company at a premium-to-net-asset value, thereby doubling the company's size. Voyager used the pooling method to account for the acquisition of Dragon; however, because of FASB changes to the Business Combination Standard, Voyager will use the acquisition method to account for the Daily acquisition.

(in millions except per share data)	Voyager Inc. (before merger)	The Daily (before merger)
Revenues	$1,800	$7,600
Operating income	$415	$998
Earnings	$200	$650
Assets	$1,900	$14,700
Debt	$200	$2,500
Equity	$1,100	$7,600
Number of shares	117.6 million	213.1 million
Stock price per share	$68	$35
Earnings per share	$1.70	$3.05
PE ratio	40.0x	11.5x

Voyager has made an all-cash offer of $45 per share to acquire The Daily. Wall Street is skeptical about the merger. While Voyager has been growing its revenues by 40% per year, The Daily's revenue growth has been less than 2% per year. Michael Renner, the CFO of Voyager, defends the acquisition by stating that The Daily has accumulated a large amount of tax losses and that the combined company can benefit by immediately increasing net income after the merger. In addition, Renner states that the new Voyager will eliminate the inefficiencies of its Internet operations and thereby boost future earnings. Renner believes that the merged companies will have a value of $17.5 billion.

In the past, The Daily's management has publicly stated its opposition to merging with any company, a position management still maintains. As a result of this situation, Voyager submitted its merger proposal directly to The Daily's board of directors, while the firm's CEO was on vacation. Upon returning from vacation, The Daily's CEO issued a public statement claiming that the proposed merger was unacceptable under any circumstances.

79. Voyager used the pooling of interests method when accounting for the 2000 acquisition of Dragon, rather than the acquisition method it would use today. Which of the following is *least likely* a feature of the pooling of interests method?
    A. Operating results for prior periods are restated as though the two firms were always combined.
    B. The pooling of interests method combines historic book values and fair values.
    C. The pooling of interests method combines historic book values.

80. Based on Renner's comments defending Voyager's acquisition of The Daily, indicate whether his comments about net income and elimination of inefficiencies are *most likely* correct.
    A. Only Renner's comment that unused tax losses will immediately translate into higher net income is correct.
    B. Only Renner's comment that the elimination of inefficiencies within the Internet operations will create additional value is correct.
    C. Both comments are correct.

81. Assuming that Renner's estimate of the value of the merged companies is correct, calculate the acquirer's gain from the merger.
    A. $7,910.5 million.
    B. $9,503.2 million.
    C. $11,634.2 million.

82. Assume that Voyager offers 63 million shares of its stock, rather than cash, to acquire The Daily. The share price of the combined company is *closest* to:
    A. $145 per share.
    B. $150 per share.
    C. $155 per share.

83. The management of The Daily is not pleased with the $45 per share offering price. Which of the following is the *most likely* takeover defense The Daily would consider in an effort to stop the acquisition?
    A. Immediately amend The Daily bylaws to establish a staggered board.
    B. File suit against Voyager for antitrust violations.
    C. Restrict the voting rights of shareholders owning more than 10% of The Daily stock.

84. Which of the following *best* characterizes Voyager's proposal to merge with The Daily?
    A. Bear hug.
    B. Proxy fight.
    C. White knight.

Use the following information to answer Questions 85 through 90.

Gary Smith, CFA, has been hired to analyze a specialty tool and machinery manufacturer, Whitmore Corporation (WMC). WMC is a leading producer of specialty machinery in the United States. At the end of 2006, WMC purchased York Tool Company (YTC), an Australian firm in a similar line of business. YTC has partially integrated its marketing functions within WMC but still maintains control of its operations and secures its own financing. Following is a summary of the income statement and balance sheet for YTC (in millions of Australian dollars – AUD) for the past three years as well as exchange rate data over the same period.

Income Statement (AUD millions)	2006	2007	2008
Revenues	765	820	870
COGS	484	520	580
SG&A	171	183	200
Depreciation expense	50	50	50
Interest expense	18	17	16
Income before tax	42	50	24
Taxes	21	25	12
Net income	**21**	**25**	**12**

Balance Sheet (AUD millions)

	2006	2007	2008		2006	2007	2008
Cash	22	25	20	Current liabilities	616	593	584
Accounts receivable	400	422	460	Long-term debt	180	170	160
Inventories	20	25	30				
Prepaid expenses	8	20	25	Common stock	50	50	50
Net Fixed assets	500	450	400	Retained earnings	104	129	141
Total assets	950	942	935	Total liabilities & equity	950	942	935

Exchange rates (AUD / USD)	2006	2007	2008
Average exchange rate	1.40	1.30	1.45
Year-end exchange rate	1.20	1.40	1.50
Historical exchange rate	1.20	1.20	1.20

Smith has discovered that WMC has a small subsidiary in Ukraine. The subsidiary follows IAS accounting rules and uses FIFO inventory accounting. The Ukrainian subsidiary was acquired ten years ago and has been fully integrated into WMC's operations. WMC obtains funding for the subsidiary whenever the company finds profitable investments within Ukraine or surrounding countries. According to forecasts from economists, the Ukrainian currency is expected to depreciate relative to the U.S. dollar over the next few years. Local currency prices are forecasted to remain stable, however.

One of the managers at WMC asks Smith to analyze a third subsidiary located in India. The manager has explained that real interest rates in India over the past three years have been 2.00%, 2.50%, and 3.00%, respectively, while nominal interest rates have been 34.64%, 29.15%, and 25.66%, respectively. Smith requests more time to analyze the Indian subsidiary.

85. Calculate the percent change in YTC net income shown on the WMC financial statements from 2007 to 2008.
     A. −52.0%.
     B. −55.2%.
     C. −56.9%.

86. If WMC uses the temporal method, YTC's net monetary liabilities leave WMC exposed to loss in the event of:
     A. currency (AUD) depreciation.
     B. currency (AUD) appreciation.
     C. either currency depreciation or currency appreciation.

87. Determine whether the translated total asset turnover for YTC for 2008 would be higher under the current rate method or under the temporal method.
     A. Temporal method.
     B. Current rate method.
     C. No difference between temporal and current rate methods.

©2012 Kaplan, Inc.

88. Determine whether the translation method appropriate for consolidating the Ukrainian subsidiary's financial statements would allow WMC to recognize unrealized and realized gains in nonmonetary assets owned by the subsidiary.
    A. WMC would only be able to recognize realized gains.
    B. WMC would only be able to recognize unrealized gains.
    C. WMC would be able to recognize unrealized and realized gains.

89. Which of the following statements regarding the consolidation of WMC's Ukrainian subsidiary for the next year is *least likely* correct? Compared to the temporal method, the Ukrainian subsidiary's translated:
    A. net income before translation gains or losses would be higher using the current rate method.
    B. debt-to-equity ratio would be higher using the current rate method.
    C. gross profit margin would be lower using the current rate method.

90. Which of the following statements related to the consolidation of WMC's Indian subsidiary is *least likely* correct?
    A. The Indian economic environment meets the criteria to be classified as a hyperinflationary economy.
    B. IFRS would allow WMC to translate the inflation-indexed value of nonmonetary assets of the Indian subsidiary at the current exchange rate.
    C. WMC can reduce potential translation losses from the Indian subsidiary by issuing debt denominated in U.S. currency and purchasing fixed assets for the subsidiary.

Use the following information to answer Questions 91 through 96.

Zi Wang is a senior buy-side equity analyst with Shandong Securities. Wang must review the work of several junior colleagues before investment recommendations go to the Shandong portfolio managers. One recommendation from a junior analyst is given in Exhibit 1.

Exhibit 1

Summary of investment characteristics for Aussie Shipping Company	
Current dividend	AUD 2.20 (AUD is Australian dollar)
Dividend growth rate	5%, perpetual
Equity beta	1.20
Risk-free rate	5.2%
Equity risk premium	4.5%
Current stock price	AUD 33.50
Estimated intrinsic value	AUD 41.25
Investment recommendation	Buy

This same junior analyst e-mailed Wang, saying "I'm in a meeting and hate to bother you. I don't have my calculator or computer with me. We have a British stock with a current £4.00 dividend that is expected to grow at 40% per year for two years and then forever after at 6%. If we assume a required return of 12%, what is the value of this stock?"

In a few minutes, Wang e-mails him back: "The British stock is worth £110.42."

The junior analyst sends back a second e-mail. "Thanks. If we can buy this stock for £90, what rate of return would we get? Assume the same dividend pattern as in my first e-mail."

Wang replies to the second e-mail: "I used trial and error and found an expected rate of return for the British stock of 12%."

One of Shandong's portfolio managers asks Wang to clarify the PVGO (present value of growth opportunities) concept for him. Wang tells him, "PVGO is the part of a stock's total value that comes from future growth opportunities. PVGO is conventionally estimated as the market value per share minus the book value per share."

The Shandong portfolio manager quickly follows up with two more requests. He says, "I need a couple of favors. First, could you describe the sustainable growth rate concept for us? We've been arguing about it among ourselves. And, second, could you review some highlighted phrases from a research report we received from one of our investment bankers? We aren't sure that the analyst who wrote this report is very competent." The highlighted phrases are:

Phrase 1: When calculating the justified P/E ratios based on a constant growth model like the Gordon model, the forward P/E should be greater than the trailing P/E.

Phrase 2: A free cash flow approach might be preferable when the company's cash flows differ substantially from dividends or when the investor takes a control perspective.

Phrase 3: When the required rate of return increases, the value of a share of stock should decrease even if the stock's dividend has a negative growth rate.

91.   Upon review, should Wang accept the estimated intrinsic value and investment recommendation for Aussie Shipping?
    A. Yes.
    B. No. The intrinsic value is AUD 39.29, although the recommendation is still a "buy."
    C. No. The intrinsic value is AUD 31.67, and the recommendation should be "do not buy."

$$\frac{D \cdot (1+g)}{r - g}$$

92.   Is Wang's estimate of the British stock price correct?
    A. Yes.
    B. No. The value is £86.90.
    C. No. The value is £121.67.

93.   Is Wang's estimate of the expected rate of return for the British stock approximately correct?
    A. Yes.
    B. No. The rate of return is closer to 13%.
    C. No. The rate of return is closer to 14%.

94.   Is Wang's description of PVGO *most likely* correct?
    A. Yes.
    B. No. PVGO is the difference between the price and the value of assets in place. The value of assets in place is estimated by dividing dividends per share by the required rate of return.
    C. No. PVGO is the difference between the price and the value of assets in place. The value of assets in place is estimated by dividing earnings per share by the required rate of return.

95. How should Wang describe sustainable growth? "The sustainable growth rate is the rate of dividend and earnings growth that can be sustained for a given return on equity, assuming that:
    A. no additional external capital is raised."
    B. additional debt capital may be raised, keeping the capital structure constant."
    C. additional equity capital may be raised proportional to the amount of earnings retained."

96. Which of the three phrases in the investment banker's report is *least likely* to be correct?
    A. Phrase 1.
    B. Phrase 2.
    C. Phrase 3.

Use the following information to answer Questions 97 through 102.

Yummy Doughnuts (YD) sells a variety of doughnuts and other related items through both company-owned locations and franchise locations. YD has experienced significant growth over the past five years. However, barriers to entry are low and competition is increasing.

Linda Haas, CFA, follows YD for Gibraltar Capital. Gibraltar Capital prides itself on its thorough fundamental analysis of investment opportunities. The company uses a bottom-up approach to the investment process. Haas's security selection process utilizes residual income models to determine a stock's intrinsic value. Haas obtains YD's 2008 financial statements shown in Exhibit 1. In addition, Haas provides supporting information about YD's financials and other related material found in Exhibit 2.

Exhibit 1: Yummy Doughnuts's 2008 Income Statement and Balance Sheet

In millions, except for per share items	2008
Revenue	$300
Cost of goods sold	$205
SG&A	$40
Depreciation expense	$6
Income from operations	$49
Interest expense	$1
Pretax income	$48
Income tax (40% tax rate)	$19
Net income	$29
Shares outstanding	18.6
EPS	$1.56

In millions	2008		2008
Assets		**Liabilities and equity**	
Cash	$15	Accounts payable	$12
Accounts receivable	$27	Accrued expenses	$26
Inventory	$16	Current liabilities	$38
Current assets	$58		
Property and equipment	$113	Total long-term debt (7% coupon, at par value)	$12
Long-term investments	$10	Equity	$131
Total assets	**$181**	**Total liabilities & equity**	**$181**

Exhibit 2: Additional Information

- YD uses the FIFO method of inventory valuation.
- 2008 cash operating taxes equal $15 million. This amount includes all appropriate tax adjustments. 2008 NOPAT was estimated to be $42 million.
- Haas believes that YD will have a 17% ROE and a 10% long-term growth rate over the foreseeable future.
- Haas estimates YD's cost of equity to be 15.0%
- YD expects annual capital expenditures to remain at about $37 million.
- YD's stock currently trades at $15.50 per share.
- YD's bonds are currently trading at par value.
- YD's total adjusted capital base was $200 million at the end of 2007.

Haas makes the following statements during her YD presentation to the investment committee:

Statement 1:   Based on ROE mean reversion, YD's continuing residual income is assumed to decline to zero over time.

Statement 2:   The residual income model states that if YD's ROE equals its equity cost of capital, then YD's intrinsic value will equal its book value per share.

97.   For this question only, a careful evaluation of YD's financial statement reveals that the decrease in value of available-for-sale securities has been reported in the other comprehensive income (OCI) section of stockholder's equity. The *most likely* impact on the computation of residual income due to this would be:
   A. a reduction in residual income due to lower ROE.
   B. a reduction in residual income due to lower ROE and book value.
   ✓ C. an increase in residual income due to higher ROE.

98. Based on Exhibits 1 and 2, YD's weighted average cost of capital (WACC) is *closest* to:
    A. 12%.
    B. 13%.
    ✓C. 15%.

99. For this question only, assume a weighted average cost of capital (WACC) of 12.0%. YD's economic value added (EVA) during the year 2008 is *closest* to:
    A. $6 million.
    ✓B. $18 million.
    C. $24 million.

100. Based on Exhibit 1, Exhibit 2, and the single-stage residual income model, YD's intrinsic value is *closest* to:
    A. $8.00 per share.
    B. $10.00 per share. ✓
    C. $12.00 per share.

101. Haas notes that the multi-stage residual equity income model captures more detail in calculating YD's intrinsic value. An assumption of the model is that ROE fades to the cost of equity over time, which is known as a persistence factor (varying from 0 to 1). Identify which characteristic indicates a higher persistence of abnormal earnings.
    ✓A. Low dividend payout.
    B. Low price-to-earnings ratio.
    C. High dividend yield.

102. Haas makes a statement about an assumption concerning residual income (Statement 1) and the residual income model (Statement 2). Which of the statements is correct?
    A. Only Statement 1 is correct.
    B. Only Statement 2 is correct.
    ✓C. Both Statements 1 and 2 are correct.

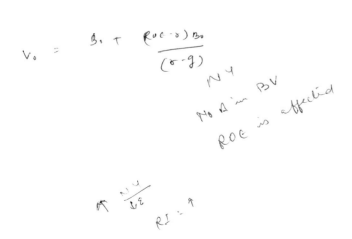

Use the following information to answer Questions 103 through 108.

Michael Thomas, CFA, is a fixed-income portfolio manager for TFC Investments. As part of his portfolio strategy for the Prosperity Fund, Thomas searches for companies that he expects to be upgraded or downgraded. Potential upgrades that he finds are added to the portfolio or, if already in the portfolio, are increased in proportion to other holdings. Potential downgrades are sold from the portfolio. Thomas's portfolio's current holdings include several bonds issued by companies in the oil and gas exploration and refining industries. Year-end rating updates are expected to occur in a few days, and Thomas is preparing to adjust his portfolio in advance of expected changes in credit ratings.

Thomas has been discussing his fixed-income strategies with fellow portfolio manager Shawna Reese. Reese suggests that while Thomas's general approach is suitable, the overall credit-analysis strategy could be improved. Reese makes the following statements to Thomas:

- Sometimes corporate credit ratings (CCRs) on different issues by the same issuer can vary significantly—especially for issuers with investment-grade corporate family ratings (CFRs).
- Your current methodology does not include special considerations related to high-yield debt. Because most high-yield issuers have a heavy dependence on short-term debt financing, analysis of the firm's debt structure is extremely important in order to determine the priority of claims on the firm's assets, as well as which source(s) of funds will be used to repay the principal. In addition, the corporate structure of high-yield issuers must be examined to determine the issuer's access to cash flows generated by its subsidiaries. A simple analysis of the parent's financial ratios will not reveal complicated corporate structures and indebtedness of subsidiaries that may restrict the issuer's ability to obtain the cash flows necessary to service its debt.
- Your current methodology does not include the specialized analysis necessary for municipal securities. Among other items, general obligation municipal bonds must be scrutinized as to the issuer's ability to maintain balanced budgets, as well as to ensure that the issue has first priority of claims to revenue from public works projects. Revenue municipal bonds require an assessment of the sufficiency of rates charged to cover expenses and debt servicing of the underlying project.

As part of his portfolio analysis, Thomas also examines yield volatility. Thomas makes the following statements:

Statement 1: Implied yield-volatility estimates are based on the assumptions that the option-pricing model is correct and that volatility is constant.

Statement 2: Yield volatility has been observed to follow patterns over time that can be modeled and used to forecast future volatility.

Thomas concludes his analysis by comparing the swap rate curve to a government bond yield curve.

103. Reese's statement about difference in CCRs is:
   A. correct.
   B. incorrect with regard to significant differences between issues of the same issuer.
   C. incorrect with regard to investment grade issuers.

104. The difference in CCRs between two bonds of the same issuer is *most likely* due to a difference in:
   A. restricted vs. non-restricted status of the issues.
   B. expected recovery rates.
   C. cross-default provisions.

105. In regard to Reese's statements about high-yield debt securities:
   A. Reese is correct only with regard to the issuer's debt structure.
   B. Reese is correct only with regard to the corporate structure of the issuer.
   C. Reese's entire statement about high-yield debt securities is correct.

106. Evaluate Reese's statements about municipal securities with respect to general obligation securities and revenue-backed securities.
   A. Reese is correct only with regard to general obligation securities.
   B. Reese is correct only with regard to revenue-backed securities.
   C. Reese is incorrect with regard to both general obligation and revenue-backed securities.

107. Which of Thomas's statements concerning yield volatility are accurate?
   A. Statement 1 only.
   B. Statement 2 only.
   C. Both statements are correct.

108. Which of the following statements regarding the choice between government bond yield curves and swap-rate curves as a benchmark interest rate curve is *most accurate*?
   A. The swap-rate curve is preferred because swap curves are comparable across countries since they reflect similar levels of credit risk.
   B. Government bond yield curves are preferred because they are based on a more complete set of market yields.
   C. Government bond yield curves are preferred because the lack of a liquid secondary market can distort swap yields compared with government bond yields.

Use the following information to answer Questions 109 through 114.

MediSoft Inc. develops and distributes high-tech medical software used in hospitals and clinics across the United States and Canada. The firm's software provides an integrated solution to monitoring, analyzing, and managing output from a variety of diagnostic medical equipment including MRIs, CT scans, and EKG machines. MediSoft has grown rapidly since its inception ten years ago, averaging 25% growth in sales over the past decade. The company went public three years ago. Twelve months after its IPO, MediSoft made two semiannual coupon bond offerings, the first of which was a convertible bond. At the time of issuance, the convertible bond had a coupon rate of 7.25%, a par value of $1,000, a conversion price of $55.56, and ten years until maturity. Two years after issuance, the bond became callable at 102% of par value. Soon after the issuance of the convertible bond, the company issued another series of bonds, which were putable but contained no conversion or call features. The putable bonds were issued with a coupon of 8.0%, a par value of $1,000, and 15 years until maturity. One year after their issuance, the put feature of the putable bonds became active, allowing the bonds to be put at a price of 95% of par value, and increasing linearly over five years to 100% of par value. MediSoft's convertible bonds are now trading in the market for a price of $947 with an estimated straight value of $917. The company's putable bonds are trading at a price of $1,052. Volatility in the price of MediSoft's common stock has been relatively high over the past few months. Currently, the stock is priced at $50 on the New York Stock Exchange and is expected to continue its annual dividend in the amount of $1.80 per share.

High-tech industry analysts for Brown & Associates, a money management firm specializing in fixed-income investments, have been closely following MediSoft ever since it went public three years ago. In general, portfolio managers at Brown & Associates do not participate in initial offerings of debt investments, preferring instead to see how the issue trades before considering taking a position in the issue. Because MediSoft's bonds have had ample time to trade in the marketplace, analysts and portfolio managers have taken an interest in the company's bonds. At a meeting to discuss the merits of MediSoft's bonds, the following comments were made by various portfolio managers and analysts at Brown & Associates:

"Choosing to invest in MediSoft's convertible bond would benefit our portfolios in many ways, but the primary benefit is the limited downside risk associated with the bond. Because the straight value will provide a floor for the value of the convertible bond, downside risk is limited to the difference between the market price of the bond and the straight value."

"Decreasing volatility in the price of MediSoft's common stock as well as increasing volatility in the level of interest rates are expected in the near future. The combined effects of these changes in volatility will be a decrease in the price of MediSoft's putable bonds and an increase in the price of the convertible bonds. Therefore, only the convertible bonds would be a suitable purchase."

109. Calculate the market conversion premium per share for MediSoft's convertible bonds.
    A. $2.61.
    B. $2.95.
    C. $5.56.

110. Assuming that portfolio managers at Brown & Associates purchased the convertible bonds, how many years would it take to recover the premium per share?
    A. 1.17.
    B. 1.32.
    C. 2.26.

111. Subsequent to purchasing one of the putable bonds for his portfolio, one of the managers at Brown & Associates realized that the bond contained a soft put. Which of the following securities cannot be used to redeem the bond in the event the bond becomes putable?
    A. Shares of MediSoft's common stock.
    B. Thirty-year Treasury notes with a coupon of 4.5%.
    C. MediSoft's 9.0% subordinated notes with a maturity of 10 years.

112. Under what circumstances will the analyst's comments regarding the limited downside risk of MediSoft's convertible bonds be accurate?
    A. Short-term and long-term interest rates are expected to remain equivalent.
    B. The Federal Reserve Bank decides to pursue a restrictive monetary policy.
    C. The convertible bond is trading in the market as a common stock equivalent.

113. Assuming the common stock of MediSoft underwent a one-for-two reverse split, how would the features of the company's bonds be adjusted? The:
    A. conversion ratio of the convertible bond would be reduced by 50%.
    B. market conversion price of the convertible bond would be doubled.
    C. conversion value of the convertible bond would be reduced by half.

114. Evaluate the portfolio managers' comments regarding the changes in the values of MediSoft's bonds resulting from changes in the volatility of the company's common stock and the volatility of interest rates. The managers were:
    A. correct only with regard to the convertible bonds.
    B. correct only with regard to the putable bonds.
    C. incorrect with regard to both securities.

Use the following information to answer Questions 115 through 120.

James Walker is the chief financial officer for Lothar Corporation, a U.S. mining company that specializes in worldwide exploration for and excavation of precious metals. Lothar Corporation generally tries to maintain a debt-to-capital ratio of approximately 45% and has successfully done so for the past seven years. Due to the time lag between the discovery of an extractable vein of metal and the eventual sale of the excavated material, the company frequently must issue short-term debt to fund its operations. Issuing these one- to six-month notes sometimes pushes Lothar's debt-to-capital ratio above its long-term target, but the cash provided from the short-term financing is necessary to complete the majority of the company's mining projects.

Walker has estimated that extraction of silver deposits in southern Australia has eight months until project completion. However, funding for the project will run out in approximately six months. In order to cover the funding gap, Walker will have to issue short-term notes with a principal value of $1,275,000 at an unknown future interest rate. To mitigate the interest rate uncertainty, Walker has decided to enter into a forward rate agreement (FRA) based on LIBOR which currently has a term structure as shown in Exhibit 1.

Exhibit 1

LIBOR Rates (t = 0)	
	LIBOR
90-day	4.28%
180-day	4.52%
240-day	5.11%
360-day	5.92%

Exhibit 2

LIBOR Rates (t = 90)	
	LIBOR
90-day	5.12%
150-day	5.96%
210-day	6.03%
300-day	6.41%

Three months after establishing the position in the forward rate agreement, LIBOR interest rates have shifted, causing the value of Lothar's FRA position to change as well. The new LIBOR term structure is shown in Exhibit 2.

While Walker is estimating the change in the value of the original FRA position, he receives a memo from the chief operating officer of Lothar, Maria Steiner, informing him of a major delay in one of the company's South African mining projects. In the memo, Steiner states the following:

"As usual, the project delay will require a short-term loan to cover the funding shortage that will accompany the extra time until project completion. I have estimated that in 210 days, we will require a 90-day project loan in the amount of $2,350,000. I would like you to establish another FRA position, this time with a contract rate of 6.95%."

115. Given data in Exhibit 1, which of the following was *closest* to the price of the FRA on the date of the contract's inception?
    A. 4.7%.
    ✓B. 6.8%.
    C. 7.2%.

116. Which of the following is *closest* to the value of the forward rate agreement three months after the inception of the contract (from Walker's perspective)? For this question only, assume that the interest rate at inception was 6.0%.
    ✓A. $2,340.
    B. −$3,266.
    C. $3,266.

117. Which of the following statements regarding the credit risk associated with Walker's original FRA contract three months after the inception of the contract is *least* accurate?
    A. Credit risk to all parties could be reduced to zero by marking the FRA to market.
    ✓B. The clearinghouse will have the greatest exposure to credit risk.
    C. Credit risk to the long position will be greater than the credit risk to the short position.

118. When the silver is removed from the mine, it will be sold to an Australian subsidiary before being exported. Walker is concerned that the price of silver and the Australian dollar will both depreciate over the next eight months. Which of the following strategies will be *most* appropriate given Walker's expectations? Establish a:
    A. short position in a silver forward contract and a short position in a U.S. dollar currency forward contract.
    B. long position in a silver forward contract and a short position in an Australian dollar currency forward contract.
    ✓C. short position in a silver forward contract and a long position in a U.S. dollar currency forward contract.

119. Which of the following is *least likely* a reason Walker has chosen to use forward contracts instead of futures contracts?
    A. Greater ability to create offsetting positions.
    B. Less scrutiny by regulatory agencies.
    C. Flexibility of contract length and level of notional principal.

120. Which of the following transactions should Walker initiate in order to comply with Steiner's request regarding the funding shortage at the South African gold mine? Establish a:
    A. long position in an off-market FRA by making a payment to the short position.
    B. short position in an off-market FRA by receiving a payment from the long position.
    C. long position in an off-market FRA by receiving a payment from the short position.

End of Afternoon Session

Exam 2
Morning Session

Question	Topic	Minutes (Points)	
1 to 6	Ethical and Professional Standards	18	
7 to 12	Economics	18	15
13 to 24	Financial Reporting and Analysis	36	23,24
25 to 42	Asset Valuation – Equity	54	
43 to 48	Asset Valuation – Fixed Income	18	44
49 to 54	Asset Valuation – Derivatives	18	50
55 to 60	Portfolio Management	18	57

Test Answers

1.	(A)	(B)	(C)		41.	(A)	(B)	(C)
2.	(A)	(B)	(C)		42.	(A)	(B)	(C)
3.	(A)	(B)	(C)		43.	(A)	(B)	(C)
4.	(A)	(B)	(C)		44.	(A)	(B)	(C)
5.	(A)	(B)	(C)		45.	(A)	(B)	(C)
6.	(A)	(B)	(C)		46.	(A)	(B)	(C)
7.	(A)	(B)	(C)		47.	(A)	(B)	(C)
8.	(A)	(B)	(C)		48.	(A)	(B)	(C)
9.	(A)	(B)	(C)		49.	(A)	(B)	(C)
10.	(A)	(B)	(C)		50.	(A)	(B)	(C)
11.	(A)	(B)	(C)		51.	(A)	(B)	(C)
12.	(A)	(B)	(C)		52.	(A)	(B)	(C)
13.	(A)	(B)	(C)		53.	(A)	(B)	(C)
14.	(A)	(B)	(C)		54.	(A)	(B)	(C)
15.	(A)	(B)	(C)		55.	(A)	(B)	(C)
16.	(A)	(B)	(C)		56.	(A)	(B)	(C)
17.	(A)	(B)	(C)		57.	(A)	(B)	(C)
18.	(A)	(B)	(C)		58.	(A)	(B)	(C)
19.	(A)	(B)	(C)		59.	(A)	(B)	(C)
20.	(A)	(B)	(C)		60.	(A)	(B)	(C)
21.	(A)	(B)	(C)					
22.	(A)	(B)	(C)					
23.	(A)	(B)	(C)					
24.	(A)	(B)	(C)					
25.	(A)	(B)	(C)					
26.	(A)	(B)	(C)					
27.	(A)	(B)	(C)					
28.	(A)	(B)	(C)					
29.	(A)	(B)	(C)					
30.	(A)	(B)	(C)					
31.	(A)	(B)	(C)					
32.	(A)	(B)	(C)					
33.	(A)	(B)	(C)					
34.	(A)	(B)	(C)					
35.	(A)	(B)	(C)					
36.	(A)	(B)	(C)					
37.	(A)	(B)	(C)					
38.	(A)	(B)	(C)					
39.	(A)	(B)	(C)					
40.	(A)	(B)	(C)					

Exam 2
Morning Session

Use the following information to answer Questions 1 through 6.

Charles Connor, CFA, is a portfolio manager at Apple Investments, LLC. Apple is a U.S.-based firm offering a wide spectrum of investment products and services. Connor manages the Biogene Fund, a domestic equity fund specializing in small capitalization growth stocks. The Biogene Fund generally takes significant positions in stocks, commonly owning 4.5–5% of the outstanding shares. The fund's prospectus limits positions to a maximum of 5% of the shares outstanding. The performance of the Biogene Fund has been superior over the last few years, but for the last two quarters the fund has underperformed its benchmark by a wide margin. Connor is determined to improve his performance numbers going forward.

The Biogene prospectus allows Connor to use derivative instruments in his investment strategy. Connor frequently uses options to hedge his fund's exposure as he builds or liquidates positions in his portfolio since Biogene's large positions often take several weeks to acquire. For example, when he identifies a stock to buy, he often buys call options to gain exposure to the stock. As he buys the stock, he sells off the options or allows them to expire. Connor has noticed that the increased volume in the call options often drives the stock price higher for a few days. He has seen a similar negative effect on stock prices when he buys large amounts of put options.

The end of the quarter is just a few days away, and Connor is considering three transactions:

Transaction A: Buying Put Options on Stock A

The Biogene Fund owns 4.9% of the outstanding stock of Company A, but Connor believes the stock is fully valued and plans to sell the entire position. He anticipates that it will take approximately 45 trading days to liquidate the entire Biogene position in Stock A.

Transaction B: Buying Call Options on Stock B

The Biogene Fund owns 5% of the outstanding stock of Company B. Connor believes there is significant appreciation potential for Stock B, but the stock price has dropped in recent weeks. Connor is hoping that by taking an option position, there will be a carryover effect on the stock price before quarter end.

Transaction C: Selling the Biogene Fund's Entire Position in Stock C

Connor believes that Stock C is still attractive, but he is selling the stock with the idea that he will repurchase the position next month. The motivation for the transaction is to capture a capital loss that will reduce the Biogene Fund's tax expense for the year.

Apple has an investment banking department that is active in initial public offerings (IPOs). George Arnold, CFA, is the senior manager of the IPO department. Arnold approached Connor about Stock D, a new IPO being offered by Apple. Stock D will open trading in two days. Apple had offered the IPO to all of its clients, but approximately 20% of the deal remained unsold. Having read the prospectus, Connor thinks Stock D would be a good fit for his fund, and he expects Stock D to improve his performance in both the short and long term. Connor is not aware of any information related to Stock D beyond that provided in the prospectus. Connor asked to purchase 5% of the IPO, but Arnold limited Biogene's share to 2%, explaining:

> "With Biogene's reputation, any participation will make the unsold shares highly marketable. Further, we may need Biogene to acquire more Stock D shares at a later date if the price does not hold up."

Connor is disappointed in being limited to 2% of the offering and suggests to Arnold in an e-mail that, given the 2% limitation, Biogene will not participate in the IPO. Arnold responded a few hours later with the following message:

> "I have just spoken with Ms. D, the CFO of Stock D. Although it is too late to alter the prospectus, management believes they will receive a large contract from a foreign government that will boost next year's sales by 20% or more. I urge you to accept the 2%—you won't be sorry!"

After reviewing Arnold's e-mail, Connor agrees to the 2% offer.

1. By executing Transaction A, Connor is:
    A. violating the Standards because his option trading can be reasonably expected to affect the price of Stock A.
    B. violating the Standards because the option position creates a profit opportunity in conflict with Biogene's clients.
    C. not violating the Standards.

2. By executing Transaction B, Connor is:
    A. violating the Standards because his option trading can be reasonably expected to affect his quarterly performance.
    B. not violating the Standards because the option position creates a profit opportunity consistent with Biogene's clients' interests.
    C. not violating the Standards because he believes there is significant appreciation potential in Stock B.

3. By executing Transaction C, Connor is:
   A. violating the Standards by executing a transaction for tax reasons only.
   B. violating the Standards by executing a transaction that provides tax benefits to the Biogene Fund.
   C. not violating the Standards.

4. By offering Biogene the opportunity to participate in the IPO of Stock D, Apple Investments has violated CFA Institute Standards relating to:
   A. priority of transactions but not independence and objectivity.
   B. independence and objectivity but not priority of transactions.
   C. neither priority of transactions nor independence and objectivity.

5. Arnold's arguments for limiting Biogene's share to 2% suggest that Apple:
   A. may engage in a liquidity pumping strategy that would be acceptable given that Biogene is a related entity.
   B. may engage in transaction-based manipulation of Stock D in the future, in violation of Standards relating to market manipulation.
   C. is violating Standards related to priority of transactions by offering the IPO to Biogene before it is fully subscribed.

6. Based upon Connor's acceptance of the 2% limitation after receiving the e-mail from Arnold:
   A. Connor has violated Standards relating to material nonpublic information, and Arnold has violated Standards relating to preservation of confidentiality.
   B. Connor has not violated Standards relating to material nonpublic information, but Arnold has violated Standards relating to preservation of confidentiality.
   C. Connor has not violated Standards relating to material nonpublic information, but Arnold has violated Standards relating to preservation of confidentiality and material nonpublic information.

Use the following information to answer Questions 7 through 12.

Alfred Farias, fixed income analyst for BNF, Inc., is analyzing the economic prospects of Procken, Krosse, Weira, and Toban, four countries in the same region. He collects the following economic and demographic statistics for the countries:

	Procken	Krosse	Weira	Toban
Current real GDP (in $ billions)	$250.0	$250.0	$4,500.00	$4,800.00
Projected real GDP in 5 years (in $ billions) based on potential GDP growth rate	$306.0	$315.0	$5,262.00	$5,778.00
Long-term growth rate of capital	4.0%	4.2%	3.2%	3.8%
Current capital base ($billions)	$782.9	$699.2	$18,750	$19,750
Imports (in $ billions)	$30.00	$60.00	$1,500.00	$900.00
Exports (in $ billions)	$32.00	$80.00	$1,000.00	$900.00
Population (in millions)	20.4	20.0	101.0	100.0
Labor growth rate	1.9%	2.9%	0.4%	0.8%
Cost of capital relative to total factor cost	32.5%	35.0%	25.0%	22.5%
Average real annual appreciation in equities (past five year)	4.0%	4.7%	4.5%	3.8%

A GDP per capita below $25,000 is considered a developing country, and a GDP per capita greater than $25,000 is considered a developed country.

Farias concludes that Weira and Toban have reached steady-state growth.

In the latest round of trade negotiations, representatives from each country discussed their efforts to foster their countries' economic development and benefit from the growth of world trade.

Procken's Representative: "We are wary of the potential for loss of domestic industries if we remove trade barriers. Given the state of our economy, I'm not certain that we can lower our trade barriers any further."

Krosse's Representative: "We in Krosse are not investing enough in infrastructure and education to increase the level of productivity and technology in our economy. We also need foreign direct investment and hence we welcome foreign investors."

Weira's Representative: "We are concerned about my country's negative trade balance. Weira needs more exports to sustain our growth."

Toban's Representative: "We seem to be at a point in Toban where the growth rate of my country's labor force may be insufficient to support our GDP growth rate."

7. Which country is *most likely* to benefit from capital deepening?
   A. Weira.
   B. Krosse.
   C. Procken.

8. For this question only, assume that the population growth rate is the same for Krosse and Procke. A possible cause for the difference in growth rate of labor is that relative to Procken, Krosse has:
   A. stricter immigration policies.
   B. a lower labor participation rate.
   C. experienced an increase in average hours worked.

9. The long-term growth rate of technology (TFP) for Toban is *closest* to:
   A. 0.4%.
   B. 2.1%.
   C. 2.3%.

10. Going forward, which country is *most likely* to experience lower stock market appreciation than that experienced over the past five years?
    A. Weira.
    B. Toban.
    C. Procken.

11. The rental price of capital in Weira is *closest* to:
    A. 4.1%.
    B. 6%.
    C. 25%.

12. Based on the information provided, which developing country is *most likely* to achieve convergence in growth rates and standard of living with their developed counterparts?
    A. Toban.
    B. Krosse.
    C. Procken.

Use the following information to answer Questions 13 through 18.

William Jones, CFA, is analyzing the financial performance of two U.S. competitors in connection with a potential investment recommendation of their common stocks. He is particularly concerned about the quality of each company's financial results in 2007–2008 and in developing projections for 2009 and 2010 fiscal years.

Adams Company has been the largest company in the industry, but Jefferson Inc. has grown more rapidly in recent years. Adams's net sales in 2004 were 33-1/3% higher than Jefferson's but were only 18% above Jefferson's in 2008. During 2008, a slowing U.S. economy led to lower domestic revenue growth for both companies. The 10-k reports showed overall sales growth of 6% for Adams in 2008 compared to 7% for 2007 and 9% in 2006. Jefferson's gross sales rose almost 12% in 2008 versus 8% in 2007 and 10% in 2006. In the past three years, Jefferson has expanded its foreign business at a faster pace than Adams. In 2008, Jefferson's growth in overseas business was particularly impressive. According to the company's 10-k report, Jefferson offered a sales incentive to overseas customers. For those customers accepting the special sales discount, Jefferson shipped products to specific warehouses in foreign ports rather than directly to those customers' facilities.

In his initial review of Adams's and Jefferson's financial statements, Jones was concerned about the quality of the growth in Jefferson's sales, considerably higher accounts receivables, and the impact of overall accruals on earnings quality. He noted that Jefferson had instituted an accounting change in 2008. The economic life for new plant and equipment investments was determined to be five years longer than for previous investments. For Adams, he noted that the higher level of inventories at the end of 2008 might be cause for concern in light of a further slowdown expected in the U.S. economy in 2009.

The accompanying table shows financial data for both companies' Form 10-k reports for 2006–2008 used by Jones for his analysis. To evaluate sales quality, he focused on trends in sales and related expenses for both companies as well as cash collections and receivables comparisons. Inventory trends relative to sales and the number of days' sales outstanding in inventory were determined for both companies. Expense trends were examined for Adams and Jefferson relative to sales growth and accrual ratios on a balance sheet and cash flow basis were developed as overall measures of earnings quality.

©2012 Kaplan, Inc.

($ in thousands)	Adams Company				Jefferson Inc.		
	2006	2007	2008		2006	2007	2008
Gross sales	32,031	34,273	36,330		25,625	27,675	30,900
Sales discounts, returns, and allowances	781	836	886		625	675	900
Net sales	31,250	33,438	35,444		25,000	27,000	30,000
Cost of goods sold —	15,312	16,384	17,367		12,250	13,250	15,500
SG&A expenses	9,028	9,660	10,240		7,222	7,800	8,200
Depreciation expense	625	669	709		500	515	516
Interest expense	400	428	454		360	366	396
Income before taxes	5,835	6,243	6,618		4,668	5,069	5,388
Taxes (tax rate 40%)	2,334	2,497	2,647		2,000	2,028	2,155
Net income	3,501	3,746	3,971		2,668	3,041	3,233
Dividends	3,000	3,180	3,307		2,460	2,760	2,880
Net addition to retained earnings	501	566	664		208	281	353
Balance Sheet							
Cash and equivalents	150	160	170		120	130	120
Short-term marketable securities	250	325	345		200	217	195
Accounts receivable (net)	15,875	16,758	17,763		12,700	13,000	15,892
Inventories —	6,500	6,850	7,800		5,200	5,200	4,500
PP&E (net of depreciation)	8,562	8,991	9,440		6,850	7,057	7,200
Total assets	31,337	33,084	35,518		25,070	25,604	27,907
Accounts payable	7,062	7,880	9,300		6,050	6,100	6,398
Other current liabilities	337	400	450		270	373	1,525
Long-term debt	7,500	7,800	8,100		6,000	6,100	6,600
Common stock	15,000	15,000	15,000		12,000	12,000	12,000
Retained earnings	1,438	2,004	2,668		750	1,031	1,384
Total liabilities and shareholders equity	31,337	33,084	35,518		25,070	25,604	27,907
% change gross sales		7.0%	6.0%			8.0%	11.7%
% change sales discounts and allowances		6.0%	6.0%			8.0%	33.3%
% change net sales		7.0%	6.0%			8.0%	11.1%
% change cost of goods sold —		7.0%	6.0%			8.0%	17.0%
% change in SG&A		6.0%	6.0%			8.0%	5.1%
% change in depreciation expense		6.0%	6.0%			3.0%	0.2%
% change in accounts receivable		6.0%	6.0%			2.0%	22.3%
% change in inventories		5.0%	13.8%			0.0%	(13.5%)
Revenues % cash collections	1.03	1.03	1.03		1.0	1.0	1.11
Days inventory outstanding	155	153	164		144	143	106
Balance sheet accrual ratio	3.4%	3.5%	3.9%		2.0%	2.4%	10.1%
Cash flow accrual ratio	3.4%	3.5%	3.8%		2.0%	2.0%	4.3%

13. Jones observed that comparisons of 2007–2008 trends in sales, accounts receivables, and cash collections showed:

A. Jefferson's higher increase in sales relative to Adams's led to improvement in cash collections indicated by the rise in the revenue/collections ratio. There was no change in Adams's cash collections in 2008.

B. Jefferson's sales growth accelerated in 2008 compared to Adams's, but cash collections declined as indicated by the rise in receivables and the revenue/collections ratio; Adams's sales, accounts receivables, and cash collections rose at similar rates in 2008. ✓

C. Jefferson's decline in cash and equivalents in 2008 resulted in lower cash collections despite strong sales growth; Adams's showed similar growth in cash and equivalents and accounts receivable relative to sales gains.

14. Jones also observed that inventory and cost of goods sold comparisons showed:

A. Jefferson's inventory increase and large increase in cost of goods sold may be related to the success of the special offer; Adams's large increase in inventories suggests possible inventory obsolescence.

B. Jefferson's inventory decline suggests possible problems in inventory management to meet the stronger customer demand from the special offer; Adams's large inventory increase suggests better inventory management to meet future sales growth.

C. Jefferson's inventory levels may be understated and sales overstated to the extent of product shipments for the special offer; Adams's inventory increase may reflect slowing product demand and possible inventory obsolescence. ✓

15. Comparisons of expense trends in 2007–2008 showed:

A. higher growth of Adams's SG&A and depreciation expense versus Jefferson's; the small change in Jefferson's depreciation may relate to the change in depreciation lives, while the slower SG&A growth may reflect expense controls imposed to offset lower gross profit margins. ✓

B. Jefferson's management appeared to have managed SG&A and depreciation expenses more effectively than Adams's; there was a small increase in Jefferson's depreciation expense and slower growth in SG&A relative to the company's previous year and compared to Adams's trends.

C. higher growth of Adams's SG&A and depreciation expense versus Jefferson's may indicate more effective expense control by Jefferson in a slowing domestic economy.

16. The quality of earnings as measured by balance-sheet-based accruals ratios showed:

  strong improvement in Jefferson's earnings quality relative to Adams's due to the sharp jump in the ratio in 2008 compared to the much smaller increase for Adams.

 decrease in Jefferson's earnings quality relative to Adams's due to the sharp jump in the ratio in 2008 compared to a much smaller increase for Adams. ✓

 both companies' earnings quality improved due to the increase in the ratio with Jefferson showing the most improvement.

17. The quality of earnings as measured by cash-flow-based accruals ratios showed:

 Jefferson's higher accruals ratio in 2008 compared to 2007 and relative to Adams's in 2008 indicates Jefferson's higher earnings quality.

 Jefferson's 2008 accrual ratio exceeded Adams's ratio for the first time in the 2006–2008 period, thus demonstrating significant improvement in earnings quality relative to Adams's.

Jefferson's 2008 accrual ratio exceeded Adams's ratio for the first time in the 2006–2008 period, indicating a decline in earnings quality compared to previous years and lower earnings quality relative to Adams's in 2008. ✓

18. Based on the financial results of Adams and Jefferson in 2007 and 2008, the company demonstrating the lower earnings quality would be:

Adams due to lower cash collection measures, possible inventory obsolescence related to higher 2008 inventories despite slowing customer demand, higher expense growth compared to Jefferson, and lower balance sheet and cash flow accrual ratios relative to Jefferson.

 Jefferson due to sharply higher accruals ratios and less conservative accounting methods indicated by the change in depreciation policies and the impact of changes in shipment terms on revenue recognition and inventories for the special overseas offer. ✓

Adams due to slower revenue growth, higher expense growth compared to Jefferson, possible inventory obsolescence related to higher 2008 inventories despite slowing customer demand, and lower balance sheet and cash flow based accrual ratios in 2008 compared to Jefferson.

Use the following information to answer Questions 19 through 24.

In 2001, Continental Supply Company was formed to provide drilling equipment and supplies to contractors and oilfield production companies located throughout the United States. At the end of 2005, Continental Supply created a wholly owned foreign subsidiary, International Oilfield Incorporated, to begin servicing customers located in the North Sea. International Oilfield maintains its financial statements in a currency known as the local currency unit (LCU). Continental Supply follows U.S. GAAP and its presentation currency is the U.S. dollar.

For the years 2005 through 2008, the weighted-average and year-end exchange rates, stated in terms of local currency per U.S. dollar, were as follows:

LCU/$US	2005	2006	2007	2008
Average	0.90	1.05	1.05	1.25
Year-end	1.00	1.10	1.00	1.50

International Oilfield accounts for its inventory using the lower-of-cost-or-market valuation method in conjunction with the first-in, first-out, cost flow assumption. All of the inventory on hand at the beginning of the year was sold during 2008. Inventory remaining at the end of 2008 was acquired evenly throughout the year.

At the beginning of 2006, International Oilfield purchased equipment totaling LCU 975 million when the exchange rate was LCU 1.00 to $1. During 2007, equipment with an original cost of LCU 108 million was totally destroyed in a fire. At the end of 2007, International Oilfield received a LCU 92 million insurance settlement for the loss. On June 30, 2008, International Oilfield purchased equipment totaling LCU 225 million when the exchange rate was LCU 1.25 to $1.

For the years 2007 and 2008, Continental Supply reported International Oilfield revenues in its consolidated income statement of $375 million and $450 million, respectively. There were no inter-company transactions. Following are International Oilfield's balance sheets at the end of 2007 and 2008:

LCU in millions	2008	2007
Cash and receivables	120.0	216.0
Inventory	631.3	650.4
Equipment	820.7	693.6
Liabilities (all monetary)	600.0	600.0
Capital stock	350.0	350.0
Retained earnings	622.0	610.0

©2012 Kaplan, Inc.

At the end of 2008, International Oilfield's retained earnings account was equal to $525 million and, to date, no dividends have been paid. All of International Oilfield's capital stock was issued at the end of 2005.

19. Assuming International Oilfield is a significantly integrated sales division and virtually all operating, investing, and financing decisions are made by Continental Supply, foreign currency gains and losses that arise from the consolidation of International Oilfield should be reported in:

A. shareholders' equity.
B. operating cash flow.
C. net income. ✔

20. Assuming that International Oilfield's equipment is depreciated using the straight-line method over ten years with no salvage value, calculate the subsidiary's 2008 depreciation expense under the temporal method.
A. $78.4 million.
B. $95.7 million. ✔
C. $104.7 million.

21. Compute the cumulative translation adjustment reported on Continental Supply's consolidated balance sheet at the end of 2008, assuming International Oilfield is a relatively self-contained and independent operation of Continental Supply.
A. –$227 million. ✔
B. –$200 million.
C. $298 million.

22. Compared to the temporal method, which of the following *best* describes the impact of the current rate method on International Oilfield's gross profit margin percentage for 2008 when stated in U.S. dollars? The gross profit margin would be:
A. lower.
B. higher. ✔
C. the same. ✏

23. When remeasuring International Oilfield's 2008 financial statements into the presentation currency, which of the following ratios is NOT affected by changing exchange rates under the temporal method?
A. Current ratio.
B. Total asset turnover.
C. Quick ratio. ✔

TM   CR

24. Assume the country where International Oilfield is operating has been experiencing 30% annual inflation over the past three years. Which of the following *best* describes the effect on Continental's consolidated financial statements for the year ended 2008?

    A. A gain is recognized in the income statement. ✓
    B. A loss is recognized in the income statement. ✗
    C. A gain is recognized as a direct adjustment to the balance sheet.

Use the following information to answer Questions 25 through 30.

Sampson Aerospace is a publicly traded U.S. manufacturer. Sampson supplies communication and navigation control systems to manufacturers of airplanes for commercial and government use. The company operates two divisions: (1) Commercial Operations, and (2) Government Operations. Revenues from the Government Operations division comprise 80% of Sampson's total company revenues. Revenues for other companies in the industry are also driven primarily by sales to the U.S. government.

Sampson has gained a reputation for offering unique products and services. Sampson's market share has been increasing, and its net profit margin is among the highest in its industry.

As part of its business strategy, Sampson seeks out opportunities to enhance internal growth by acquiring smaller companies that possess new technologies that would allow Sampson to offer unique products and services. To this end, Drew Smith, CEO, recently asked his acquisitions team to consider the purchase of a controlling interest in either NavTech or Aerospace Communications, both software applications firms. Smith provides his acquisitions team with an aerospace analyst's industry report that addresses many key issues within the industry. Selected passages from the report are reproduced below:

> Sales in the aerospace electronics industry depend primarily on government military spending, which, in turn, depends on defense budgets. Sales depend on commercial travel to a much lesser extent. The government defense spending budget outlook is fairly bleak as the current administration is looking for ways to reduce the budget deficit. We feel the commercial airline segment has more upside than downside, especially as the global economy improves, so we might see a gradual shift in industry focus toward the commercial airline sector. Companies that already have a foothold in the commercial sector are well positioned to grow during the global recovery. Even so, companies in this industry will remain highly sensitive to government spending for their revenues. Research and development costs are high and the industry is highly capital intense. While there are only a few companies in this industry, good opportunities exist, especially for companies that have developed sustainable profits through wise acquisitions, cost containment, and the ability to secure long-term government contracts.

> Sampson Aerospace recently announced that it is reducing its investment return assumption on its pension assets from 6% to 5%, and that it has entered negotiations to possibly acquire controlling equity interests in communications software firms, NavTech and Aerospace Communications. NavTech recently has decided to capitalize a significant portion of its research and development expense, and Aerospace Communications has restructured and reclassified many of its leases from operating to financial

leases. Sampson CEO Drew Smith recently announced that Sampson had dropped out of negotiations with Knowledge Technologies, claiming it was likely not a sustainable business model.

Consensus forecasts for NavTech and Aerospace Communications are presented in Exhibit 1.

Exhibit 1: Selected Financial Data for NavTech and Aerospace Communications

	NavTech	Aerospace Comm.
Expected year-end dividend per share	$1.07	$0.55
Expected year-end free cash flow to equity per share	$0.80	$1.25
Weighted average cost of capital	10%	9%
Required return on equity	12%	12%
Current stock price	$21.40	$25

25. Which of the following is *most likely* a negative factor in assessing the profitability of Sampson over the medium to long term?
    A. Bargaining power of suppliers.
    B. Bargaining power of customers. ✓
    C. New entrants to the industry.

26. It would be *most* appropriate to characterize Sampson's generic strategy for achieving superior performance as:
    A. focus. ✗
    B. differentiation. ✓
    C. cost leadership.

27. The *most* appropriate approach for Sampson Aerospace's valuation of NavTech and Aerospace Communications is the:
    A. dividend discount model.
    B. free cash flow model. ✓
    C. relative value model.

28. Regarding the financial statement information provided in the analyst's report, the quality of financial statements has improved *least* for:
    A. Sampson.
    B. NavTech. ✓
    C. Aerospace Communications.

29. By claiming that Knowledge Technologies is "not a sustainable business model," Sampson CEO Drew Smith would *most likely* estimate Knowledge Technologies's value using:
   A. balance sheet value.
   B. going concern value.
   C. liquidation value. ✓

30. Assuring that NavTech is valued according to the constant growth dividend model, the market expectation of dividend growth implied by NavTech's current stock price is *closest* to:
   A. 5%.
   B. 7%. ✓
   C. 9%.

Use the following information to answer Questions 31 through 36.

Richard Grass, the healthcare analyst for Furmon Investments, is reviewing the investment merits of the developing hospice industry. The hospice industry has a short history in the public market; however, several companies in the sector have recently completed initial public offerings. Hospice services offer symptom and pain management to patients diagnosed with terminal illnesses as an alternative to aggressive medical management. The use of hospice services at skilled nursing facilities and assisted-living facilities is forecasted to continue its recent growth. The program was added to the Medicare benefit package in the early 1980s, and Medicare is the primary source of funding for hospice services, accounting for 85% of the approximately $7 billion in industry revenues. Any state-certified hospice facility can participate in the Medicare program. Growth in the sector has only recently accelerated due to the emergence of a number of for-profit companies. The caregiver provides a plan for each admitted patient, and care is given in any number of healthcare environments, including the patient's home.

Grass's analysis of the hospice industry has uncovered several facts:

- The annual growth rate in industry's revenue rate has increased from 14% in the late 1990s to 25% in 2013.
- The average length of stay at facilities for hospice patients is increasing.
- Labor costs account for 75% of total expenses, drugs for 15% of total expenses, and medical supplies for 10%.
- More than 80% of hospice patients are above 65 years old and 30% are above 85 years old.
- Based on the U.S. Census Bureau's statistics, over the next six years (2014–2020), the number of people in the 65 and older age group will increase annually by 1.4%.
- The Medicare hospice benefit is still underutilized by the terminally ill population, according to MedPac (an independent advisory committee for the U.S. Congress on healthcare issues).
- Only 30% of Medicare beneficiaries enroll in the hospice benefit before they die.
- In recent years, the U.S. government has approved rate increases for the sector compared to flat or declining rate trends for other healthcare services.
- The Medicare hospice program has a beneficiary cap, which cannot exceed approximately $18,000 per person annually.
- The top six for-profit providers account for about half of the segment's sales.
- The overall hospice provider market is roughly divided into 55% non-profit, 10% U.S. government, and 35% for-profit.
- New patient monitoring systems are expected to reduce labor cost by 8%.

Grass is evaluating Hope Care, Inc., ("Hope"), a small privately held chain of hospice care facilities in the Southwest. Hope is almost entirely equity financed and is profitable. Grass is evaluating a potential acquisition of Hope in a leveraged buyout. He makes several adjustments to Hope's financial statements as detailed below:

Adjustment 1: Hope's owner/CEO received a compensation package of $1.2 million including bonus. This is consistent with compensation packages at other firms. Grass considers the current management team to be very competent and does not anticipate any major changes; however, he increases the compensation estimate to $1.5 million.

Adjustment 2: Hope has long-term leases on all of its facilities. The lease rates were negotiated before the real estate market collapsed recently. Grass adjusts the leasing cost downward by $3 million.

Adjustment 3: Hope has purchased fractional ownership in a corporate jet for the CEO. The benefit with an annual cost of $350,000 is deemed to be excessive by market standards and Grass adjusts the cost estimates by that amount.

Exhibit 1 shows projections of selected financial data for Hope for the next year.

Exhibit 1: Selected Financial Information (Estimates) for Hope Care, Inc.

Item	$ Millions
Normalized EBITDA	32
Depreciation	11
SG&A expense	8
Net income	15
Capital expenditure	6
Working capital expense	5
Interest expense	2

Note: Hope's tax rate is expected to be 25%.

31.   The cost structure of the hospice industry *most likely* indicates evidence of low:
        A. threat of substitutes.
        B. bargaining power of suppliers.
        C. rivalry among existing competitors.

32. Grass is concerned about potential risks that could impact the investment merits of the hospice industry. Based on the facts presented and Porter analysis, the *most likely* risk for the hospice industry is:
    A. increased competition among the for-profit companies, which could lower profit margins (rivalry among competitors).
    B. suppliers could force the hospice industry to pay higher prices for medical supplies (bargaining power of suppliers).
    C. Medicare could reduce its benefit program for hospice services (bargaining power of buyers).

33. The market share of the top six for-profit providers, together with the presence of non-profit and government providers, *most likely* indicates that the:
    A. rivalry among existing competitors is high.
    B. power of suppliers is low in the hospice industry.
    C. threat of substitutes is high in the hospice industry.

34. Cost savings due to implementation of patient monitoring systems is *most accurately* characterized as a:
    A. factor that will influence the bargaining power of suppliers.
    B. fleeting factor.
    C. factor that will influence the threat of new entrants.

35. Regarding Grass's adjustments to Hope's financial statements, the *most appropriate* adjustment is:
    A. Adjustment 1.
    B. Adjustment 2.
    C. Adjustment 3.

36. For valuation purposes, Hope's expected (first year) FCFF is *closest* to:
    A. $15 million.
    B. $16 million.
    C. $20 million.

Use the following information to answer Questions 37 through 42.

Ivan Johnson is reviewing the investment merits of BioTLab, a fast-growing biotechnology company. BioTLab has developed several drugs, which are being licensed to major drug companies. BioTLab also has several drugs in phase III trials (phase III trials are the last testing stage before FDA approval). Johnson notes that two drugs recently received approval which should provide BioTLab solid revenue growth and generate predictable cash flow well into the future. Based on the potential for the two drugs, BioTLab's estimated annual cash flow growth rate for the next two years is 25%, and long-term growth is expected to be 12%. Because of BioTLab's attractive investment opportunities, the company does not pay a dividend. BioTLab's current weighted average cost of capital is 15% and its stock is currently trading at $50 per share. Financial information for BioTLab for the most recent 12 months is provided below:

- Net working capital excluding cash increased from $7,460,000 to $9,985,000.
- Book value increased from $81,250,000 to $101,250,000.
- BioTLab currently has no debt.
- Research facilities and production equipment were purchased for $8,450,000.
- BioTLab held non-operating assets in the amount of $875,000.
- Net income for the 12 months was $20,000,000.
- BioTLab has a marginal tax rate of 40%.
- Noncash charges for depreciation and restructuring for the 12 months were $1,250,000.

BioTLab's management has indicated an interest in establishing a dividend and will fund new drug research by issuing additional debt.

Johnson also reviews a competitor to BioTLab, Groh Group, which has a larger segment operating in a highly cyclical business. The Groh Group has a debt to equity ratio of 1.0 and pays no dividends. In addition, Groh Group plans to issue bonds in the coming year.

37.   Johnson prefers to use free cash flow analysis to value investments. Which of the statements below is *least* accurate in describing the advantages of free cash flow valuation models?
    A. Accounting issues limit the usefulness of reported earnings, while free cash flow is adjusted for these issues.
    B. Determining free cash flow is easier than dividends. ✓
    C. A company must generate free cash flow to grow in the long run.

38. Using a two-stage, free cash flow to the firm model, determine which of the following is *closest* to the value of BioTLab.
    A. $419 million.
    B. $436 million.
    C. $477 million. ✓

39. If BioTLabs establishes a dividend and issues additional debt, the *most likely* effect on FCFF will be:
    A. no effect. ✓
    B. a decrease in FCFF.
    C. an increase in FCFF.

40. Which model would be *most* appropriate in valuing the Groh Group?
    A. FCFF model. ✓
    B. FCFE model.
    C. Dividend Discount model.

41. Ten years have passed and BioTLab's drug pipeline has generated the expected growth. To support BioTLab's growth, the company levered its balance sheet to a debt-to-equity ratio of 35%. The company recently started paying a dividend equaling 10% of earnings. The company's current return on assets is 10%, with a tax rate of 40% and pretax interest rate of 6%. BioTLab's FCFE equals $20,000,000 and FCFF equals $24,000,000. The company's WACC equals 11% and the required rate of return on equity equals 13%. The FCFE model calculates a value for BioTLab of $1,110,000,000 and the FCFF model calculates a value of $1,308,000,000. Calculate BioTLab's new expected growth rate using the FCFF model.
    A. 9%. ✓
    B. 10%.
    C. 11%. ✓

42. Which of the following statements regarding free cash flow models is *least likely* correct?
    A. Sensitivity analysis indicates that the FCFE model's valuation of BioTLab's common stock is most sensitive to the company's growth rate.
    B. FCFE is net income plus depreciation minus net capital expenditures minus the increase in working capital plus net new debt financing.
    C. FCFF can be inflated by increasing capital expenditures relative to depreciation. ✓

Use the following information to answer Questions 43 through 48.

Mike Diffle has been asked to evaluate the bonds of Hardin, Inc. The specific issue Diffle is considering has an 8% annual coupon and matures in two years. The bonds are currently callable at 101, and beginning in six months, they are callable at par. Bratton Corporation, Hardin's competitor, also has bonds outstanding which are identical to Hardin's except that they are not callable. Diffle believes the AA rating of both bonds is an accurate reflection of their credit risk. Diffle is wondering if the Bratton bonds might be a better investment than the Hardin bonds. Assume that the following 1-year interest rate tree is used to value bonds with a maturity of up to three years (this tree assumes interest rate volatility of 10%).

Today	Year 1	Year 2
		9.324%
	8.530%	
7.250%		7.634%
	6.983%	
		6.250%

Also, assume that the appropriate spot rates for securities maturing in one, two, and three years are 7.25%, 7.5%, and 7.80%, respectively.

Diffle believes he should begin his analysis with the option-free Bratton bonds. He decides to consider two different approaches to valuing the Bratton Bonds—one that uses the current spot rate curve and another that uses the interest rate tree given above.

For the next step in his analysis, Diffle has decided to calculate the value of the Hardin bonds using the interest rate tree. His assumption is that the bond will be called at any node of the tree where the calculated value exceeds the call price. Diffle summarizes the results of his bond valuation analysis in a memo to his supervisor, Luke Puldo. In this memo, Diffle makes the following statements:

Statement 1: The value of the option embedded in the Hardin bonds can be derived by simply subtracting the interest rate tree value of the Hardin bonds from the interest rate tree value of the Bratton bonds.

Statement 2: I am concerned that the 10% volatility assumption used to develop the interest rate tree might be too low. A higher volatility assumption would result in a lower value for the Hardin bonds.

After reviewing Diffle's analysis, Puldo notes that Diffle has not included any information on the option adjusted spread (OAS) for the Hardin bonds. Puldo suggests that Diffle should evaluate the OAS in order to get an idea of the liquidity risk of the Hardin bonds. Diffle counters that the OAS may not be very informative in this case, since he is uncertain as to the reliability of the interest rate volatility assumption.

To finish his analysis, Diffle would like to use his binomial model to evaluate the interest rate risk of both the Hardin bonds and the Bratton bonds. Diffle has shocked interest rates by 25 basis points throughout the interest rate tree he has been using to value the two bond issues. Using the new rates, Diffle has calculated values for the bonds assuming a 25-basis-point increase or decrease in rates. He plans to use these values as inputs into the following formulas for duration and convexity:

$$\text{duration} = \frac{V_- - V_+}{2 \times V_0 \times \Delta y} \qquad\qquad \text{convexity} = \frac{V_+ + V_- - 2V_0}{2 \times V_0 \times (\Delta y)^2}$$

43. Calculate the value of the Bratton bonds using the interest rate tree.
    A. 100.218.
    B. 100.378.
    C. 100.915. ✓

44. Using the interest rate tree, and assuming that the bonds will be called at any node of the tree where the calculated value exceeds the call price, which of the following is *closest* to the value of the Hardin bonds?
    A. 100.378.
    B. 100.472. ✓
    C. 100.915.

45. Indicate whether the statements made by Diffle in his memo regarding the value of the embedded option and the effect of the volatility assumption are correct.
    A. Only the statement regarding the value of the embedded option is correct.
    B. Only the statement regarding the effect of the volatility assumption is correct.
    C. Both statements are correct. ✓

46. Which of the following *most* accurately critiques the OAS discussion between Diffle and Puldo? Puldo is:
    A. correct that the OAS will provide insight into the liquidity risk of the Hardin bonds, and Diffle is correct that different volatility assumptions would change the OAS. ✓
    B. correct that the OAS will provide insight into the liquidity risk of the Hardin Bonds, but Diffle is incorrect since OAS implicitly adjusts for the volatility of interest rates.
    C. incorrect that the OAS will provide insight into the liquidity risk of the Hardin Bonds, but Diffle is correct that different volatility assumptions would change the OAS. ✗

47. Puldo still believes that Diffle must include the OAS for the Hardin bonds in his report. Puldo points out that a proper benchmark is critical to any OAS analysis. Which of the following statements regarding benchmark interest rates and OAS is *most* accurate? Since liquidity risk is a critical issue, the OAS calculation for the Hardin bonds should:
    A. use on-the-run U.S. Treasury rates as a benchmark in order to isolate the credit risk of the Hardin bonds.
    B. use on-the-run interest rates for other callable Hardin bonds as a benchmark in order to isolate the liquidity risk of the 2-year bond issue. ✓
    C. be based on a benchmark that has no credit risk.

48. Which of the following statements is *most* accurate regarding Diffle's calculation of duration and convexity?
    A. The duration estimate will be inaccurate since it does not account for any change in cash flows due to the call option embedded in the Hardin bond.
    B. The duration estimate for the Bratton bonds will reflect the projected percentage change in price for a 100-basis-point change in interest rates. ✓
    C. The estimates for both duration and convexity will be inaccurate because the Δy term includes the OAS.

X > S +

Use the following information to answer Questions 49 through 54.

Charles Mabry manages a portfolio of equity investments heavily concentrated in the biotech industry. He just returned from an annual meeting among leading biotech analysts in San Francisco. Mabry and other industry experts agree that the latest industry volatility is a result of questionable product safety testing methodologies. While no firms in the industry have escaped the public attention brought on by the questionable safety testing, one company in particular is expected to receive further attention—Biological Instruments Corporation (BIC), one of several long biotech positions in Mabry's portfolio. Several regulatory agencies as well as public interest groups have heavily criticized the rigor of BIC's product safety testing.

In an effort to manage the risk associated with BIC, Mabry has decided to allocate a portion of his portfolio to options on BIC's common stock. After surveying the derivatives market, Mabry has identified the following European options on BIC common stock:

BIC Call Options				BIC Put Options			
	Strike	Maturity	Premium		Strike	Maturity	Premium
Call A	40	October	3.51	Put D	30	November	2.31
Call B	50	October	1.98	Put E	40	November	4.14
Call C	60	October	1.42	Put F	50	November	9.21

Mabry wants to hedge the large BIC equity position in his portfolio, which closed yesterday (June 1) at $42 per share. Since Mabry is relatively inexperienced with utilizing derivatives in his portfolios, Mabry enlists the help of an analyst from another firm, James Grimell.

Mabry and Grimell arrange a meeting in Boston where Mabry discusses his expectations regarding the future returns of BIC's equity. Mabry expects BIC equity to make a recovery from the intense market scrutiny but wants to provide his portfolio with a hedge in case BIC has a negative surprise. Grimell makes the following suggestion:

"If you want to avoid selling the BIC position and are willing to earn only the risk-free rate of return, you should sell calls and buy puts on BIC stock with the same market premium. Alternatively, you could buy put options to manage the risk of your portfolio. I recommend waiting until the vega on the options rises, making them less attractive and cheaper to purchase."

49. Which of the following statements regarding the delta of the BIC options is correct? (Assume that the largest delta is defined as the delta furthest from zero.)

   A. Call C has the largest delta of all the BIC options. *less to 1*
   B. Put D has the smallest delta of all the BIC options. *b/w -1 and 0*
   C. Put F has the largest delta of all the BIC options. ✓

50. If the gamma of Put E is equal to 0.081, which of the following correctly interprets the option's gamma?

   A. The sensitivity of Put E's price to changes in BIC's stock price is very likely to change. ✓
   B. A dynamic hedging strategy using Put E would require infrequent rebalancing.
   C. A $1.00 increase in BIC's stock price will increase Put E's premium by $0.081.

   Δ in delta to Δ in SP.
   G is g^v for at the money, near expiration

51. Assuming that on October 15, the closing price of BIC common stock is $40 per share, how would the delta of Put F have changed from June 1?

   A. The delta on Put F will move closer to –1. ✓
   B. The delta on Put F will move closer to 0.
   C. The delta on Put F will move closer to 1.

   Delta = $\frac{\Delta C}{\Delta S}$
   ΔP (N(d) –1) (ΔS) = ΔP
   (n-1)(

52. If the premium on Put D on November 1 is $3.18, which of the following has *most likely* occurred?

   A. The price of BIC stock has decreased to $26.82.
   B. BIC had a negative earnings surprise. ✓
   C. Volatility of BIC stock has decreased.

53. Given Mabry's assessment of the risks associated with BIC, which option strategy would be the *most* effective in delta-neutral hedging the risk of BIC stock?

   A. Add put options to the portfolio as the put option delta moves closer to zero.
   B. Add call options to the portfolio as the call option delta moves further away from zero.
   C. Add put options to the portfolio as the put option delta moves toward –1. ✓

54. Which of the following correctly analyzes Grimell's comments regarding earning the risk-free rate by selling calls and buying puts, and regarding waiting for the option vegas to increase?

   A. Only Grimell's statement regarding earning the risk-free rate is correct.
   B. Only Grimell's statement regarding waiting for vega to rise is correct.
   C. Neither of Grimell's statements is correct.

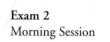
Use the following information to answer Questions 55 through 60.

Samuel Edson, CFA, portfolio manager for Driver Associates, employs a multifactor model to evaluate individual stocks and portfolios. Edson examines several possible risk factors and finds two that are priced in the marketplace. These two factors are investor sentiment (IS) risk and business cycle (BC) risk. Edson manages three equity portfolios (A, B, and C) and derives the following relationships for each portfolio, as well as for the S&P 500 stock market index:

$$R_A \quad = 0.1750 + 2.0F_{IS} + 1.5F_{BC} \quad\quad (1)$$

$$R_B \quad = 0.0940 + 0.5F_{IS} + 0.8F_{BC} \quad\quad (2)$$

$$R_C \quad = 0.1550 + 1.25F_{IS} + 1.15F_{BC} \quad\quad (3)$$

$$R_{S\&P} \quad = 0.1475 + 1.5F_{IS} + 1.25F_{BC} \quad\quad (4)$$

where:
R_A, R_B, R_C, and $R_{S\&P}$ = the returns for portfolios A, B, C, and the S&P 500 market index, respectively

Portfolios A and B are well-diversified, while C is a less than fully diversified, value-oriented portfolio. F_{IS} is the surprise in investor sentiment, and F_{BC} is the surprise in the business cycle. Surprises in the risk factors are defined as the difference between the actual value and the predicted value.

Exhibit 1 provides data for the actual and predicted values for the investor sentiment and business cycle risk factors.

Exhibit 1: Risk Factor Values

Factor	Actual Value	Predicted Value
Investor sentiment	1%	2%
Business cycle	2%	3%

Driver Associates also provides Edson with the following multifactor equations on three additional portfolios (D, E, and Z):

$$E(R_D) \quad = R_F + 1.0F_{IS} + 0.0F_{BC} = 9\% \quad\quad (5)$$

$$E(R_E) \quad = R_F + 0.0F_{IS} + 1.0F_{BC} = 8\% \quad\quad (6)$$

$$E(R_Z) \quad = R_F + 1.5F_{IS} + 1.25F_{BC} = 16\% \quad\quad (7)$$

Driver Associates uses a two-factor Arbitrage Pricing Model to develop equilibrium expected returns for individual stocks and portfolios:

$$E(R) = \text{risk-free rate} + b_1\lambda_1 + b_2\lambda_2 \qquad (8)$$

where:
b_1 = sensitivity of the portfolio return to changes in risk factor 1
b_2 = sensitivity of the portfolio return to changes in risk factor 2
λ_1 = risk premium associated with risk factor 1
λ_2 = risk premium associated with risk factor 2

At the time of Edson's analysis, the long-term government bond yield was 5%.

55.   Equations (1) through (4) are examples of:
       A. macroeconomic factor models. ✓
       B. fundamental factor models.
       C. statistical factor models.

56.   Edson's supervisor, Rosemary Valry, asks Edson to interpret the intercept of the multifactor equation for Portfolio A (0.175). Edson should respond that the intercept equals:
       A. the expected return for Portfolio A, assuming no surprises in the macroeconomic variables. ✓
       B. the expected return for Portfolio A, assuming the macroeconomic variables (investor sentiment and business cycle) equal zero.
       C. the expected abnormal return for Portfolio A.

57.   Valry is concerned that the economy did not perform as originally predicted by Driver Associates. She informs Edson that the returns for all the portfolios will likely differ from their expected returns. Use the multifactor equation (1) and the data provided in Exhibit 1 to find the revised returns for Portfolio A.
       A. 12.5%.
       B. 14.0%. ✓
       C. 21.0%.

58.   Driver Associates uses portfolios D, E, and Z as part of their risk management strategies. Which of these portfolios are factor portfolios?
       A. Portfolios D and E. ✓
       B. Portfolios D and Z.
       C. Portfolio Z only.

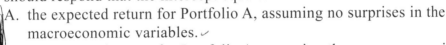
① −0.5

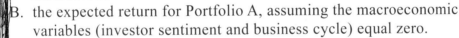
② −0.25

⑤

59. Valry instructs Edson to use the two-factor Arbitrage Pricing Model to examine Driver Associates's well-diversified balanced Portfolio P, which has an Investor Sentiment factor sensitivity equal to 1.25 and a Business Cycle factor sensitivity equal to 1.10. According to Driver Associates's Arbitrage Pricing Model, the expected return for Portfolio P equals:
   A. 8.3%.
   B. 10.8%.
   C. 13.3%.

60. Assuming Driver Associates uses the S&P 500 index as their performance benchmark, which of the following portfolios is expected to have the *least* active factor risk?
   A. Portfolio D.
   B. Portfolio E.
   C. Portfolio Z.

$$ E(R_p) = RF + \beta_1(\lambda_1) + \beta_2(\lambda_2) $$

End of Morning Session

$$ 0.05 + 0.5(1.25) + 0.5(1.10) $$
$$ + 0.55 $$

59. $\text{Risk premium}_1 = ER_1 - RF$
$$ = 4\% $$

$$ RP_2 = ER_2 - RF $$
$$ = 8 - 5 = 3\% $$

$$ 0.05 + 0.04(1.25) + 0.03(1.10) $$

Exam 2
Afternoon Session

Question	Topic	Minutes (Points)
61 to 66	Ethical and Professional Standards	18
67 to 72	Quantitative Analysis	18
73 to 78	Economics	18
79 to 90	Corporate Finance	36
91 to 96	Portfolio Management	18
97 to 102	Asset Valuation – Alternative Investments	18
103 to 108	Asset Valuation – Equity	18
109 to 114	Asset Valuation – Fixed Income	18
115 to 120	Asset Valuation – Derivatives	18

61.	(A)	(B)	(C)
62.	(A)	(B)	(C)
63.	(A)	(B)	(C)
64.	(A)	(B)	(C)
65.	(A)	(B)	(C)
66.	(A)	(B)	(C)
67.	(A)	(B)	(C)
68.	(A)	(B)	(C)
69.	(A)	(B)	(C)
70.	(A)	(B)	(C)

71.	(A)	(B)	(C)
72.	(A)	(B)	(C)
73.	(A)	(B)	(C)
74.	(A)	(B)	(C)
75.	(A)	(B)	(C)
76.	(A)	(B)	(C)
77.	(A)	(B)	(C)
78.	(A)	(B)	(C)
79.	(A)	(B)	(C)
80.	(A)	(B)	(C)

81.	(A)	(B)	(C)
82.	(A)	(B)	(C)
83.	(A)	(B)	(C)
84.	(A)	(B)	(C)
85.	(A)	(B)	(C)
86.	(A)	(B)	(C)
87.	(A)	(B)	(C)
88.	(A)	(B)	(C)
89.	(A)	(B)	(C)
90.	(A)	(B)	(C)

91.	(A)	(B)	(C)
92.	(A)	(B)	(C)
93.	(A)	(B)	(C)
94.	(A)	(B)	(C)
95.	(A)	(B)	(C)
96.	(A)	(B)	(C)
97.	(A)	(B)	(C)
98.	(A)	(B)	(C)
99.	(A)	(B)	(C)
100.	(A)	(B)	(C)

101.	(A)	(B)	(C)
102.	(A)	(B)	(C)
103.	(A)	(B)	(C)
104.	(A)	(B)	(C)
105.	(A)	(B)	(C)
106.	(A)	(B)	(C)
107.	(A)	(B)	(C)
108.	(A)	(B)	(C)
109.	(A)	(B)	(C)
110.	(A)	(B)	(C)

111.	(A)	(B)	(C)
112.	(A)	(B)	(C)
113.	(A)	(B)	(C)
114.	(A)	(B)	(C)
115.	(A)	(B)	(C)
116.	(A)	(B)	(C)
117.	(A)	(B)	(C)
118.	(A)	(B)	(C)
119.	(A)	(B)	(C)
120.	(A)	(B)	(C)

Exam 2
Afternoon Session

Use the following information to answer Questions 61 through 66.

Pat Wilson, CFA, is the chief compliance officer for Excess Investments, a global asset management and investment banking services company. Wilson is reviewing two investment reports written by Peter Holly, CFA, an analyst and portfolio manager who has worked for Excess for four years. Holly's first report under compliance review is a strong buy recommendation for BlueNote Inc., a musical instrument manufacturer. The report states that the buy recommendation is applicable for the next 6 to 12 months with an average level of risk and a sustainable price target of $24 for the entire time period. At the bottom of the report, an e-mail address is given for investors who wish to obtain a complete description of the firm's rating system. Among other reasons supporting the recommendation, Holly's report states that expected increases in profitability, as well as increased supply chain efficiency, provide compelling support for purchasing BlueNote.

Holly informs Wilson that he determined his conclusions primarily from an intensive review of BlueNote's filings with the SEC but also from a call to one of BlueNote's suppliers who informed Holly that their new inventory processing system would allow for more efficiency in supplying BlueNote with raw materials. Holly explains to Wilson that he is the only analyst covering BlueNote who is aware of this information and that he believes the new inventory processing system will allow BlueNote to reduce costs and increase overall profitability for several years to come.

Wilson must also review Holly's report on BigTime Inc., a musical promotion and distribution company. In the report, Holly provides a very optimistic analysis of BigTime's fundamentals. The analysis supports a buy recommendation for the company. Wilson finds one problem with Holly's report on BigTime related to Holly's former business relationship with BigTime Inc. Two years before joining Excess, Holly worked as an investment banker and received 1,000 restricted shares of BigTime as a result of his participation in taking the company public. These facts are not disclosed in the report but are disclosed on Excess Investment's Web site. Wilson decides, however, that the timeliness of the information in the report warrants overlooking this issue so that the report can be distributed.

Just before the report is issued, Holly mentions to Wilson that BigTime unknowingly disclosed to him and a few other analysts who were waiting for a conference call to begin that the company is planning to restructure both its sales staff and sales strategy and may sell one of its poorly performing business units next year.

Three days after issuing his report on BigTime, which caused a substantial rise in the price of BigTime shares, Holly sells all of the BigTime shares out of both his performance fee-based accounts and asset-based accounts and then proceeds to sell all of the BigTime shares out of his own account on the following day. Holly obtained approval from Wilson before making the trades.

Just after selling his shares in BigTime, Holly receives a call from the CEO of BlueNote who wants to see if Holly received the desk pen engraved with the BlueNote company logo that he sent last week and also to offer two front row tickets plus limousine service to a sold-out concert for a popular band that uses BlueNote's instruments. Holly confirms that the desk pen arrived and thanks the CEO for the gift and tells him that before he accepts the concert tickets, he will have to check his calendar to see if he will be able to attend. Holly declines the use of the limousine service should he decide to attend the concert.

After speaking with the CEO of BlueNote, Holly constructs a letter that he plans to send by e-mail to all of his clients and prospects with e-mail addresses and by regular mail to all of his clients and prospects without e-mail addresses. The letter details changes to an equity valuation model that Holly and several other analysts at Excess use to analyze potential investment recommendations. Holly's letter explains that the new model, which will be put into use next month, will utilize Monte Carlo simulations to create a distribution of stock values, a sharp contrast to the existing model which uses static valuations combined with sensitivity analysis. Relevant details of the new model are included in the letter, but similar details about the existing model are not included. The letter also explains that management at Excess has decided to exclude alcohol and tobacco company securities from the research coverage universe. Holly's letter concludes by stating that no other significant changes that would affect the investment recommendation process have occurred or are expected to occur in the near future.

61. According to CFA Institute Research Objectivity Standards (ROS), which of the following statements is *most* accurate with regard to the rating system used by Holly in his investment report on BlueNote Inc.? The rating system:
    - A. has appropriately incorporated the three recommended rating system elements from the ROS.
    - B. should not have included a price target as it makes an implicit guarantee of investment performance.
    - C. should not have included a time frame, as it misrepresents the level of certainty of the recommendation.

62. Did Holly violate any CFA Institute Standards of Professional Conduct with respect to his report on BlueNote or BigTime, as it relates to potential use of material nonpublic information?
    A. Holly has violated Standard on material nonpublic information in the case of both reports.
    B. There is a violation regarding the BlueNote report, but no violation with the BigTime report.
    C. There is a violation regarding the BigTime report, but no violation with the BlueNote report.

63. According to CFA Institute Research Objectivity Standards (ROS), which of the following statements is *most* accurate with regard to Holly's disclosure of his ownership of BigTime restricted shares and past investment banking relationship with BigTime? The disclosure:
    A. is not required or recommended by the ROS since the shares are restricted.
    B. complies with the ROS recommended procedures for disclosing conflicts of interest.
    C. should have been made in the research report itself and not just on Excess's Web site.

64. According to CFA Institute Standards of Professional Conduct, which of the following statements is *most likely* correct with regard to Holly's report and subsequent sale of his and his clients' shares of BigTime common stock? Holly has:
    A. violated the Standard by attempting to manipulate the market price of BigTime stock.
    B. not violated the Standard since he first obtained approval to make the trades from his compliance officer.
    C. not violated the Standard since he acted in the best interest of his clients by realizing gains on BigTime stock.

65. According to CFA Institute Standards of Professional Conduct, which of the following *best* describes the actions Holly should take with regard to the desk pen and the concert tickets offered to him by the CEO of BlueNote? Holly:
    A. must not accept the desk pen or the concert tickets.
    B. may accept both the desk pen and the concert tickets.
    C. may accept the desk pen but should not accept the concert tickets.

66. In his letter to clients explaining the change in the valuation model, did Holly violate any CFA Institute Standards of Professional Conduct?
    A. No.
    B. Yes, because he did not treat all clients fairly in his dissemination of the letter.
    C. Yes, because he failed to include details of the current valuation model to contrast with the new model.

Use the following information to answer Questions 67 through 72.

Lena Pilchard, research associate for Eiffel Investments, is attempting to measure the value added to the Eiffel Investments portfolio from the use of 1-year earnings growth forecasts developed by professional analysts.

Pilchard's supervisor, Edna Wilrus, recommends a portfolio allocation strategy that overweights neglected firms. Wilrus cites studies of the "neglected firm effect," in which companies followed by a small number of professional analysts are associated with higher returns than firms followed by a larger number of analysts. Wilrus considers a company covered by three or fewer analysts to be "neglected."

Pilchard also is aware of research indicating that, on average, stock returns for small firms have been higher than those earned by large firms. Pilchard develops a model to predict stock returns based on analyst coverage, firm size, and analyst growth forecasts. She runs the following cross-sectional regression using data for the 30 stocks included in the Eiffel Investments portfolio:

$$R_i = b_0 + b_1 COVERAGE_i + b_2 LN(SIZE_i) + b_3(FORECAST_i) + e_i$$

where:
R_i	= the rate of return on stock i
$COVERAGE_i$	= one if there are three or fewer analysts covering stock i, and equals zero otherwise
$LN(SIZE_i)$	= the natural logarithm of the market capitalization (stock price times shares outstanding) for stock i, units in millions
$FORECAST_i$	= the 1-year consensus earnings growth rate forecast for stock i

Pilchard derives the following results from her cross-sectional regression:

Exhibit 1: Results of Pilchard's Cross-Sectional Regression

Variable	Coefficient	T-statistic
Constant	0.060	1.56
COVERAGE	0.050	3.20
LN(SIZE)	−0.003	−2.50
FORECAST	0.200	2.85

The standard error of estimate in Pilchard's regression equals 1.96 and the regression sum of squares equals 400.

©2012 Kaplan, Inc.

Wilrus provides Pilchard with the following values for analyst coverage, firm size, and earnings growth forecast for Eggmann Enterprises, a company that Eiffel Investments is evaluating.

Exhibit 2: Coverage, Firm Size, and Earnings Growth Forecast for Eggmann Enterprises

Number of analysts	5
Firm size	$500 million
Earnings growth forecast	50%

Pilchard uses the following table to conduct some of her hypothesis tests.

Exhibit 3: Critical Values for Student t-Distribution

Degrees of Freedom	Area in Upper Tail				
	0.10	0.05	0.025	0.01	0.005
26	1.315	1.706	2.056	2.479	2.779
27	1.314	1.703	2.052	2.473	2.771
28	1.313	1.701	2.048	2.467	2.763
29	1.311	1.699	2.045	2.462	2.756
30	1.310	1.697	2.042	2.457	2.750

67. Wilrus asks Pilchard to derive the lowest possible value for the coefficient on the FORECAST variable using a 99% confidence interval. The appropriate lower bound for the FORECAST coefficient is *closest* to:
    - A. 0.0055. ✓
    - B. 0.0628.
    - C. 0.1300.

68. Wilrus asks Pilchard to assess the overall significance of her regression. To address the question, Pilchard calculates the R-square. She also decides to run a test of the significance of the regression as a whole. Determine the appropriate test statistic she should use to test the overall significance of the regression.
    - A. F-statistic. ✓
    - B. t-statistic.
    - C. Chi-square statistic.

$$\hat{b_1} \pm \left(t_c \times S_b \right)$$

69. Pilchard is asked whether her regression indicates that small firms outperform large firms, after controlling for analyst coverage and consensus earnings growth forecasts. Pilchard determines the appropriate hypothesis test to answer the question. Eiffel Investments uses a 0.01 level of significance for all hypothesis tests. Given the results of her regression, Pilchard should make which of the following decisions after controlling for analyst coverage and consensus earnings forecasts?
    A. Not reject the hypothesis that $b_2 \geq 0$, and conclude that large firms significantly outperformed small firms.
    B. Reject the hypothesis that $b_2 \geq 0$, and conclude that large firms significantly outperformed small firms.
    C. Reject the hypothesis that $b_2 \geq 0$, and conclude that small firms significantly outperformed large firms.

70. Holding firm size and consensus earnings growth forecasts constant, the estimated average difference in stock returns between neglected and non-neglected firms equals:
    A. 3%.
    ✓ B. 5%.✓
    C. 7%.

71. Pilchard derives the ANOVA table for her regression. In her ANOVA table, the degrees of freedom for the regression sum of squares and total sum of squares should equal:
    A. 3 and 30, respectively.
    B. 4 and 29, respectively.
    ✓ C. 3 and 29, respectively.

72. Using the inputs for Eggmann Enterprises provided in Exhibit 2, the predicted stock return for Eggmann Enterprises is *closest* to:
    A. 4%.
    ✓ B. 14%.
    C. 18%.

Use the following information to answer Questions 73 through 78.

Debbie Angle and Craig Hohlman are analysts for a large commercial bank, Arbutus National Bank. Arbutus has extensive dealings in both the spot and forward foreign exchange markets. Angle and Hohlman are providing a refresher course on foreign exchange relationships for its traders.

Angle uses a three country example from North America to illustrate foreign exchange parity relations. In it, the Canadian dollar is expected to depreciate relative to the U.S. dollar and the Mexican peso. Nominal, 1-year interest rates are 7% in the United States and 13% in Mexico. From this data and using the uncovered interest rate parity relationship, Angle forecasts future spot rates.

During their presentation, Hohlman discusses the effect of monetary and fiscal policies on exchange rates. He cites a historical example from the United States, where the Federal Reserve shifted to an expansionary monetary policy to stimulate economic growth. This shift was largely unanticipated by the financial markets because the markets thought the Federal Reserve was more concerned with inflationary pressures. Hohlman states that the effect of this policy was an increase in economic growth and an increase in inflation. The cumulative effect on the dollar was unchanged, however, because, according to the Mundell-Fleming model, an expansionary monetary policy would strengthen the dollar whereas under relative purchasing power parity, an increase in inflation would weaken the dollar.

Regarding U.S. fiscal policies, Hohlman states that if these were unexpectedly expansionary, real interest rates would increase, which would produce an appreciation of the dollar. Hohlman adds that a sustained increase in the federal budget would attract foreign capital such that the long-run effect would be an increase in the value of the dollar.

Hohlman makes the following statements about parity conditions:

Statement 1: If relative purchasing power parity holds, we can say that uncovered interest rate parity also holds.

$$E(S_t)$$
$$= S_0 \left(\frac{1 + R_A}{1 + R_B} \right)^t$$

Statement 2: For uncovered interest rate parity to hold, the forward rate must be an unbiased predictor of the future spot rate.

Angle next discusses the foreign exchange expectations. While examining Great Britain and Japan, she states that it appears the 4-year forward rate, which is currently ¥200/£, is an accurate predictor of the expected future spot rate. Furthermore, she states that uncovered interest rate parity and relative purchasing power parity hold. In the example for her presentation, she uses the following figures for the two countries.

$$E(S_t) = S_0 \left(\frac{1 + R_A}{1 + R_B} \right)^t$$

$$F = S_0 \left(\frac{1 + \text{inf}_A}{1 + \text{inf}_B} \right)^t \quad F = S_0 \left[\frac{1 + R_A \left(\frac{\text{days}}{360} \right)}{1 + R_B \left(\frac{\text{days}}{360} \right)} \right]$$

	Great Britain	Japan
Real interest rates	3.20%	1.90%
Expected GDP growth	2.50%	1.80%
Nominal 1-year interest rates	9.70%	6.40%
Growth in exports	3.90%	5.70%

As a follow-up to Angle's example, Hohlman discusses the use and evidence for purchasing power parity. He makes the following statements.

Statement 3: Absolute purchasing power parity is based on the law of one price, which states that a good should have the same price throughout the world. Absolute purchasing power parity is not widely used in practice to forecast exchange rates.

Statement 4: Although relative purchasing power parity is useful as an input for long-run exchange rate forecasts, it is not useful for predicting short-run currency values.

73. Using Angle's analysis, what is the nominal 1-year interest rate in Canada?
     A. Less than 7%.
     B. Between 7% and 13%.
     C. Greater than 13%. ✓

74. Are Hohlman's statements regarding the effect of monetary policies on the dollar correct?
     A. Yes, they are correct.
     B. No, under the Mundell-Fleming model, expansionary monetary policy in the U.S. would weaken the dollar. ✓
     C. No, the dollar value would be unchanged, but under the asset market model and not the Mundell-Fleming model.

75. What additional condition must be satisfied for Hohlman's Statement 1 to be valid?
     A. Covered interest parity must hold. ✗
     B. The forward exchange rate must be an unbiased predictor of the future spot rate. ✗
     C. The international Fisher relation must hold. ✓

76.   Hohlman's Statement 2 is:
       A. correct. ✓
       B. incorrect as uncovered interest rate parity holds only if real interest rate parity holds.
       C. incorrect as uncovered interest rate parity holds only if covered interest rate parity holds.

77.   Which of the following is *closest* to the current ¥/£ spot rate, using relative purchasing power parity? Use the exact methodology in your calculations.
       A. ¥186/£.
       B. ¥215/£. ✓
       C. ¥226/£.

78.   Regarding the statements made by Hohlman on purchasing power parity, are both statements correct?
       A. Yes. ✓
       B. No, only Statement 4 is correct.
       C. No, both statements are incorrect.

$$S_t = S_0 \left(\frac{1 + \text{inflation A}}{1 + \text{inflation B}} \right)^t$$

(S_t)

Use the following information to answer Questions 79 through 84.

Engineered Packaging Inc. (EPI) is a manufacturer of industrial and consumer packaging products. The company's products include composite and plastic rigid packaging, flexible packaging, as well as metal and plastic ends and closures. In January 2008, EPI entered into a joint venture with BMI Enterprises. EPI contributed ownership of five plants, while BMI contributed a new manufacturing technology. The joint venture is known as EP/BM LLC. EPI owns 50% of EP/BM LLC and uses the equity method to account for its investment. The following information for 2008 is provided:

In Millions, Year-End 2008	EPI	EP/BM LLC
Revenue	$3,115	$421
Cost of goods sold	$2,580	$295
SG&A	$316	$50
Interest expense	$47	$8
Equity in earnings of EP/BM	$22	
Pretax income	$194	$68
Income tax	$60	$24
Net income	$134	$44

In Millions, December 31, 2008	EPI	EP/BM LLC
Assets		
Cash	$118	$13
Accounts receivable	$390	$50
Inventory	$314	$41
Property	$1,007	$131
Investment	$38	
Total	$1,867	$235

Liabilities and Equity		
Accounts payable	$274	$35
Long-term debt	$719	$125
Equity	$874	$75
Total	$1,867	$235

79. Had EPI used the proportionate consolidation method instead of the equity method to account for its joint venture investment, which of the following statements is the *most* correct?
    A. Net income would have been the same and total assets would have been lower.
    B. Equity would have been the same and total liabilities would have been lower.
    C. Revenue would have been higher and expenses would have been higher. ✓

80. Based on the proportionate consolidation method, calculate EPI's current ratio for 2008 (use the financial information provided).
    A. 1.8.
    B. 2.6.
    C. 3.0. ✓

81. Based on the proportionate consolidation method, calculate EPI's interest coverage ratio for 2008 (use the financial information provided).
    A. 3.6.
    B. 4.0.
    C. 5.0. ✓

82. Had EPI used the proportionate consolidation method instead of the equity method to account for its joint venture investment, EPI's long-term debt-to-equity ratio would have been:
    A. higher. ✓
    B. lower.
    C. the same.

83. For this question only, assume EPI increases its ownership of the joint venture to more than 50% in 2009. In this case, EPI should:
    A. report its investment at fair value.
    B. use the acquisition method unless circumstances indicate that EPI is unable to exercise control over the joint venture. ✓
    C. use the uniting-of-interest method.

84. In January 2009, EPI decides to sell its interest in EP/BM LLC. This is the fifth divesture in the last five years. Which of the following statements is *least likely* regarding this sale? The divestiture:
   A. may be signaling a poor operating choice and prior bad acquisitions.
   B. could be used to manage earnings by lowering the company's overall debt level. ✗
   C. is sending a positive signal that management is able to sell assets at a good price. ✓

Use the following information to answer Questions 85 through 90.

GigaTech, Inc., is a large U.S.-based technology conglomerate. The firm has business units in three primary categories: (1) hardware manufacturing, (2) software development, and (3) consulting services. Because of the rapid pace of technological innovation, GigaTech must make capital investments every two to four years. The company has identified several potential investment opportunities for its hardware manufacturing division. The first of these opportunities, Tera Project, would replace a portion of GigaTech's microprocessor assembly equipment with new machinery expected to last three years. The current machinery has a book value of $120,000 and a market value of $195,000. The Tera Project would require purchasing machinery for $332,000, increasing current assets by $190,000, and increasing current liabilities by $80,000. GigaTech has a tax rate of 40%. Additional pro forma information related to the Tera Project is provided in the following table:

	Existing Equipment	Tera Project
Annual sales	$523,000	$708,000
Cash operating expenses	$352,000	$440,000
Annual depreciation	$40,000	$110,667
Accounting salvage value	$0	$0
Expected salvage value (after three years)	$90,000	$113,000

Analysts at GigaTech have noted that investment in the Tera Project can be delayed for up to nine months if managers at the company decide this is necessary. However, once the capital investment is made, the project will be necessary to maintain continuing operations. Tera Project can be scaled up with more equipment requiring less capital than the original investment if results are meeting expectations. In addition, the equipment used in Tera Project can be used in shift work if brief excess demand is expected.

GigaTech is also considering expanding its software development operations in India. Software development equipment must be continually replaced to maintain efficiency as newer and faster technology is developed. The company has identified two mutually exclusive potential expansion projects, Zeta and Sigma. Zeta requires investing in equipment with a 3-year life, while Sigma requires investing in equipment with a 2-year life. GigaTech has estimated real capital costs for the two projects at 10.58%. GigaTech expects inflation to be approximately 4.0% for the foreseeable future. Nominal cash flows and net present values for the Zeta and Sigma projects are provided in the following table:

	Annual Cash Flows				
Project	0	1	2	3	NPV
Zeta	−$360,000	$250,000	$220,000	$190,000	$148,671
Sigma	−$470,000	$330,000	$390,000	$0	$111,853

Recently, GigaTech's board of directors has become concerned with the firm's capital budgeting decisions and has asked management to provide a detailed explanation of the capital budgeting process. After reviewing the report from management, the board makes the following comments in a memo:

- The capital rationing system being utilized is fundamentally flawed since, in some instances, projects that do not increase earnings per share are selected over projects that do increase earnings per share.
- The cash flow projections are flawed since they fail to include costs incurred in the search for projects or the economic consequences of increased competition resulting from highly profitable projects.
- We are making inappropriate investment decisions since the discount rate used to evaluate all potential projects is the firm's weighted average cost of capital.

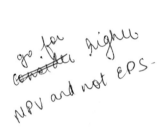

go for higher NPV and not EPS-

85. Assuming that working capital will be recaptured at the end of the project, which of the following is *closest* to the final period after-tax cash flow for the Tera Project?
   A. $196,467.
   B. $210,267. ✓
   C. $219,467.

86. Which of the following *best* describes how GigaTech should implement scenario analysis to analyze the Tera Project?
   A. Generate a base case, high, and low estimate of NPV by changing only the most sensitive cash flow variable.
   B. Generate a base case, high, and low estimate of NPV by changing only the discount rate applicable to the project.
   C. Generate a base case, high, and low estimate of NPV by simultaneously changing sales, expense, and discount rate assumptions for each case. ✓

87. Which of the following is *least likely* to be a real option available to GigaTech with regard to the Tera Project?
   A. Abandonment option. ✓
   B. Expansion option. ✗
   C. Flexibility option. ✗

88.   Using the least common multiple of lives approach, determine whether
      the Zeta Project or the Sigma Project will increase the value of
      GigaTech by a greater amount.
      A. Zeta Project.
      B. Sigma Project. ✓
      C. Both projects increase GigaTech's value by the same amount.

89.   Determine whether the board of director's memo is correct with regard
      to its statements about GigaTech's capital rationing system and its
      method of projecting project cash flows.
      A. Only the statement regarding capital rationing is correct.
      B. Only the statement regarding cash flow projections is correct.
      C. Neither the statement regarding capital rationing nor the statement
          regarding cash flow projections is correct. ✓

90.   Which of the following would *best* correct GigaTech's discount rate
      problem described in the board of director's memo?
      A. Use the firm's marginal cost of capital to evaluate all potential
          projects.
      B. Use a beta specific to each potential project to determine the
          appropriate discount rate. ✓
      C. Use the cost of the firm's equity capital to discount the cash flows
          of all potential projects.

Use the following information to answer Questions 91 through 96.

Sharon Foster, 56, is an executive at a large Biotech firm. Foster plans to retire in five years to travel and spend time with her grandchildren. Foster is in excellent health, although her husband died several years ago. Foster's only significant asset is her employer's 401(k) retirement plan. Her salary is more than adequate to cover her living expenses until she retires, but she does not anticipate that she will accumulate any additional savings beyond her retirement account. The balance in her account currently is $3.2 million, but Foster estimates that by the time she retires the account will have grown to $4.5 million. She expects that her living expenses, including a liberal travel budget, will be $150,000 per year, beginning when she retires. She is willing to take risk to achieve her financial goals. Her retirement account is currently invested 80% in stocks and 20% in bonds. Foster estimates her post-retirement income tax rate to be 35%, which is about the same as her current tax rate.

As she is starting to plan her retirement, Foster has turned to her longtime friend, Don Welch, CFA, who is a portfolio manager at Scientific Investments, LLC. Welch is considering three different mutual funds for Foster's account. All three are well-diversified funds of large capitalization stocks. The expected returns and standard deviations of each fund are shown below in Exhibit 1. Welch assumes a risk-free rate of return of 3.0%.

Exhibit 1

Fund	$E(r_p)$	Standard Deviation (σ_p)
A	8.0%	6.0%
B	10.0%	8.0%
C	12.0%	10.0%

Welch believes in stock market efficiency, but he also believes that individual securities are mispriced by the market from time to time. He has recently reviewed research related to the Treynor-Black (TB) model of security selection and portfolio optimization. Welch refers to a prospectus from Fund D, which uses the TB framework in developing its portfolios. In discussing their use of the TB model, the prospectus cites an example where an active portfolio of five stocks is combined with a passive, index portfolio. The portfolio weights of the stocks are in Exhibit 2.

Exhibit 2

Portfolio	Weighting	Alpha
Stock 1	50%	6%
Stock 2	–25%	–6%
Stock 3	50%	8%
Stock 4	50%	7%
Stock 5	–25%	–4%

Welch further notes that the beta of the active portfolio is 0.90, although the standard deviation of the portfolio's returns is high. Of the five stocks shown in the portfolio, three have positive alphas, and two have negative alphas. A footnote to the sample data states that the sample assumes that the analysts' alpha forecasts are perfect.

Welch is reviewing Foster's account, together with the mutual fund data, in an attempt to develop a long-term investment plan for Foster.

91. In preparing an investment policy statement for Foster, which of the following *best* describes her post-retirement risk tolerance?
    A. Resolution needed.
    B. Below average.
    C. Above average. ✓

92. In preparing an investment policy statement for Foster, her time horizon would *most likely* be described as:
    A. short-term and single stage.
    B. long-term and multi-stage. ✓
    C. long-term and single stage.

93. Foster has been reading some investment literature provided by her employer regarding her retirement account. That literature mentions the Sharpe ratio as a meaningful method to compare investment managers' performance results. If Welch were to select a mutual fund from the alternatives shown in Exhibit 1 based solely on the Sharpe ratio, which fund would he *most likely* select?
    A. Fund A.
    B. Fund B.
    C. Fund C.

94. Welch is interested in how the Treynor-Black model combines active and passive portfolios in an attempt to earn incremental returns. Which of the following *best* describes the advantages of optimizing active and passive portfolios?

    A. If securities with negative alphas can be identified, these securities will allow the investor to move further down the capital market line.

    B. Active and passive portfolios are best optimized when the returns of the active portfolio are perfectly correlated with the returns of the passive portfolio.

    C. If securities with a positive alpha can be identified, the active portfolio comprised of these securities can be combined with the market portfolio to create a portfolio with superior risk-adjusted returns.

95. In evaluating the Fund D prospectus, Welch was concerned about the large weightings of the individual securities, as well as the relatively low beta of the active portfolio. Which of the following statements *best* describes the effects of these large asset weights and the low beta of the active portfolio?

    A. The large asset weights are required to offset the low relative returns of the market portfolio, while the low beta represents the combination of long and short positions in the active portfolio.

    B. The large asset weights will fall to reasonable levels as the active and passive portfolios are combined, while the low beta represents the combination of long and short positions in the active portfolio.

    C. The large asset weights, either positive or negative, are a result of combining long and short positions in the active portfolio, while the low beta reflects that the active portfolio is well diversified before being combined with the market portfolio.

96. If Welch was to ban short sales from the 5-stock portfolio and equally weight the remaining stocks, indicate the amount of performance lost due to a ban on short sales.

    A. 2.50%.

    B. 3.50%.

    C. 6.00%.

Use the following information to answer Questions 97 through 102.

Bill Henry, CFA, is the CIO of IS University Endowment Fund located in the United States. The Fund's total assets are valued at $3.5 billion. The investment policy uses a total return approach to meet the return objective that includes a spending rate of 5%. In addition, the policy constraints established make tax-exempt instruments an inappropriate investment vehicle. The Fund's current asset mix includes an 18% allocation to private equity. The private equity allocation is shown in Exhibit 1.

Exhibit 1: IS University Endowment Fund's Private Equity Investments

Private Equity	Percentage Allocation
Venture capital	12%
Buyouts	56%
Special situations	32%

The private equity allocation is a mixture of funds with different vintages. For example, within the venture capital category, investments have been made in five different funds. Exhibit 2 provides details about the Alpha Fund with a vintage year of 2006 and committed capital of $195 million. The distribution waterfall calls for 20% carried interest when NAV before distributions exceeds committed capital.

Exhibit 2: $195 million Venture Capital Alpha Fund *(\$Millions)*

Year	Called-Down	Management Fees	Operating Results
2006	$30	$0.45	−$10
2007	$25	$0.83	$55
2008	$75	$1.95	$75

The Alpha Fund is considering a new investment in Targus Company. Targus is a start-up biotech company seeking $9 million of venture capital financing. Targus's founders believe that, based on the company's new drug pipeline, a company value of $300 million is reasonable in five years. Management at Alpha Fund views Targus Company as a risky investment (15% risk of failure) and is using a discount rate of 40%.

97. Which of the following risk factors will *most likely* impact the private equity portion of the IS University Endowment?
    A. Lack of diversification.
    B. Illiquid investments.
    C. Taxation risk.

98. Using Exhibit 2, calculate the 2008 percentage management fee of the Alpha Fund.
    A. 1.5%.
    B. 2.0%.
    C. 2.5%.

99. Alpha Fund's 2008 dollar amount of carried interest is *closest* to:
    A. $0 million.
    B. $10 million.
    C. $20 million.

100. Which of the following is *most likely* a characteristic of a venture capital investment?
    A. The typical investment uses leverage.
    B. Measureable risk.
    C. Increasing capital requirements.

101. Using the single period NPV method (venture capital method), the post-money valuation of Targus Company is *closest* to:
    A. $48 million.
    B. $50 million.
    C. $55 million.

102. For this question only, assuming that the founders will hold 2.5 million shares, and the post money valuation is $90 million, the price per share for the venture capital investor is *closest* to:
    A. $27.48.
    B. $32.33.
    C. $36.00.

Use the following information to answer Questions 103 through 108.

Sentinel News is a publisher of more than 100 newspapers around the country, with the exception of the Midwestern states. The company's CFO, Harry Miller, has been reviewing a number of potential candidates (both public and private companies) that would provide Sentinel News entrance into the Midwestern market. Recently, the founder of Midwest News, a private newspaper company, passed away. The founder's family members are inclined to sell their 80% controlling interest. The family members are concerned that Midwest News's declining newspaper circulation is not cyclical, but rather permanent. The family members would reinvest the cash proceeds from the sale of Midwest News into a diversified portfolio of stocks and bonds. Miller's staff collects the financial information shown in Exhibit 1.

Exhibit 1: Midwest News's Financial Information

Total assets	$92.5 million
Total debt	$0
Total equity	$79.5 million
Shares outstanding	1.5 million
Revenues	$251.5 million
Net income (next year's forecast)	$19.5 million

$$\frac{15,000,000,000}{375,000,000}$$

Miller noted that Midwest News does not pay a dividend, nor does the company have any debt. The most comparable publicly traded stock is Freedom Corporation. Freedom, however, has significant radio and television operations. Freedom's estimated beta is 0.90, and 40% of the company's capital structure is debt. Freedom is expected to maintain a payout ratio of 40%. Analysts are forecasting the company will earn $3.00 per share next year and grow their earnings by 6% per year. Freedom has a current market capitalization of $15 billion and 375 million shares outstanding. Freedom's current market value equals its intrinsic value.

$\frac{40}{100} \times$

6b

Miller's staff uses current expectations to develop the appropriate equity risk premium for Midwest News. The staff uses the Gordon growth model (GGM) to estimate Midwest's equity risk premium. The equity risk premium calculated by the staff is provided in Exhibit 2.

Miller believes the best method to estimate the required return on equity of Midwest News is the build-up method. All relevant information to determine Midwest News's required return on equity is presented in Exhibit 2.

Exhibit 2: Required Return Estimate Factors

Risk-free rate	3.5%
Equity risk premium	4.0%
Small size premium	3.5%
Specific-company premium	2.0%
Beta	1.2
Growth rate	3.0%

The specific-company premium reflects concerns about future industry performance and business risk in Midwest News. Miller makes two statements concerning the valuation methodology used to value Midwest News's equity.

Statement 1: The required return estimate that is calculated from Exhibit 2 reflects all adjustments needed to make an accurate valuation of Midwest News.

Statement 2: It is better to use the free cash flow model to value Midwest News than a dividend discount model.

Miller considered two different valuation models to determine the price of Midwest News's equity: a single-stage free cash flow model and a single-stage residual income model.

103.   Using Freedom Corporation as a comparable, the estimated beta for Midwest News is *most likely*:
A. greater than 0.90. ⌣
B. less than 0.90.
C. equal to 0.90.

104.   The required return estimate of Freedom Corporation is *closest* to:
A. 6%.
B. 9%. ✓
C. 12%.

105.   Which of the following is NOT an input used to estimate Midwest News's equity risk premium based on the Gordon growth model (GGM)?
A. Dividend yield on the market index.
B. Current long-term government bond yield.
C. Expected growth in the market index's P/E ratio. ⌁

106. Based on Exhibit 2 and using the build-up method, Midwest News's required return on equity is *closest* to:
    A. 13.0%. ✓
    B. 13.8%.
    C. 15.8%.

107. Using the single-stage residual income model and assuming the required return on equity is 15%, the value of Midwest News is *closest* to: (use information in Exhibits 1 and 2)
    A. $75 per share.
    B. $95 per share. ✓
    C. $115 per share.

108. Miller has made two statements, one concerning the required return estimate and the other concerning the relative merits of the free cash flow model versus the dividend discount model. Are Miller's statements correct?
    A. Only Statement 1 is correct.
    B. Only Statement 2 is correct.
    C. Both Statements 1 and 2 are correct.

$$\frac{D_1}{P_0} + g - r$$

Use the following information to answer Questions 109 through 114.

Christopher Robinson, chairman of the board of directors for a private endowment fund, believes that the endowment fund for which he is responsible has diverged too far from its stated objectives. Over several years, the board has increased the size of the fund's equity position beyond the stated limits of the investment policy statement. In an effort to realign the fund's investments, Robinson has elected to choose a mortgage-backed security (MBS) for inclusion in the endowment's portfolio. After surveying the MBS market, Robinson has selected four MBS securities to present as potential investments at the next investment committee meeting. Details on the selected MBS securities are presented below:

MBS	Initial Principal ($millions)	Coupon Rate	Underlying Maturity (years)	Nominal Spread	OAS	Z-spread
W	250	7.0%	30	1.21%	0.28%	0.79%
X	175	7.8%	25	1.43%	0.49%	1.16%
Y	225	7.2%	20	1.62%	0.31%	1.12%
Z	190	8.0%	30	1.59%	0.40%	1.14%

At the investment committee meeting, a fellow board member raises his concerns over the potential MBS investments stating, "While we all agree that the fixed-income proportion of the endowment is much too small, I am not sure the suggested MBS securities will fulfill the cash flow requirements of the endowment. What risks are we taking on by allocating a portion of the portfolio to these investments? We cannot afford to end up with a timing mismatch between the cash needs of the endowment and the cash provided from its investments. Also, we have given no consideration to commercial mortgage-backed securities (CMBS). Isn't our analysis incomplete if we fail to give proper discussion of potential CMBS investment opportunities?"

Robinson responded to his fellow board member by addressing the board member's concerns as follows:

"Because the cash requirements of the endowment fund fluctuate directly with interest rates, the cash flows provided from the MBS will provide adequate protection against cash shortfalls arising from differences in the timing of cash needs and cash sources. In addition, we can further reduce uncertainty surrounding the timing of cash flows by purchasing planned amortization class CMOs, which are securities issued against pools of MBS. CMBS were not presented due to the unacceptable risk profile of the comparable CMBS trading in the marketplace."

109. Determine the single month mortality rate for MBS-X for Month 20 using 200 PSA.
    A. 0.0043.
    B. 0.0069. ✓
    C. 0.0080.

110. Assuming that the outstanding principal of MBS-Z is $183 million at the beginning of Month 20 and the total mortgage principal payment for the month is $0.42 million, the expected prepayment for Month 20 using 125 PSA is *closest* to:
    A. $0.525 million.
    B. $0.785 million. ✓
    C. $0.984 million.

111. Of the four MBS securities under consideration, which MBS will add the *most* value relative to the risk associated with the security assuming the effective durations of the MBS securities is approximately the same?
    A. MBS-W.
    B. MBS-X. ✓
    C. MBS-Y.

112. Which of the following statements regarding the difference between the risk profiles of MBS-W and a comparable CMBS is *least* accurate?
    A. Relatively illiquid CMBS properties will increase the degree of balloon risk to the investor.
    B. Contraction risk for a CMBS is significantly lower if the issue contains a defeasance provision.
    C. Shortfalls in cash flow from the underlying properties of a CMBS can be augmented by the sale of the properties or the borrowers' other assets. ✓

113. Which of the following factors would *most likely* increase the rate of prepayments on any of the listed MBS securities?
    A. The Federal Reserve increases the reserve requirement for domestic banks.
    B. Annualized GDP growth, on an inflation adjusted basis, increases from last year. ✓
    C. Interest rates hit a low of 5.2% for the second time in the same year.

114. Robinson commented that the MBS cash flows would match the cash needs of the endowment, and also that planned amortization class CMOs also help mitigate cash flow timing risk. Are Robinson's comments correct?

   A. Only the comment about the MBS matching the cash flow needs of the endowment is correct.
   B. Only the comment about planned amortization class CMOs and cash flow timing risk is correct.
   C. Both comments are correct.

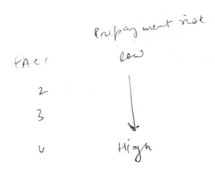

©2012 Kaplan, Inc.

Use the following information to answer Questions 115 through 120.

Rock Torrey, an analyst for International Retailers Incorporated (IRI), has been asked to evaluate the firm's swap transactions in general, as well as a 2-year fixed for fixed currency swap involving the U.S. dollar and the Mexican peso in particular. The dollar is Torrey's domestic currency, and the exchange rate as of June 1, 2009, was $0.0893 per peso. The swap calls for annual payments and exchange of notional principal at the beginning and end of the swap term and has a notional principal of $100 million. The counterparty to the swap is GHS Bank, a large full-service bank in Mexico.

The current term structure of interest rates for both countries is given in the following table:

Time Period	U.S. Interest Rates	Mexican Interest Rates
360 days	4.0%	5.0%
720 days	4.5%	5.2%

Torrey believes the swap will help his firm effectively mitigate its foreign currency exposure in Mexico, which stems mainly from shopping centers in high-end resorts located along the eastern coastline. Having made this conclusion, Torrey begins writing his report for the management of IRI. In addition to the terms of the swap, Torrey includes the following information in the report:

- Implicit in the currency swap under consideration is a swap spread of 75 basis points over 2-year U.S. Treasury securities. This represents a 10 basis point narrowing of the spread compared to this time last year. Thus, we can assume that the credit risk of the global credit market has decreased. Unfortunately, the decline provides no insight into the credit risk of the individual currency swap with GHS Bank, which could have increased.
- In order to decrease the counterparty default risk on the currency swap, we will need to utilize credit derivatives between the beginning and midpoint of the swap's life when this particular risk is at its highest. This is a significantly different strategy than we normally use with interest rate swaps. For interest rate swaps, counterparty default risk peaks at the middle of the swap's life, at which point we utilize credit derivative countermeasures to offset the risk.
- Because currency swaps almost always include netting agreements and interest rate swaps can be structured to include mark-to-market agreements, we can significantly reduce the credit risk of these swap instruments by negotiating swap contracts that include these respective features. When negotiating these features is not possible, credit risk can be reduced by using off-market swaps that do not require an initial payment from IRI.

Six months have passed (180 days) since Torrey issued his report to IRI's management team, and the current exchange rate is now $0.085 per peso. The new term structure of interest rates is as follows:

Time Period	U.S. Interest Rates	Mexican Interest Rates
180 days	4.2%	5.0%
540 days	4.8%	5.2%

115. For the currency swap that Torrey is evaluating, calculate the annual payments that will be required of International Retailers Incorporated.
    A. 29.1 million pesos.
    B. 56.8 million pesos. ✓
    C. 105.5 million pesos.

116. Which of the following statements correctly assesses the excerpt from Torrey's report regarding the swap spread on the currency swap under consideration?
    A. Torrey's statement is correct. ✔
    B. Torrey's statement is incorrect—the decline in the swap spread also indicates a decrease in the credit risk of the currency swap with GHS Bank.
    C. Torrey's statement is incorrect—the decline in the swap spread does not provide insight into the global credit risk level but does indicate a decrease in the credit risk of the currency swap with GHS Bank.

117. Determine whether the excerpt from Torrey's report regarding the timing of peak credit risk is correct with regard to currency swaps and interest rate swaps.
    A. Torrey is only correct regarding currency swaps.
    B. Torrey is only correct regarding interest rate swaps. ✓
    C. Torrey is correct regarding both currency and interest rate swaps.

118. Evaluate Torrey's statements regarding IRI's ability to mitigate the credit risk inherent in currency swaps and interest rate swaps. Torrey is only correct regarding:
    A. netting agreements.
    B. mark-to-market agreements. ✔
    C. off-market swap contracts.

119. Calculate the present value of the dollar fixed payments for the 2-year currency swap six months after Torrey's initial analysis.
    A. $93.28 million.
    B. $101.69 million.
    C. $108.80 million.

©2012 Kaplan, Inc.

120. Calculate the value of the 2-year currency swap from the perspective of the counterparty paying dollars six months after Torrey's initial analysis.
   A. –$0.72 million.
   B. –$3.21 million.
   C. –$4.21 million.

End of Afternoon Session

Exam 3
Morning Session

Question	Topic	Minutes (Points)
1 to 6	Ethical and Professional Standards	18
7 to 12	Quantitative Analysis	18
13 to 18	Economics	18
19 to 30	Financial Reporting and Analysis	36
31 to 42	Asset Valuation – Equity	36
43 to 48	Asset Valuation – Alternative Investments	18
49 to 54	Asset Valuation – Fixed Income	18
55 to 60	Asset Valuation – Derivatives	18

Test Answers

1.	(A)	(B)	(C)
2.	(A)	(B)	(C)
3.	(A)	(B)	(C)
4.	(A)	(B)	(C)
5.	(A)	(B)	(C)
6.	(A)	(B)	(C)
7.	(A)	(B)	(C)
8.	(A)	(B)	(C)
9.	(A)	(B)	(C)
10.	(A)	(B)	(C)

11.	(A)	(B)	(C)
12.	(A)	(B)	(C)
13.	(A)	(B)	(C)
14.	(A)	(B)	(C)
15.	(A)	(B)	(C)
16.	(A)	(B)	(C)
17.	(A)	(B)	(C)
18.	(A)	(B)	(C)
19.	(A)	(B)	(C)
20.	(A)	(B)	(C)

21.	(A)	(B)	(C)
22.	(A)	(B)	(C)
23.	(A)	(B)	(C)
24.	(A)	(B)	(C)
25.	(A)	(B)	(C)
26.	(A)	(B)	(C)
27.	(A)	(B)	(C)
28.	(A)	(B)	(C)
29.	(A)	(B)	(C)
30.	(A)	(B)	(C)

31.	(A)	(B)	(C)
32.	(A)	(B)	(C)
33.	(A)	(B)	(C)
34.	(A)	(B)	(C)
35.	(A)	(B)	(C)
36.	(A)	(B)	(C)
37.	(A)	(B)	(C)
38.	(A)	(B)	(C)
39.	(A)	(B)	(C)
40.	(A)	(B)	(C)

41.	(A)	(B)	(C)
42.	(A)	(B)	(C)
43.	(A)	(B)	(C)
44.	(A)	(B)	(C)
45.	(A)	(B)	(C)
46.	(A)	(B)	(C)
47.	(A)	(B)	(C)
48.	(A)	(B)	(C)
49.	(A)	(B)	(C)
50.	(A)	(B)	(C)

51.	(A)	(B)	(C)
52.	(A)	(B)	(C)
53.	(A)	(B)	(C)
54.	(A)	(B)	(C)
55.	(A)	(B)	(C)
56.	(A)	(B)	(C)
57.	(A)	(B)	(C)
58.	(A)	(B)	(C)
59.	(A)	(B)	(C)
60.	(A)	(B)	(C)

Exam 3
Morning Session

Use the following information to answer Questions 1 through 6.

For the past 15 years, Susan Luna, CFA, Kyle Lawson, CFA, and Matt Miller, CFA, have worked together as equity analysts and then equity portfolio managers in the investment management division (BIMCO) of Broadway Life Insurance Company. For the past five years, the three associates have worked together managing the BIMCO Aggressive Growth Fund (BAGF). During their management tenure, the BAGF had excellent performance and was well recognized in the financial press.

Just over one year ago, Broadway Life was acquired by a larger company, Gobble Insurance, and as part of the consolidation process, BIMCO was closed. The closure allowed Luna, Lawson, and Miller to start their own investment management firm, Trio Investment Management LLC (TIM). TIM focuses on the small capitalization growth equities area. This is the same investment focus as the BAGF, but TIM will have individually managed accounts. Several cases have arisen calling for interpretation as to consistency with CFA Institute Standards of Professional Conduct.

Case 1

TIM markets its investment management services by contracting with small, local bank trust departments. One of the newest bank trust clients for TIM is Shadow Mountain Bank and Trust. Judy Sampson, CFA, the trust officer for Shadow Mountain, has scheduled a meeting with a potential client. When Lawson arrives for the client meeting, he finds that all the TIM marketing material, including biographies of TIM portfolio managers, has been relabeled by Sampson as the Shadow Mountain Wealth Management Team. Sampson has also added the performance of BAGF into the current TIM Equity Composite Index portfolio and relabeled the resultant combined graph, the Shadow Mountain Equity Composite Index. Sampson states that making such changes would probably please clients and improve the chances of acquiring additional trust management accounts for Shadow Mountain and TIM. Lawson goes along and makes the presentation to the potential client using the Shadow Mountain marketing material and the relabeled BAGF/TIM equity performance record.

Case 2

Susan Luna of TIM is meeting with Sol Wurtzel, an institutional salesman for Turn Byer, a large national brokerage firm. Luna complains that TIM's technology costs are too high, especially their outside software services costs. TIM currently subscribes to two investment-related software services. The first software vendor is StockCal Software Services (StockCal), which provides valuation and stock-charting capabilities that TIM uses in its equity research and selection process. The other vendor is Add-Invest Software (Add-Invest), a software program providing account management and performance evaluation reporting, which TIM uses in developing monthly reports for all clients. In response to Luna, Wurtzel suggests that Turn Byer has an excellent soft dollar trading desk and would be willing to offer to cover TIM's StockCal and Add-Invest expenses through soft dollar commissions. Luna then reviews TIM's projected commission dollars for the year and decides there are more than enough soft dollars to pay the StockCal, AGF, and Add-Invest Software bills combined. Luna believes she can be assured of excellent trade execution from Turn Byer and improved profitability for TIM because of the increased use of soft dollars. Luna then directs that the StockCal and Add-Invest software services be paid for with soft dollar or client brokerage dollars.

Case 3

Sol Wurtzel, the equity salesman for Turn Byer, has referred several clients to TIM over the past year. In fact, Wurtzel referrals currently account for almost 20% of the assets managed by TIM. The principals of TIM decide to reward Wurtzel, either by doubling the commissions paid on trades executed through Turn Byer on Wurtzel's referral accounts, or by paying Wurtzel a cash referral fee for each additional TIM account opened by a Wurtzel referral. The principals agree that any cash referral fee would need to be disclosed to clients in advance.

Case 4

Luna notes that her clients have become increasingly aware of the directed client brokerage/soft dollar commissions issue. At a recent meeting with one of her large pension clients, Service Workers Union Local No. 1418, the subject of directed commissions came up. Upon learning of the commission dollars available to their account, the Union trustees directed Luna to use their client brokerage of approximately $25,000 to donate to a think tank called the Hoover Study Center of Unions at Samford University. Service Workers trustees believe the Hoover study will increase the public awareness of the benefits unions offer to their members and increase union membership. Luna concurs with the trustee's judgment on increasing union enrollment as a great goal, and follows the client's instructions and makes the $25,000 contribution to the Hoover Study Center. Another client, Rosa Lutz, has asked Luna to credit the soft dollar client brokerage proceeds from her personal retirement accounts to Roswell Academy, to update their computer lab. Luna agrees that a new computer lab for Roswell Academy is greatly needed, and she allocates $10,000 of Lutz's commission dollars to Roswell Academy.

1. Did Sampson and/or Lawson violate the CFA Institute Standards of Professional Conduct with respect to presenting the TIM biographies to the client?
    A. Yes, both Sampson and Lawson violated the Standards.
    B. Yes, Sampson violated the Standards, while Lawson did not.
    C. Neither Sampson nor Lawson violated the Standards, because such outsourcing is permitted.

2. Sampson's use of the relabeled BAGF investment performance record violates CFA Institute Standards:
    A. only if Sampson fails to include written disclosures as to the true source and nature of the performance record.
    B. only if Sampson does not have written permission from Gobble Insurance to use the performance data.
    C. unless Sampson includes written disclosures as to the true source and nature of the performance record and has written permission from Gobble Insurance to use the performance data.

3. Did Luna violate the CFA Institute Standards of Professional Conduct and the CFA Institute Soft Dollar Standards by using soft dollar commissions to pay TIM's software subscription costs to StockCal and/or Add-Invest?
    A. Both StockCal and Add-Invest software services may be paid for with soft dollars.
    B. Neither StockCal nor Add-Invest software may be paid for with soft dollars.
    C. It is acceptable to use soft dollars to pay for the StockCal software but not the Add-Invest software.

4. Would either compensation arrangement to reward Wurtzel for client referrals violate the CFA Institute Standards of Professional Conduct?
    A. Both compensation arrangements would be violations, regardless of any disclosures to clients.
    B. The increased commissions plan would be a violation, while the cash referral fees would not be a violation.
    C. Both compensation arrangements are allowed, as long as they are fully disclosed, in advance, to all clients and prospective clients.

5. Is the use of client brokerage to make the $25,000 educational contribution to the Hoover Study Center of Unions a violation of the CFA Institute Standards of Professional Conduct?
   A. Yes, because TIM must ensure that client brokerage fees are directed to the benefit of the client.
   B. Yes, because client brokerage must only be used to pay for goods and services directly related to the investment decision-making process.
   C. No, because the client brokerage has been spent at the specific direction of the client.

6. Is the use of client brokerage to make the $10,000 contribution to the Roswell Academy a violation of the CFA Institute Standards of Professional Conduct?
   A. Yes, because client brokerage must only be used to pay for goods and services directly related to the investment decision-making process.
   B. Yes, because client brokerage of tax-deferred accounts cannot be used to make charitable contributions.
   C. No, because the client brokerage has been spent at the specific direction of the client.

Use the following information to answer Questions 7 through 12.

William Shears, CFA, has been assigned the task of predicting sales for the specialty retail industry. Shears finds that sales have been increasing at a fairly constant rate over time and decides to estimate the linear trend in sales for the industry using quarterly data over the past 15 years, starting with Quarter 1 of 1994 and ending with Quarter 4 of 2008. On January 1, 2009, Shears estimates the following model:

$$sales_t = b_0 + b_1t + e_t \quad (1)$$

where:
sales = quarterly sales (measured in $ millions) for the specialty retail industry
b_0 = intercept term
b_1 = slope
t = time variable (quarter number)
e = random error

Exhibit 1 provides the results of the linear trend regression.

Exhibit 1: Linear Trend Regression

	Coefficient	Standard Error
Intercept	10.0	3.50
Trend	16.0	6.55

Shears also estimates an autoregressive model of order one, AR(1), using the changes in quarterly sales data for the industry from the first quarter of 1994 through the fourth quarter of 2008. He obtains the following results for his AR(1) model:

$$\Delta sales_t = b_0 + b_1\Delta sales_{t-1} + e_t$$

Exhibit 2: AR(1) Model for Changes in Industry Sales

	Coefficient	Standard Error
Intercept	20.00	2.15
Lag 1	0.10	0.04

The autocorrelations for the first four lags from Shears's AR(1) model are provided in Exhibit 3:

Exhibit 3: Autocorrelations from the AR(1) Model

Lag	Autocorrelation	p-Value
1	−0.032	0.38
2	−0.200	0.16
3	−0.065	0.23
4	0.470	0.02

Shears also derives a regression using the residuals from the AR(1) model. He regresses the squared residuals (or estimated errors) against the lagged squared residuals. The results of this regression are reported in Exhibit 4.

Exhibit 4: Squared Residuals Regression

	Coefficient	Standard Error	p-Value
Intercept	3.00	0.577	0.01
Lagged residual squared	0.28	0.185	0.31

Quarterly sales for the Specialty Retail Industry during 2008 were:

Exhibit 5: 2008 Quarterly Industry Sales

Quarter	Sales (in millions)
Quarter 1, 2008	900
Quarter 2, 2008	925
Quarter 3, 2008	950
Quarter 4, 2008	1,000

7. Shears's supervisor, Sam Kite, expresses concern that equation (1) might be misspecified. Specifically, Kite refers to the finding that "sales have been increasing at a fairly constant rate over time."

    Which of the following data transformations should be applied to the dependent variable in equation (1) to best address Kite's concern?
    A. Lagged transformation.
    B. Logarithmic transformation. ✓
    C. First difference transformation.

8. Using the results for the linear trend equation in Exhibit 1, the specialty retail industry sales forecast for Quarter 1 of 2009 is *closest* to:
    A. $26 million.
    B. $976 million.
    C. $986 million. ✓

9. Assuming the AR(1) model in Exhibit 2 is appropriate, Shears should conclude that the Quarter 1, 2009, change in sales is *most likely* to:
    A. fall from Quarter 4, 2008, change in sales. ✓
    B. rise from Quarter 4, 2008, change in sales. ✗
    C. remain unchanged from Quarter 4, 2008, change in sales.

10. Regarding seasonality, given a 5% level of significance, Shears should use Exhibit 3 to conclude he should add the following lag to his autoregressive model:
    A. no lag.
    B. the 3rd lag.
    C. the 4th lag. ✓

11. From the data provided in Exhibit 4, for a 5% level of significance, Shears should conclude that his AR(1) model exhibits:
    A. no autocorrelation.
    B. no autoregressive conditional heteroskedasticity (ARCH). ✓
    C. no multicollinearity.

12. Using the historical data provided in Exhibit 5, the two-period-ahead forecast of the change in industry sales is *closest* to:
    A. $5 million.
    B. $22.5 million. ✓ $b_1 - ?$
    C. $120 million.

Use the following information to answer Questions 13 through 18.

Tristanya is a developed country with three states, West Tristanya (West), Central Tristanya (Central), and East Tristanya (East). Tristanya is a stable democracy with elected representatives, appointed judges, and an elected prime minister. All three states have approximately the same population and geographical area. Tristanya's savings rates are above the global average, and economic development has been mostly financed with domestic savings. The currency in Tristanya is the Tristanya dollar with a symbol of T$. The financial markets are highly liquid and function efficiently. Tristanya's foreign trade is a significant part of the economy, and because of this, Tristanya has continued to push for lower trade barriers. Similar to other developed nations, population growth rate in Tristanya is low and capital stock is high.

The three states adhere to all federal regulations but differ significantly on some policies that are not covered by federal laws. The states also have their own agencies for regional administration of state-specific regulations. Any jurisdictional issue is resolved in federal courts.

The government of Tristanya is increasing its efforts to boost labor productivity. Some of the proposals under consideration include:

1. Increased education funding for elementary and middle schools.

2. Increased tax credits for private research and development expenditures.

3. Increased depreciation allowances for tax purposes.

At a recent congressional hearing, Mr. Adel Mahi, the chief economic adviser to the prime minister, stated that Tristanya's capital accumulation affects the size of the Tristanyan GDP but not its growth rate.

All commercial and financial market regulations are the domain of federal agencies and government recognized self-regulatory organizations (SROs). In this regard, the federal government tends to set minimum standards and allows each state to create agencies to enforce their regulations.

Fuel costs have become an issue in Tristanya as demand for gasoline is expected to increase. Mandated fuel additives, specifically corn ethanol, are used to increase supply, and minimum fuel economy standards have been imposed to curtail demand.

East has the highest obesity rates among the three states. To control the state government's health care expenditure, East's government is implementing an additional tax on all sweet snack foods manufactured in the state. The tax is also known as the "sweet tax." Another regulation, the "supersize drinks ban," will prohibit restaurants in East from selling large portion sizes of carbonated beverages.

The most common form of sweetener in Tristanya is corn syrup. The agricultural industry has benefited from excess demand for corn to produce corn syrup and ethanol. Even after implementation of the "sweet tax", the demand for corn is expected to remain high.

West has the highest gasoline usage per capita, and reducing gasoline consumption is a policy goal for that state's government. West also has the most stringent environmental regulations and has recently raised their standards for minimum fuel economy for automobiles.

Juanita Estrada, an analyst, is assigned to assess the impact of all the regulatory changes on economic growth. Estrada lists the following findings from her analysis:

Finding 1: The snack food industry is in the process of relocating manufacturing of sweet snack foods to West and Central and relocating manufacturing of salty snack foods to East.

Finding 2: After West raised that state's fuel economy standards, the average miles driven per capita increased.

13. Based on finding 1, the snack food industry is engaging in regulatory:
   A. capture.
   B. arbitrage. ✓
   C. competition.

14. Which Tristanyan industry is *most likely* to shrink due to the regulatory changes in the East?
   A. Snacks.
   B. Agriculture.
   C. Carbonated beverages. ✓

15. The cost associated with finding 2 is a:
   A. component of the regulatory burden.
   B. component of the implementation cost.
   C. justification for sunset provisions. ✓

16. The government proposal that would *most likely* lead to the highest increase in labor productivity is:
   A. Proposal 1. ✗
   B. Proposal 2. ✓
   C. Proposal 3.

17. Mahi's statement is consistent with:
   A. classical growth theory. ✗
   B. endogenous growth theory.
   C. neoclassical growth theory.

18. The objectives of regulators in financial markets is *least likely* to include:
    A. low inflation. ✓
    B. prudential supervision.
    C. promotion of economic growth.

Use the following information to answer Questions 19 through 24.

Viper Motor Company, a publicly traded automobile manufacturer located in Detroit, Michigan, periodically invests its excess cash in low-risk fixed-income securities. At the end of 2009, Viper's investment portfolio consisted of two separate bond investments: Pinto Corporation and Vega Incorporated.

On January 2, 2009, Viper purchased $10 million of Pinto's 4% annual coupon bonds at 92% of par. The bonds were priced to yield 5%. Viper intends to hold the bonds to maturity. At the end of 2009, the bonds had a fair value of $9.6 million.

On July 1, 2009, Viper purchased $7 million of Vega's 5% semiannual coupon mortgage bonds at par. The bonds mature in 20 years. At the end of 2009, the market rate of interest for similar bonds was 4%. Viper intends to sell the securities in the near term in order to profit from expected interest rate declines.

Neither of the bond investments were sold by Viper in 2009.

On January 1, 2010, Viper purchased a 60% controlling interest in Gremlin Corporation for $900 million. Viper paid for the acquisition with shares of its common stock.

Exhibit 1 contains Viper's and Gremlin's preacquisition balance sheet data.

Exhibit 1: Preacquisition Balance Sheet Data

in millions	Viper		Gremlin	
	Book Value	Fair Value	Book Value	Fair Value
Current assets	$9,000	$9,000	$500	$700
Noncurrent assets	7,500	7,800	900	950
	$16,500		$1,400	
Current liabilities	$3,000	$3,000	$250	$250
Long-term debt	7,700	7,500	400	300
Stockholders' equity	5,800		750	
	$16,500		$1,400	

Exhibit 2 contains selected information from Viper's financial statement footnotes.

Exhibit 2: Selected Footnote Information—Viper Motor Company

In millions

At the end of 2010, the carrying value of Viper's investment in Gremlin was $1,425, including goodwill. On that date, the fair value of Gremlin was $1,475, and the fair value of Gremlin's identifiable net assets was $1,350. The recoverable amount was estimated at $1,430.

19.   The carrying value of Viper's investment portfolio as of December 31, 2009, is *closest* to:
    A. $16.6 million.
    B. $17.2 million.
    C. $17.5 million.

20.   If Viper had initially classified its Vega bond investment as available for sale, which of the following *best* describes the *most likely* effect for the year ended 2009?
    A. Lower asset turnover.
    B. Higher return on equity.
    C. Lower net profit margin. ✓

21.   What is the appropriate adjustment, if any, if the Pinto bonds are reclassified as available-for-sale securities during 2010?
    A. The difference between the fair value and the carrying value on the date of reclassification is recognized in Viper's other comprehensive income. ✓
    B. Any unrealized gain or loss, as of the date of reclassification, is immediately recognized in Viper's net income.
    C. No adjustment is necessary because reclassification to/from available for sale is strictly prohibited under U.S. GAAP and IFRS.

22.   The amount of goodwill Viper should report in its consolidated balance sheet immediately after the acquisition of Gremlin is *closest* to:
    A. $250 million under the partial goodwill method.
    B. $350 million under the pooling method.
    C. $400 million under the full goodwill method.

23.   According to U.S. GAAP, Viper's long-term debt-to-equity ratio, calculated immediately after the acquisition, is *closest* to:
    A. 1.07.
    B. 1.10.
    C. 1.12.

24. Using only the information contained in Exhibit 2, which of the following statements is *most* accurate when presenting Viper's consolidated income statement for the year ended 2010?
   A. An impairment loss of $5 million should be recognized under IFRS.
   B. An impairment loss of $275 million should be recognized under U.S. GAAP.
   C. No impairment loss is recognized under U.S. GAAP or IFRS.

Use the following information to answer Questions 25 through 30.

Delicious Candy Company (Delicious) is a leading manufacturer and distributor of quality confectionery products throughout Europe and Mexico. Delicious is a publicly traded firm located in Italy and has been in business over 60 years. Delicious complies with International Financial Reporting Standards (IFRS).

Caleb Scott, an equity analyst with a large pension fund, has been asked to complete a comprehensive analysis of Delicious in order to evaluate the possibility of a future investment.

Scott compiles the selected financial data found in Exhibit 1 and learns that Delicious owns a 30% equity interest in a supplier located in the United States. Delicious uses the equity method to account for its investment in the U.S. associate. The associate prepares its financial statements in accordance with U.S. Generally Accepted Accounting Principles (GAAP).

Exhibit 1: Selected Financial Data—Delicious Candy Company

In millions	2009	2008
Income Statement		
Revenue	€60,229	€55,137
Earnings before interest and tax	7,990	7,077
Earnings before tax	7,570	6,779
Income from associate[a]	354	270
Net income	6,501	5,625
Balance sheet		
Total assets[b]	€56,396	€53,111
Investment in associate	5,504	5,193
Stockholders' equity[c]	30,371	29,595

[a] Not included in EBIT or EBT.

[b] Total assets were €45,597 at the end of 2007.

[c] Stockholders' equity was €27,881 at the end of 2007.

Scott reads the Delicious's revenue recognition footnote found in Exhibit 2.

Exhibit 2: Revenue Recognition Footnote

In millions
Revenue is recognized, net of returns and allowances, when the goods are shipped to customers and collectibility is assured. Several customers remit payment before delivery in order to receive additional discounts. Delicious reports these amounts as unearned revenue until the goods are shipped. Unearned revenue was €7,201 at the end of 2009 and €5,514 at the end of 2008.

Delicious operates two geographic segments: Europe and Mexico. Selected financial information for each segment is found in Exhibit 3.

Exhibit 3: Selected Financial Information by Segment

In millions	*EBIT*	*Revenue*	*Total CapEx*	*Total Assets*
Europe	€7,203	€50,463	€4,452	€36,642
Mexico	€787	€9,766	€8,269	€14,250

At the beginning of 2009, Delicious entered into an operating lease for manufacturing equipment. At inception, the present value of the lease payments, discounted at an interest rate of 10%, was €300 million. The lease term is six years, and the annual payment is €69 million. Similar equipment owned by Delicious is depreciated using the straight-line method and no residual values are assumed.

Scott gathers the information in Exhibit 4 to determine the implied "stand-alone" value of Delicious without regard to the value of its U.S. associate.

Exhibit 4: Selected 2009 Market Capitalization Data

In millions except exchange rates	*Delicious*	*Associate*
Market capitalization	€97,525	$32,330
Current exchange rate (€ per $)	€0.70	
Average exchange rate (€ per $)	€0.73	

Associate financial statements include an investment of $60 million in debt securities, which are reported as designated at fair value.

25. When applying the financial analysis framework to Delicious, which of the following is the *best* example of an input Scott should use when establishing the purpose and context of the analysis?
    A. The audited financial statements of Delicious prepared in conformance with either U.S. GAAP or IFRS.
    B. Ratio analysis adjusted for differences between U.S. accounting standards and international accounting standards.
    C. Review of the pension fund's guidelines related to developing the specific work product.

26. If the associate reported the investment in debt securities as held for trading instead of designated at fair value, the impact on Delicious's financial statement would be:
    A. to decrease total assets.
    B. to increase total assets.
    C. no change to total assets.

27. Using the data found in Exhibit 1 and Exhibit 2, which of the following *best* describes the impact on Delicious's financial leverage in 2009 as compared to 2008?
    A. Financial leverage increased, but the true nature of the leverage decreased.
    B. Financial leverage increased, and the true nature of the leverage increased.
    C. Financial leverage and the true nature of the leverage were unchanged.

28. The data found in Exhibit 3 indicates that Delicious may be over-allocating resources to the:
    A. Europe segment.
    B. Mexico segment.
    C. Europe segment and the Mexico segment.

29. If Delicious were to treat the operating lease as a finance lease, its interest coverage ratio for 2009 would be *closest* to:
    A. 16.9.
    B. 17.8.
    C. 19.0.

30. Using the data found in Exhibit 1 and Exhibit 4, Delicious's implied P/E multiple without regard to its U.S. associate is *closest* to:
    A. 14.0.
    B. 14.8.
    C. 15.1.

Use the following information to answer Questions 31 through 36.

Rogert Markets is the nation's third-largest retail grocery chain and usually has the largest or second-largest market share in every city in which it competes. In its most successful large cities, Rogert has as much as a 25% market share, although its share is sometimes greater in small cities. Rogert is known for its excellent customer service and has a wide variety of grocery selections in almost every part of its stores. Its profit margins on sales are slightly above industry averages, and its return on assets and return on equity are above average.

Rogert has an equity beta of 0.78 and a debt-to-capital ratio of approximately 50%. Recent economic difficulties, including higher commodity prices and higher unemployment, resulted in lower profit margins for Rogert. Still, Rogert's decline in profit margin was less than that of its competitors. Rogert did not experience substantial losses of sales from customers switching to lower-priced competitors because its market share remained essentially unchanged.

Zephine Markets is one of Rogert's smaller competitors. Zephine operates in roughly 15% of the same cities as Rogert. Zephine is publicly traded, and one of the members of Rogert's board of directors has asked the staff to evaluate an acquisition of Zephine. The staff believes that Zephine is slightly underpriced and that it could be acquired for a 20% premium over its current price. In recommending against the acquisition, staff member Pierre Chiraq says:

> "I agree that eliminating Zephine as a rival would probably enhance our profit margins. However, I am skeptical about this acquisition. First, because our market share is almost never dominant, much of the benefit of eliminating a smaller rival will be shared by our other rivals. They will free-ride on our investment. Second, if our profit margins do increase, we will eventually attract new rivals into our markets. And finally, our cost of capital should increase substantially because the firm will be diversifying horizontally instead of vertically, increasing the firm's risk."

Over the past several years, grocery industry growth has tended to follow the general economy. The competitors in the industry, like Rogert, compete for market share in a stable industry. The industry's cyclical behavior has shown stable performance in both the ups and downs of the business cycle.

In assessing Rogert's competitive position, Chiraq comments about the threat of new entrants:

"My concern about new entrants into our business is low for several reasons. Economies of scale are achievable at a low size of operations relative to that of our firm. Our brand identity is high in the markets in which we compete. And, finally, access to distribution channels is difficult to achieve in the grocery business. While there are many competitive forces that concern me, threat of new entrants is low on my list."

Finally, the staff discusses industry changes that might have a negative effect on Rogert's industry position. The following three phenomena are mentioned as possibly having such an effect:

1. Industry growth rates are low and declining.

2. Several suppliers are sponsoring national television advertisements for their products.

3. The government has approved a new method of extending the shelf life of fruits and vegetables.

31. Which of Porter's five forces *most likely* account for Rogert's above-average profitability?
    A. High threat of new entrants.
    B. High threat of substitutes.
    C. Low bargaining power of buyers.

32. Which of the following is *least likely* to relate to rivalry among existing competitors in Rogert's industry?
    A. A high degree of operating or financial leverage.
    B. A short product shelf life.
    C. High switching costs.

33. Which of Chiraq's reasons for opposing the acquisition of Zephine Markets is *least likely* to be correct?
    A. The free-rider argument.
    B. The risk of new rivals argument.
    C. The cost of capital argument.

34. Which of the following is *least likely* to relate to the threat of new entrants for Rogert?
    A. Threat of forward integration.
    B. Product differences and identity.
    C. Cost and/or quality advantages.

35. Chiraq's concerns about new entrants into Rogert's business is *least likely* correct regarding:
    A. economies of scale.
    B. brand identity.
    C. access to distribution channels.

36. Which industry change mentioned by the staff is *least likely* to reduce Rogert's profitability?
    A. Lower industry growth rates.
    B. The national advertising campaign by suppliers.
    C. The approval of a method for extending the shelf life of fruits and vegetables.

Use the following information to answer Questions 37 through 42.

George Armor, CFA, is a new stock analyst for Pedad Investments. One tool that Pedad uses to compare stock valuations is the dividend discount model (DDM). In particular, the firm evaluates stocks in terms of "justified" multiples of sales and book value. These multiples are based on algebraic manipulation of the DDM. Over time, these multiples seem to provide a good check on the market valuation of a stock relative to the company's fundamentals. Any stock that is currently priced below its value based on a justified multiple of sales or book value is considered attractive for purchase by Pedad portfolio managers. Exhibit 1 contains financial information from the year just ended for three stable companies in the meatpacking industry: Able Corporation, Baker, Inc., and Charles Company, from which Armor will derive his valuation estimates.

Exhibit 1: Selected Financial Information

	Able Corporation	Baker, Inc.	Charles Company
Revenue/share	$115.00	$52.80	$25.75
EPS	$2.50	$4.80	$4.00
DPS	$1.00	$1.60	$2.50
ROE	25%	15%	8%
Book value per share	$10.00	$32.00	$50.00
Stock price per share (current)	$60.00	$70.00	$35.50
Required return	20%	12%	10%

One of Pedad's other equity analysts, Marie Swift, CFA, recently held a meeting with Armor to discuss a relatively new model the firm is implementing to determine the P/E ratios of companies that Pedad researches. Swift explains that the model utilizes a cross-sectional regression using the previous year-end data of a group of comparable companies' P/E ratios against their dividend payout ratios (r), sustainable growth rates (g), and returns on equity (ROE). The resulting regression equation is used to determine a predicted P/E ratio for the subject company using the subject company's most recent year-end data. Swift has developed the following model, which has an R-squared of 81%, for the meatpacking industry (16 companies):

Predicted P/E = 2.74 + 8.21(r) + 14.21(g) + 2.81(ROE)

(STD error)   (2.11) (6.52) (9.24)   (2.10)

After Swift presents the model to Armor, she points out that models of this nature are subject to limitations. In particular, multicollinearity, which appears to be present in the meatpacking industry model, can create great difficulty in interpreting the effects of the individual coefficients of the model. Swift continues by stating that in spite of this limitation, models of this nature generally have known and significant predictive power across different periods, although not across different stocks.

37. Based on Exhibit 1, select the stock that is the *most* undervalued by applying the justified price-to-book value method.
    A. Able Corporation.
    B. Baker, Inc.
    C. Charles Company.

38. Based on Exhibit 1, the justified price-to-sales ratio of Baker, Inc. is *closest* to:
    A. 1.5.
    B. 1.7.
    C. 1.9.

39. If valuation is based on the justified price-to-sales ratio, Armor should conclude that Able Corporation is:
    A. overvalued; the stock trades at more than double its value based on a justified price-to-sales ratio.
    B. overvalued relative to Baker, but undervalued relative to Charles.
    C. undervalued; the stock trades at less than half its value based on a justified price-to-sales ratio.

40. Armor has been asked to identify the relative valuation merits of the three stocks. Which of the following statements is correct?
    A. Able Corporation is the best investment because it has the highest ROE.
    B. Charles Company is the best investment because the stock is priced below book value.
    C. Able Corporation's earnings should grow the fastest due to its high ROE and retention ratio.

41. Based on Exhibit 1, indicate the company that has the lowest predicted P/E utilizing the meatpacking industry model presented by Swift.
    A. Able Corporation.
    B. Baker, Inc.
    C. Charles Company.

42. Evaluate Swift's comments regarding multicollinearity and predictive power. Which of the following comments is correct?
    A. Only the comment about multicollinearity is correct.
    B. Only the comment about predictive power is correct.
    C. Both comments are correct.

Use the following information to answer Questions 43 through 48.

Karen Westin, Kei Shinoya, and Carlos Perez, partners at PacRim Investment Consultants, are advising a client, the West Lundia Government Employees Pension Plan (WLGE), a large public pension fund. In a previous meeting with the pension board of WLGE, the PacRim team made a recommendation to increase the fund's exposure to domestic real estate. Because of the WLGE plan's large size and in-house expertise, the pension fund has the capacity to invest in and manage a wide variety of real estate investments. The currency in West Lundia is the West Lundian Dollar (WL$).

West Lundian Commercial Real Estate Market Expectations

Commercial real estate prices have experienced a moderate increase over the past year after a decade of unusually slow growth. Demand is expected to exceed supply over the next 10 years. The current average commercial mortgage rate of 3.75% is low by historical standards and is expected to stay relatively low for at least seven more years. The West Lundian economy is expected to enjoy an above average growth rate.

Exhibit 1: West Lundia's Economic Outlook

	Expected Annual Growth Rate	Relative to Other Developed Countries
Job Creation	3.0%	High
Population	1.8%	High
Retail Sales	1.5%	Low
Inflation	0.5%	Low

Because of the favorable real estate conditions, the consensus was to consider equity investments in real estate. Three options under consideration are:

Option 1: Direct investment, in an existing office building.

Option 2: Investment in a public equity REIT.

Option 3: Equity investment in a public REOC.

Option 1: Direct Investment	
Expected NOI Years 1–7	WL$ 7.0 MM
Expected NOI Year 8	WL$ 8.5 MM
Required return on equity investment	10%
NOI growth rate after 8 years	3.25%

Option 2: REIT	
Recent NOI	WL$ 140.0 MM
Non-cash rents	WL$ 5.0 MM
Full year adjustment for acquisition	WL$ 5.0 MM
Other assets	WL$ 50.0 MM
Total liabilities	WL$ 300.0 MM
Current market price per share	WL$ 125.00
Shares outstanding	15 MM
Going-in cap rate	7.00%
NOI growth rate	2.50%

Option 3: REOC	
Expected AFFO in Year 8	WL$ 13.5 MM
Holding Period	7 years
Present value of all dividends for 7 years	WL$ 39.7 MM
Shares outstanding	1.0 MM
Cap rate	7.0%
Growth rate (from Year 8)	2.50%

Additional Information:

1. The office building under consideration has existing tenants with long-term leases that will expire in seven years.

2. The REOC terminal value at the end of seven years is to be based on a price-to-AFFO multiple of 12x.

43. Based on the information in Exhibit 1, the REIT sector that represents the *least desirable* investment is:
    A. industrial.
    B. office.
    C. apartments.

44. The estimated value of the office building (Option 1) using the discounted cash flow approach is *closest* to:
    A. WL$ 89 million.
    B. WL$ 93 million.
    C. WL$ 99 million.

45. Based on its estimated value using the asset value approach, the REIT identified in Option 2 is:
    A. fairly priced.
    B. selling at a discount.
    C. selling at a premium.

46. The *most appropriate* reason to choose Option 1 (direct investment) over Options 2 and 3 is that Option 1 is likely to have the ability to:
    A. use higher leverage.
    B. provide greater tax advantages.
    C. avoid structural conflicts of interest.

47. The estimated value per share of Option 3, REOC, using the discounted cash flow approach is *closest* to:
    A. WL$ 125.50.
    B. WL$ 140.60.
    C. WL$ 162.00.

48. Option 3 would be preferred over Option 2 if:
    A. liquidity of the investment is critical.
    B. the investment must be efficient in terms of corporate taxes.
    C. capital appreciation is more highly valued than current income.

Use the following information to answer Ques▮

Martha Garret, CFA, manages fixed-income portfolios ▮
Inc. (JBI). JBI has been in the portfolio management bus▮
years and provides investors with access to actively manage▮
fixed-income portfolios. All of JBI's fixed-income portfolios a▮
using U.S. debt instruments. Garret's primary portfolio responsib▮
the Quasar Fund and the Nova Fund, both of which are long fixed-i▮
portfolios consisting of Treasury securities in all maturity ranges. The ▮
Fund holdings as of March 15 are provided in Exhibit 1. A comparison of▮
rate durations for the Quasar Fund and Nova Fund is provided in Exhibit 2.

Exhibit 1: Quasar Fund

Bond	Maturity (years)	Coupon	Yield	Par Value	Market Value	Duration
A	2	5.0%	5.0%	4,000,000	4,000,000	1.86
B	5	4.5%	6.0%	3,500,000	3,278,851	4.32
C	15	8.0%	7.0%	2,750,000	3,000,468	8.90
D	30	6.5%	4.0%	6,450,000	9,238,340	15.90

Exhibit 2: Key Rate Durations for Quasar Fund & Nova Fund

Fund	Maturity (years)			
	2	5	15	30
Quasar Fund	0.90	1.20	1.80	6.10
Nova Fund	0.40	2.50	3.40	1.10

Of particular importance to Garret and her colleagues is the degree of interest rate risk exposure unique to each portfolio under JBI's management. Driving the increased awareness of the portfolios' interest rate exposure is the double-digit growth in assets under management that JBI's fixed-income portfolios have experienced in the past five years. Interest in the company's fixed-income portfolios continues to grow and as a result, all portfolio managers are required to attend weekly meetings to discuss key portfolio risk factors. At the last meeting, Miranda Walsh, a principal at JBI, made the following comments:

> "The variance of daily interest rate changes has been trending higher over the past three months, leading us to believe that a period of high volatility is approaching in the next 12 to 18 months. However, the reliability is questionable because the volatility estimates were derived using an option pricing model, which assumes constant interest rates."

ntly has a similar shape to the
s, which according to the market
structure, indicates a relatively
intermediate term securities.
ng to move into other maturity
unities for arbitrage."

ncipals met to discuss a new
's suggestion, the principals
r for the new fund, which will
portfolio managers, Greg
ize the LIBOR swap curve
han using local government
y claiming that "the lack of
1akes swap rates and curves
ries despite fewer maturity points
2d to a government yield curve.
1f various countries is similar,
/ith different levels of sovereign
Intrigued by the idea of using the
1thering a range of current and

ions 49 through 54.

for Jones Brothers,
ness for over 23
d equity and
e constructed
lities are
come
uasar
key

49. Assume that Bond A is currently callable at 105 and will be callable at 103 in six months. If the yield curve experiences a negative butterfly shift over the next month, which of the following results is *most likely* to be observed?
A. The bond will experience a larger price decrease than Bond C.
B. The bond will become attractive to long-term investors.
C. The bond will experience price compression.

50. Calculate the effect of a 75 basis point decrease in the 15-year interest rate and a 50 basis point increase in the 2-year interest rate on the value of the Nova Fund.
A. 1.40%.
B. 2.35%.
C. 2.55%.

51. Which of the following statements regarding the effects of interest rate changes on the Quasar Fund and Nova Fund is *most* accurate? The value of the:
    A. Nova Fund would enjoy a smaller percentage gain from a negative butterfly yield curve shift in which all interest rates decrease than would the Quasar Fund.
    B. Quasar Fund would suffer a smaller percentage loss from a steepening twist of the yield curve in which all interest rates increased than would the Nova Fund.
    C. Quasar Fund would suffer a smaller percentage loss from a positive butterfly yield curve shift in which all interest rates increase than would the Nova Fund.

52. Which of the following factors would have the most explanatory power for the historical returns of the Quasar Fund? Changes in the:
    A. level of interest rates.
    B. slope of the yield curve.
    C. curvature of the yield curve.

53. Evaluate Walsh's comments regarding the method used to estimate the expected increase in interest rate volatility and the term structure of interest rates.
    A. Walsh is correct only with respect to interest rate volatility.
    B. Walsh is correct with respect to both interest rate volatility and term structure.
    C. Walsh is incorrect with respect to both interest rate volatility and term structure.

54. Which of the following *best* evaluates Terry's justification for using the swap curve as the benchmark for the Atlantic Fund? Terry's justification is:
    A. correct.
    B. incorrect because there are actually more maturity points to construct the swap curve.
    C. incorrect because there are different levels of credit risk in the swap curves of different countries.

Use the following information to answer Questions 55 through 60.

William Bow, CFA, is a risk manager for GlobeCorp, an international conglomerate with operations in the technology, consumer products, and medical devices industries. Exactly one year ago, GlobeCorp, under Bow's advice, entered into a 3-year payer interest rate swap with semiannual floating rate payments based on the London interbank offered rate (LIBOR) and semiannual fixed-rate payments based on an annual rate of 2.75%. At the time of initiation, the swap had a value of zero and the notional principal was set equal to $150 million. The counterparty to GlobeCorp's swap is NVS Bank, a commercial bank that also serves as a swap dealer. Exhibit 1 below summarizes the current LIBOR term structure.

Exhibit 1: Current LIBOR Term Structure

	Days							
	90	180	270	360	450	540	630	720
LIBOR	2.25%	2.45%	3.20%	3.75%	4.20%	3.80%	3.10%	2.40%

Upper management at GlobeCorp feels that the original swap has served its intended purpose but that circumstances have changed and it is now time to offset the firm's exposure to the swap. Because they cannot find a counterparty to an offsetting swap transaction, management has asked Bow to come up with alternative measures to offset the swap exposure. Bow created a report for the management team that outlines several strategies to neutralize the swap exposure. Two of his strategies are included in Exhibit 2.

Exhibit 2: Swap Neutralization Strategies

Strategy 1	Strategy 2
Establish short positions in a series of off-market LIBOR forward rate agreements with the price of each FRA equal to the swap fixed rate and with a notional principal of $150 million for each contract.	Sell a floating-rate note with a semiannual coupon payment based on 180-day LIBOR, a maturity of two years, and a par value of $150 million.

After examining its long-term liabilities, NVS Bank has decided that it currently needs to borrow $100 million over the next two years to finance its operations. For this type of funding need, NVS generally issues quarterly coupon short-term floating-rate notes based on 90-day LIBOR. NVS is concerned, however, that interest rates may shift upward and the LIBOR curve may become upward sloping. To manage this risk, NVS is considering utilizing interest rate derivatives. Managers at the bank have collected quotes on over-the-counter interest rate caps and floors from a well known securities dealer. The quotes, which are based on a notional principal of $100 million, are provided in Exhibit 3.

Exhibit 3: Interest Rate Caps and Floors

Term (Years)	LIBOR	Settlement	Interest Rate Cap		Interest Rate Floor	
			Rate	Price	Rate	Price
1	90-day	Quarterly	3.50%	$2,000,000	2.55%	$1,900,000
1	180-day	Semiannual	3.50%	$2,000,000	2.55%	$1,900,000
2	90-day	Quarterly	3.65%	$2,200,000	2.70%	$2,090,000
2	180-day	Semiannual	3.65%	$2,200,000	2.70%	$2,090,000

One of the managers at NVS Bank, Lois Green, has expressed her distrust of the securities dealer quoting prices on the caps and floors. In a memo to the CFO, Green suggested that NVS use an alternative but equivalent approach to manage the interest rate risk associated with its 2-year funding plan. Following is an excerpt from Green's memo:

"Rather than using a cap or floor, NVS Bank can effectively manage its exposure to interest rates resulting from the 2-year funding requirement by taking long positions in a series of put options on fixed-income instruments with expiration dates that coincide with the payment dates on the floating-rate note."

"As a cheaper alternative, NVS can effectively manage its exposure to interest rates resulting from the 2-year funding requirement by creating a collar using long positions in a series of call options on interest rates and long positions in a series of call options on fixed-income instruments, all of which would have expiration dates that coincide with the payment dates on the floating-rate note."

55. Which of the following statements regarding the GlobeCorp swap initiated one year ago is *most likely* correct?
    A. NVS Bank has greater current credit risk than GlobeCorp.
    B. The value of the swap to GlobeCorp has increased since initiation.
    C. Globecorp's upcoming payment will be lower than its previous payment.

56. GlobeCorp is concerned with its exposure to the interest rate swap initiated one year ago. Evaluate the strategies recommended by Bow in Exhibit 2.
    A. Only Strategy 1 will neutralize GlobeCorp's interest rate swap exposure.
    B. Only Strategy 2 will neutralize GlobeCorp's interest rate swap exposure.
    C. Either Strategy 1 or Strategy 2 will neutralize GlobeCorp's interest rate swap exposure.

57. Determine which of the interest rate derivatives in Exhibit 3 is appropriate to manage the interest rate risk associated with NVS Bank's $100 million debt obligation, and calculate the payoff from this derivative 360 days after the contract initiation if LIBOR at that time is expected to be 3.75%.
    A. $25,000.
    B. $50,000.
    C. $100,000.

58. Calculate the expected payoff after 720 days from a short position in the 2-year semiannual interest rate floor in Exhibit 3 if LIBOR at that time is expected to be 2.40%.
    A. −$150,000.
    B. −$75,000.
    C. $0.

59. Which of the following combinations of interest rate derivatives from Exhibit 3 would effectively limit the maximum and minimum interest cost associated with NVS Bank's $100 million floating rate notes?
    A. Sell a 2-year semiannual settlement interest rate floor and buy a 2-year semiannual settlement interest rate cap.
    B. Sell a 1-year quarterly settlement interest rate floor and buy a 1-year quarterly settlement interest rate cap.
    C. Sell a 2-year quarterly settlement interest rate floor and buy a 2-year quarterly settlement interest rate cap.

60. Evaluate Green's comments in her memo to the managers at NVS Bank. State whether Green is correct regarding the effectiveness of the alternative to using an interest rate cap or floor and regarding the effectiveness of creating an artificial interest rate collar.
    A. Green is only correct with respect to the artificial collar.
    B. Green is only correct with respect to the cap or floor alternative.
    C. Green is correct with respect to both the artificial collar and the cap or floor alternative.

End of Morning Session

Exam 3
Afternoon Session

Question	Topic	Minutes (Points)
61 to 66	Ethical and Professional Standards	18
67 to 72	Quantitative Analysis	18
73 to 78	Financial Reporting and Analysis	18
79 to 90	Corporate Finance	36
91 to 102	Asset Valuation – Equity	36
103 to 108	Asset Valuation – Fixed Income	18
109 to 114	Asset Valuation – Derivatives	18
115 to 120	Portfolio Management	18

61.	(A)	(B)	(C)	
62.	(A)	(B)	(C)	
63.	(A)	(B)	(C)	
64.	(A)	(B)	(C)	
65.	(A)	(B)	(C)	
66.	(A)	(B)	(C)	
67.	(A)	(B)	(C)	
68.	(A)	(B)	(C)	
69.	(A)	(B)	(C)	
70.	(A)	(B)	(C)	

71.	(A)	(B)	(C)
72.	(A)	(B)	(C)
73.	(A)	(B)	(C)
74.	(A)	(B)	(C)
75.	(A)	(B)	(C)
76.	(A)	(B)	(C)
77.	(A)	(B)	(C)
78.	(A)	(B)	(C)
79.	(A)	(B)	(C)
80.	(A)	(B)	(C)

81.	(A)	(B)	(C)
82.	(A)	(B)	(C)
83.	(A)	(B)	(C)
84.	(A)	(B)	(C)
85.	(A)	(B)	(C)
86.	(A)	(B)	(C)
87.	(A)	(B)	(C)
88.	(A)	(B)	(C)
89.	(A)	(B)	(C)
90.	(A)	(B)	(C)

91.	(A)	(B)	(C)
92.	(A)	(B)	(C)
93.	(A)	(B)	(C)
94.	(A)	(B)	(C)
95.	(A)	(B)	(C)
96.	(A)	(B)	(C)
97.	(A)	(B)	(C)
98.	(A)	(B)	(C)
99.	(A)	(B)	(C)
100.	(A)	(B)	(C)

101.	(A)	(B)	(C)
102.	(A)	(B)	(C)
103.	(A)	(B)	(C)
104.	(A)	(B)	(C)
105.	(A)	(B)	(C)
106.	(A)	(B)	(C)
107.	(A)	(B)	(C)
108.	(A)	(B)	(C)
109.	(A)	(B)	(C)
110.	(A)	(B)	(C)

111.	(A)	(B)	(C)
112.	(A)	(B)	(C)
113.	(A)	(B)	(C)
114.	(A)	(B)	(C)
115.	(A)	(B)	(C)
116.	(A)	(B)	(C)
117.	(A)	(B)	(C)
118.	(A)	(B)	(C)
119.	(A)	(B)	(C)
120.	(A)	(B)	(C)

Exam 3
Afternoon Session

Use the following information to answer Questions 61 through 66.

Chester Brothers, LLC, is an investment management firm with $200 million in assets under management. Chester's equity style is described to clients as a large-cap core strategy. One year ago, Chester instituted a new compensation plan for its equity portfolio managers. Under this new plan, each portfolio manager receives an annual bonus based upon that manager's quarterly performance relative to the S&P 500 index. For each quarter of out-performance, the manager receives a bonus in the amount of 20% of his regular annual compensation. Chester has not disclosed this new plan to clients. Portfolio managers at Chester are not bound by non-compete agreements.

James Rogers, CFA, and Karen Pierce, CFA, are both portfolio managers affected by the new policy. Rogers out-performed the S&P 500 index in each of the last three quarters, largely because he began investing his clients' funds in small-cap securities. Chester has recently been citing Rogers's performance in local media advertising, including claims that "Chester's star manager, James Rogers, has outperformed the S&P 500 index in each of the last three quarters." The print advertising associated with the media campaign includes a photograph of Rogers, identifying him as James Rogers, CFA. Below his name is a quote apparently attributable to Rogers saying "as a CFA charterholder, I am committed to the highest ethical standards."

A few weeks after the advertising campaign began, Rogers was approached by the Grumpp Foundation, a local charitable endowment with $3 billion in assets, about serving on its investment advisory committee. The committee meets weekly to review the portfolio and make adjustments as needed. The Grumpp trustees were impressed by the favorable mention of Rogers in the marketing campaign. In making their offer, they even suggested that Rogers could mention his position on the advisory committee in future Chester marketing material. Rogers has not informed Chester about the Grumpp offer, but he has not yet accepted the position.

Pierce has not fared as well as Rogers. She also shifted into smaller-cap securities, but due to two extremely poor performing large-cap stocks, her performance lagged the S&P 500 index for the first three quarters. After an angry confrontation with her supervisor, Pierce resigned. Pierce did not take any client information with her, but when she left, she did take a copy of a computer model she developed while working at Chester, as well as the most recent list of her buy recommendations, which was created from the output of her computer valuation model. Pierce soon accepted a position at a competing firm, Cheeri Group. On her first day at Cheeri, she contacted each of her five largest former clients, informing them of her new employment and asking that they consider moving their accounts from Chester to Cheeri. During both telephone conversations and e-mails with her former clients, Pierce mentioned that Chester had a new compensation program that created incentives for managers to shift into smaller-cap securities.

Cheeri has posted Pierce's investment performance for the past five years on its Web site, excluding the three most recent quarters. The footnotes to the performance information include the following two statements:

Statement 1:   Includes large capitalization portfolios only.

Statement 2:   Results reflect manager's performance at previous employer.

61.   Chester's new compensation plan for awarding bonuses to individual portfolio managers:
    A. is consistent with CFA Institute Standards and does not require disclosure.
    B. is consistent with CFA Institute Standards only if fully disclosed to clients.
    C. is consistent with CFA Institute Standards, but any bonuses awarded under the plan must be fully disclosed to clients.

62.   Assuming Rogers would like to accept the offer to serve on the Grumpp investment advisory committee, Rogers's obligations under the CFA Institute Standards require that he:
    A. refuse to serve on the Grumpp committee.
    B. accept the Grumpp committee position only after disclosing the offer to his supervisor.
    C. accept the Grumpp committee position and disclose his acceptance as soon as possible to his supervisor.

63. Chester's advertising campaign includes claims about Rogers's investment performance, as well as Rogers's use and reference to the CFA charter. Is Chester's advertising campaign consistent with the CFA Institute Standards?
    A. Chester's performance claims are inconsistent with CFA Institute Standards, but his use and reference to the CFA designation is appropriate.
    B. Both the performance claim and the reference to the CFA charter are violations.
    C. Neither the performance claims nor the use and reference to the CFA designation are violations.

64. When Pierce left her position at Chester, her behavior was inconsistent with the CFA Institute Standards in that:
    A. taking the computer model was a violation, but taking the recommended list was not a violation.
    B. taking the list of her recommendations was a violation, but taking the computer model was not a violation.
    C. both the computer model and the recommended list were Chester property that Pierce should not have taken.

65. Pierce's behavior upon assuming her new position at Cheeri can *best* be described as violating CFA Institute Standards because she:
    A. encouraged her former clients to leave Chester.
    B. should not have contacted her former clients at all.
    C. disclosed Chester's new compensation program.

66. Cheeri's presentation of Pierce's investment performance is inconsistent with CFA Institute Standards because:
    A. the results were not calculated under GIPS.
    B. performance from a previous employer should not be included.
    C. the results misrepresent Pierce's large cap performance.

Use the following information to answer Questions 67 through 72.

Austin Clark, CFA, has been asked to analyze White Goods Corporation, a $9 billion company that owns a nationwide chain of stores selling appliances and other electronic goods. As part of his analysis of the White Goods Corporation, Clark's supervisor, David Horvath, asks Clark to forecast White Goods' 2009 sales using multiple regression analysis. The following model was developed:

sales = 20.1 + 0.001 GDP + 1,000.6 TR + 0.1 CC − 3.2 PC − 40.3 UR
t-values: (1.1)   (2.3)   (1.75)   (3.2)   (−0.48)   (−0.9)

Number of observations:	76
Standard error estimate:	15.67
Unadjusted R^2:	0.96
Regression sum of squares:	412,522
Error sum of squares:	17,188

Independent Variable Descriptions

GDP = gross domestic product
TR   = average coupon rate on 5-year U.S. Treasury securities
CC   = most recent quarter end consumer confidence index value
PC   = previous year's sales of personal computers
UR   = most recent quarter end unemployment rate

Variable Estimates for 2009

GDP = 8,000
TR   = 0.05
CC   = 97
PC   = 60,000
UR   = 0.055

Critical Values For Student's *t*-Distribution

Degrees of Freedom	Level of Significance for One-Tailed Test			
	10%	5%	2.5%	1%
	Level of Significance for Two-Tailed Test			
	20%	10%	5%	2%
5	1.476	2.015	2.571	3.365
15	1.341	1.753	2.131	2.602
25	1.316	1.708	2.060	2.485
50	1.299	1.676	2.009	2.403
60	1.296	1.671	2.000	2.390
70	1.294	1.667	1.994	2.381

Clark's supervisor asks him to prepare a report explaining the implications of the regression analysis results. Clark writes the following conclusions concerning regression analysis in his report:

Interpreting the results of regression analysis can be problematic if certain assumptions of the ordinary least squares framework are violated. The regression output for White Goods Corporation is unreliable for the following reasons:

Finding 1: The correlation between regression errors across time is very close to 1.

Finding 2: There is a strong relationship between the regression error variance and the regression independent variables.

67. Using his multiple linear regression, Clark's sales forecast for 2009 is *closest* to:
A. –$191,914.
B. $18.
C. $192,090.

68. Is the regression coefficient of the 5-year U.S. Treasury interest rate statistically significantly different from zero at the 10% level of significance?
A. Yes, because 1.75 > 1.29.
B. Yes, because 1.75 > 1.67.
C. No, because 1.75 < 1.99.

69. In this multiple regression equation, a potential statistical issue is:
A. the coefficient of determination indicates a weak model.
B. that sales cannot be statistically modeled.
C. the PC variable is not a statistically significant variable.

70. What is the *F*-value that tests the hypothesis that all of the coefficients are equal to zero?
A. 42.0.
B. 101.0.
C. 336.0.

71. In his report to his supervisor, Clark's test of serial correlation indicates that the *t*-statistics for the regression estimates likely are:
A. biased upward.
B. biased downward.
C. unbiased.

72. Clark's two documented findings related to his examination of the regression errors should lead to the conclusion that Clark's regression equation exhibits strong evidence of:
A. conditional heteroskedasticity.
B. multicollinearity.
C. unit roots.

Use the following information to answer Questions 73 through 78.

Curtis Fox, an equity analyst for Altex Investments, is reviewing financial statements for Hope Manufacturing and Levitt Industries. Hope Manufacturing has recently stated its intention to acquire a 20% stake in Levitt Industries for $185 million cash. Both companies are U.S. companies that follow U.S. GAAP.

Fox wants to consolidate his pro-forma financial statements for the two companies to see the effects of the proposed acquisition. Following are the most recent balance sheets and the pro-forma income statements developed by Fox before taking into account the acquisition.

Pre-Acquisition Balance Sheets (in million $) December 31, 2010	Hope	Levitt
Current assets	13,900	716
PP&E	26,977	108
Total assets	40,877	824
Current liabilities	10,363	220
Other liabilities	11,121	8
Common stock	6,127	108
Retained earnings	13,266	488
Total liabilities and equity	40,877	824

Pro-Forma Income Statements (in million $) for Year Ending December 31, 2011	Hope	Levitt
Revenue	66,176	2,176
Expenses	63,515	2,068
Net income	2,661	108
Dividends	1,525	0

Fox is concerned about the effect that the choice of accounting method will have on the earnings and financial ratios of Hope. Fox consults with Jeffery Gordon, who tells him, "Since Levitt is profitable and pays no dividends, the equity method will result in higher net income than proportionate consolidation. Additionally, the equity method will result in lower return on assets (ROA) than the acquisition method with partial goodwill."

73. Assuming the acquisition goes through at the beginning of 2011, and that Hope will have a significant influence on Levitt, Hope's total assets after acquisition would be *closest* to:
    A. $40,877.
    B. $41,062.
    C. $41,701.

74. Fox estimates that the fair value of Levitt's PP&E is $250 million. The amount allocated to goodwill would be *closest* to:
    A. $20.2 million.
    B. $37.4 million.
    C. $65.8 million.

75. For this question only, assume that as a result of the acquisition, Hope must depreciate an additional $50 million over a 10-year period to zero salvage value. Levitt's contribution to Hope's EBT for 2011 is projected to be *closest* to:
    A. $16.6 million.
    B. $18.8 million.
    C. $21.6 million.

76. For this question only, assume the acquisition occurs on December 31, 2010, and that there is no additional depreciation expense as a result of the acquisition. Compared to its beginning of year investment balance, the balance for Hope's investment in Levitt on December 31, 2011, will be:
    A. lower.
    B. higher.
    C. unchanged.

77. Is Gordon's statement regarding the effects of the choice of accounting method on net income and ROA correct?
    A. Yes.
    B. No, he is incorrect regarding the effect on ROA.
    C. No, he is incorrect regarding the effect on net income and ROA.

78. If Fox were to follow IFRS instead of U.S. GAAP, the accounting method prescribed for this type of investment would *most likely* be:
    A. the equity method.
    B. the acquisition method.
    C. proportionate consolidation.

Use the following information to answer Questions 79 through 84.

Fashion, Inc., is a major U.S. distributor of high-quality women's jewelry and accessories. The company's growth in recent years has been moderately above the industry average. However, competition is intensifying as a number of overseas competitors have entered this mature market. Although Fashion has been a publicly held company for many years, members of senior management and their families control 20% of the outstanding common stock. Martin Silver, the chief executive officer, has been under intense pressure from both internal and external large shareholders to find ways to increase the company's future growth.

Silver has consulted with the company's investment bankers concerning possible merger targets. The most promising merger target is Flavoring International, a distributor of a broad line of gourmet spices in the United States and numerous other countries. In recent years, Flavoring's earnings growth rate has been above competitors' and also has exceeded Fashion's experience. Superior income growth is projected to continue over at least the next five years. Silver is impressed with the appeal of the company's products to upscale customers, its strong operating and financial performance, and Flavoring's dynamic management team. He is contemplating retirement in three years and believes that Flavoring's younger, more aggressive senior managers could boost the combined company's growth through increasing Fashion's operating efficiency and expanding Fashion's product line in countries outside the United States. Alan Smith, who is Silver's key contact at the investment banking firm, indicates that a key appeal of this merger to Flavoring would be Fashion's greater financial flexibility and access to lower cost sources of financing for expansion of its products in new geographic areas. Fashion has a very attractive performance based stock option plan. Flavoring's incentive plan is entirely based on cash compensation for achieving performance goals. Additionally, the 80% of Fashion's stock not controlled by management interests is very widely held and trades actively. Flavoring became a publicly held company three years ago and doesn't trade as actively.

Silver has asked Smith to prepare a report summarizing key points favoring the acquisition and an acceptable acquisition price. In preparing his report, Smith relies on the following financial data on Fashion, Flavoring, and four recently acquired food and beverage companies.

Exhibit 1: Financial and Market Data for Fashion, Inc. and Flavoring International

Financial/Price Data	Fashion	Flavoring
Sales	$400 million	$105 million
Net income	$80 million	$22 million
Cash flow	$140 million	$42 million
Book value	$320 million	$72 million
Number of common shares outstanding	50 million	20 million
Current market price of common stock	$30.50	$20.00
Recent market price range	$34–26	$22–18

Exhibit 2: Transaction Data for Food and Beverage Industry

Valuation Variables	Jones Foods	Dale, Inc.	Hill Brands	Lane Co.	Mean Multiple
Acquisition stock price	$24	$32	$40	$46	—
Price/sales per share	5.0	3.7	4.0	3.8	4.13
Price/book value per share	6.9	5.5	5.8	5.6	5.95
Price/earnings per share	20.0	22.1	18.0	19.0	19.78
Price/cash flow per share	11.8	13.0	10.5	11.0	11.58

79. The strongest motivations for Fashion to acquire Flavoring would *most likely* be:
    A. the potential to increase Fashion's growth and market power.
    B. the potential to create synergies and increase market power.
    C. Fashion management's incentives and diversification.

80. The *least likely* reason that Flavoring's management would favor an acquisition by Fashion would be:
    A. Flavoring management's incentives.
    B. opportunities to utilize Fashion's larger financial resources to increase market share of both companies.
    C. opportunities to utilize Fashion's financial resources to expand the combined company's product line into the higher volume moderately priced market segment.

81. If Fashion issues common stock at the current market price and uses the proceeds to acquire Flavoring's outstanding common stock, the bootstrap earnings effect on post merger earnings would *most likely* occur if Flavoring's acquisition price:
    A. is $20 or lower.
    B. is $20 or higher.
    C. is $20 or lower and Fashion's post merger P/E remains at the current level.

82. Using the comparable transaction approach based on the four recently acquired companies, Smith determines an estimated takeover value based on equally weighted key valuation variables. The estimated takeover value would be *closest* to:
    A. $20.27.
    B. $21.76.
    C. $22.30.

83. Based on pre-acquisition prices of $20 for Jones Foods, $26 for Dale, Inc., $35 for Hill Brands, and $40 for Lane Co., the mean takeover premium for Flavoring would be *closest* to:
    A. 12.50%.
    B. 15.25%.
    C. 18.10%.

84. To justify his use of the comparable transaction approach to establish a fair acquisition for Flavoring, Smith would like to conclude his report with the most important reason for choosing this approach. Which of the following rationales would Smith *most likely* use?
    A. The fair acquisition price developed for Flavoring reflects a market based valuation approach, an advantage compared to discounted cash flow valuations, which are based on assumptions that do not incorporate market valuations.
    B. The acquisition prices for recently acquired companies provide a reasonable approximation of their realistic intrinsic values.
    C. The fair acquisition price developed for Flavoring is a realistic estimate of potential value to Fashion given that forecasts of future performance are unavailable.

Use the following information to answer Questions 85 through 90.

James Kelley is the CFO of X-Sport, Inc., a manufacturer of high-end outdoor sporting equipment. Using both debt and equity, X-Sport has been acquiring small competitor companies rather rapidly over the past few years, leading Kelley to believe that the firm's capital structure may have drifted from its optimal mix. Kelley has been asked by the board of directors to evaluate the situation and provide a presentation that includes details of the firm's capital structure as well as a risk assessment. In order to assist with his analysis, Kelley has collected information on the current financial situation of X-Sport. He has also projected the financial information for alternative financing plans. This information is presented in Exhibit 1.

Exhibit 1

	X-Sport, Inc.					Industry Average
	Current	Plan A	Plan B	Plan C	Plan D	
Debt/equity	1.50	2.33	1.86	1.22	0.82	1.27
K_d (after-tax)	5.0%	8.5%	6.2%	4.4%	3.9%	5.9%
K_e	12.0%	16.0%	13.5%	11.2%	10.9%	12.8%
Expected EPS	$5.67	$6.00	$6.33	$5.47	$4.89	$6.31
Payout ratio	45%					42%
Growth rate	6.1%					5.9%
Stock price	$43					

After carefully analyzing the data, Kelley writes his analysis and proposal and submits the report to Richard Haywood, the chairman and CEO of X-Sport. Excerpts from the analysis and proposal follow:

- In selecting a refinancing plan, we must not push our leverage ratio too high. An overly aggressive leverage ratio will likely cause debt rating agencies to downgrade our debt rating from its current Baa rating, causing our cost of debt to rise dramatically. This effect is explained using the static trade-off capital structure theory, which states that if our debt usage becomes high enough, the marginal increase in the interest tax shield will be more than the marginal increase in the costs of financial distress. However, using some additional leverage will benefit the company by reducing the net agency costs of equity required to align the interests of X-Sport management with its shareholders.

- In the event that X-Sport decides to proceed with a recapitalization plan, I recommend Plan D because it is the most consistent with the shareholders' interests.

Haywood reviews the report and calls Kelley into his office to discuss the proposal. Haywood suggests that Plan B would be the most appropriate choice for adjusting X-Sport's capital structure. Before Kelley can argue, however, the two are interrupted by a previously scheduled meeting with a supplier.

Haywood takes Kelley's data and proposes to the board of directors that X-Sport pursue one of three alternatives to restructure the company. The first alternative is Plan B from Kelley's analysis. The second alternative involves separating GearTech, one of the companies acquired over the last few years, from the rest of the company by issuing new GearTech shares to X-Sport common shareholders. The third alternative involves creating a new company, Euro-Sport, out of the firm's European operations and selling 35% of the new Euro-Sport shares to the public while retaining 65% of the shares within X-Sport. After some persuading, Haywood convinces the 7-member board (two of whom were former executives at GearTech) to accept the second alternative, which he had favored from the beginning. The board puts together an announcement to its shareholders as well as the general public, detailing the terms and goals of the plan.

One of the board members, Michael Ponting, points out that there are several theories of optimal capital structure. Ponting makes the following statements:

Statement 1: Miller and Modigliani Proposition II (without taxes) states that cost of equity is not affected by capital structure changes.

Statement 2: Pecking order theory states that debt financing is preferable to all equity financing.

Statement 3: Static trade-off theory states that all firms have an optimal level of debt.

A group of shareholders, upset about the board's plan, submit a formal objection to X-Sport's board as well as to the SEC. In the objection, the shareholders state that the independence of the board has been compromised to the detriment of the company and its shareholders. The objection also states that:

- The value of X-Sport's common stock has been impaired as a result of the poor corporate governance system.
- The liability risk of X-Sport has increased due to the increased possibility of future transactions that benefit X-Sport's directors, without regard to the long-term interests of shareholders.
- The asset risk of X-Sport has increased due to the inability of investors to trust the GearTech financial disclosures necessary to value the division.

85. Using the information in Exhibit 1, calculate X-Sport's weighted average cost of capital for the optimal capital structure.
    A. 7.46%.
    B. 7.75%.
    C. 8.76%.

86. Determine whether Kelley's report is correct with regard to the statements made about the static trade-off theory of capital structure and the net agency costs of equity.
    A. Kelley is only correct with respect to the static trade-off theory.
    B. Kelley is only correct with respect to the net agency cost of equity.
    C. Kelley is incorrect with respect to the static trade-off theory and the net agency cost of equity.

87. Which of the following *best* explains the difference between X-Sport's current cost of debt and the cost of debt associated with Plan A?
    A. Decreased tax advantage with Plan A.
    B. Increased liquidity risk for Plan A bond purchasers.
    C. Increased probability of bankruptcy with Plan A.

88. Which of the statements made by Ponting is correct?
    A. Only Statement 1 is correct.
    B. Only Statement 2 is correct.
    C. Only Statement 3 is correct.

89. Which of the following statements with regard to the alternative plans proposed to X-Sport's board of directors by Haywood is correct?
    A. The GearTech plan is an example of a spin-off transaction, while the Euro-Sport plan is an example of a carve-out transaction.
    B. The GearTech plan is an example of a carve-out transaction, while the Euro-Sport plan is an example of a spin-off transaction.
    C. Both the GearTech plan and the Euro-Sport plans are examples of spin-off transactions.

90. Evaluate the three statements in the shareholders' formal objection submitted to X-Sport's board of directors. The objection is correct with regard to:
    A. asset risk.
    B. liability risk.
    C. the value impact.

Use the following information to answer Questions 91 through 96.

Marie Williams, CFA, and David Pacious, CFA, are portfolio managers for Stillwell Managers. Williams and Pacious are attending a conference held by Henri Financial Education on the fundamentals of valuation for common stock, preferred stock, and other assets.

During the conference, the presenter uses an example of four different companies to illustrate the valuation of common stock from the perspective of a minority shareholder.

- Firm A is a noncyclical consumer products firm with a 50-year history. The firm pays a $1.80 dividend per share and attempts to increase dividends by 4% a year. Earnings and dividends have steadily increased for the past 20 years.
- Firm B is a technology firm. It has never paid a dividend and does not expect to in the near future. Furthermore, due to large investments in new factories and equipment, the firm is not expected to generate positive free cash flow in the foreseeable future.
- Firm C is an industrial firm with currently very little competition and a dividend growth rate of 9% a year. However, the profits in its product market have started to attract competitors and it is expected that Firm C's profits will slowly decline such that the dividend growth steadily falls each year until it reaches a growth rate of 4% a year.
- Firm D is a pharmaceutical firm that is currently enjoying high profits and paying dividends. However, the firm's strongest selling drug is coming off patent in three years. With no other drugs in the pipeline, the firm's dividend growth rate is expected to drop abruptly in three years and settle at a lower growth rate.

The next day, Pacious decides to put what he learned into practice. The stock he is valuing, Maple Goods and Services, currently pays a dividend of $3.00. The dividend growth rate is 25% and is expected to steadily decline over the next eight years to a stable rate of 7% thereafter. Given its risk, Pacious estimates that the required return is 15%.

Williams analyzes the value of Mataka Plastics stock. Its dividend is expected to grow at a rate of 18% for the next four years, after which it will grow at 4%. This year's dividend is $5.00 and Williams estimates the required return at 15%.

$$\frac{D_0(1+g_L)}{r-g_L} + \frac{4 \, D_0 (g_S - g_L)}{r - g_L}$$

From the seminar, Pacious learned that a firm's health can be gauged by the present value of its future investment opportunities (PVGO). Tackling a calculation, he uses the following example for Wood Athletic Supplies:

Stock price	$90.00
Current earnings	$5.50
Expected earnings	$6.00
Required return on stock	15%

Pacious and Williams discuss the characteristics of firms in various stages of growth, where firms experience an initial growth phase, a transitional phase, and a maturity phase in their life. They both agree that the Gordon Growth Model is not always appropriate. Pacious makes the following statements.

Statement 1: For firms in the initial growth phase, earnings are rapidly increasing, there are little or no dividends, and there is heavy reinvestment. The return on equity is, however, higher than the required return on the stock, the free cash flows to equity are positive, and the profit margin is high.

Statement 2: When estimating the terminal value in the 3-stage dividend growth model, it can be estimated using the Gordon Growth Model or a price-multiple approach.

91.   Which of the following *best* describes the appropriate valuation models for the Henri presentation scenarios?
A. Firm A should be valued using a free cash flow model. Firm B should be valued using a free cash flow model.
B. Firm A should be valued using a dividend discount model. Firm B should be valued using a residual income model.
C. Firm A can be valued using either a free cash flow model or a dividend discount model. Firm B should be valued using a residual income model.

92.   Which of the following *best* describes the appropriate valuation techniques for the Henri presentation scenarios?
A. Firm C should be valued using a 2-stage dividend discount model. Firm D should be valued using an H dividend discount model.
B. Firm C should be valued using an H dividend discount model. Firm D should be valued using a 2-stage dividend discount model.
C. Both Firms C and D should be valued using the H dividend discount model.

©2012 Kaplan, Inc.

93. Which of the following is *closest* to the current value for Maple Goods and Services stock?
    A. $15.90.
    B. $49.13.
    C. $67.13.

94. Which of the following is *closest* to the current value for Mataka Plastics stock?
    A. $62.49.
    B. $73.73.
    C. $81.60.

95. Which of the following is *closest* to the percent of Wood Athletic Supplies leading P/E related to PVGO?
    A. 56%.
    B. 59%.
    C. 69%.

96. Regarding Pacious's statements on the stages of growth and the Gordon Growth Model, are both statements correct?
    A. Yes.
    B. No, only Statement 2 is correct.
    C. No, both statements are incorrect.

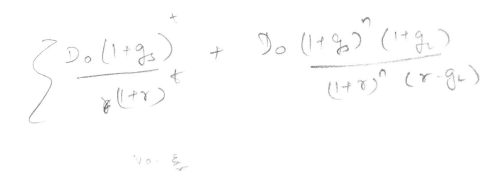

Use the following information to answer Questions 97 through 102.

Asante Bizou is an equity analyst for Alpha, Inc., a boutique consulting firm in San Jose, CA. Alpha is providing consulting services to Prizm's board in evaluating the performance of Prizm's management. Bizou reviews Prizm's key financial data for the past three years.

Selected information from Prizm's financial statements is given in Exhibit 1.

Exhibit 1: Selected Prizm Financial Data

Income Statement	20X4	20X5	20X6
	$m	$m	$m
Sales	40.2	42.3	43.9
Cost of goods sold	(11.6)	(12.3)	(12.8)
Gross profit	28.6	30.0	31.1
Administrative expenses	(10.0)	(10.0)	(3.0)
Earnings before interest and tax	18.6	20.0	28.1
Interest	(6.3)	(6.3)	(4.2)
Earnings before tax	12.3	13.7	23.9
Tax	(5.1)	(5.6)	(11.4)
Net income	7.2	8.1	12.5
Dividends	(3.0)	(3.1)	(3.2)
Retained income	4.2	5.0	9.3

$$EBITDA(1-T) - \$WACC$$

$$28.1(1-0.45) - 12.5\% \cdot (16 + 20 + 10)$$

Exhibit 1: Selected Prizm Financial Data (continued)

Balance Sheet at 31 December	20X3	20X4	20X5	20X6
	$m	$m	$m	$m
Working capital	24.0	25.6	27.2	32.4
Fixed assets	76.0	78.6	82.0	78.1
Total assets	100.0	104.2	109.2	110.5
Liabilities	24.0	24.0	24.0	16.0
Common stock	20.0	20.0	20.0	20.0
Additional paid up capital	10.0	10.0	10.0	10.0
Retained income	46.0	50.2	55.2	64.5
	100.0	104.2	109.2	110.5
Market value of equity (31 December)	167	203	199	145

Other information:

- Beta of firm = 1.
- Debtholders' required rate of return: 5%.
- Equityholders' required rate of return: 15%.
- After tax WACC: 12.5%.
- Tax rate: 45%.

Notes:

1. Depreciation included in cost of goods sold and administrative expenses is 12m, 10.5m, and 9.6m for 20X6, 20X5, and 20X4, respectively.

2. $8m of debt was redeemed at the beginning of 20X6.

3. Other than the debt redeemed in 20X6, Prizm's liabilities consist mostly of long-term debt valued approximately at book value.

4. Replacement value of assets is roughly equal to book value minus 4%.

97. In computing EVA®, which of the following adjustments made by an analyst would be *least appropriate*?
    A. Add LIFO reserve to invested capital.
    B. Expense R&D instead of capitalizing it.
    C. Eliminate deferred taxes and consider only cash taxes as an expense.

98.   Prizm's EVA® for 20X6 based on end-of-year figures is *closest* to:
        A. Negative $1.3 million.
        B. Negative $1.2 million.
        C. Positive $1.6 million.

99.   Prizm's residual income for 20X6 based on end-of-year figures is *closest* to:
        A. –$1.7 million.
        B. $0.7 million.
        C. $2.5 million.

100.   Prizm's Market Value Added (MVA) for 20X6 is *closest* to:
        A. $9.3 million
        B. $12.5 million
        C. $50.5 million

101.   Prizm's free cash flow to equity (FCFE) for 20X6 is *closest* to:
        A. 3 million.
        B. 13 million.
        C. 15 million.

102.   For this question only, assume that the chairman has drawn up budgetary forecasts for 20X7 that suggest that residual income will be $5m for the year ahead. You believe that this will increase by 5% per year for the foreseeable future.

        Using the residual income method, the value of Prizm's equity as of 31st December 20X6 is *closest* to:
        A. $144.5 million.
        B. $147.0 million.
        C. $177.2 million.

©2012 Kaplan, Inc.

Use the following information to answer Questions 103 through 108.

Mary Pierce, CFA, has just joined The James Group as a fixed income security analyst. Pierce has taken over for Katy Williams, who left The James Group to start her own investment firm. Pierce has been reviewing Williams's files, which include data on a number of securities that Williams had been reviewing.

The first file had information on several different asset-backed securities. A summary schedule that Williams had prepared is shown in Exhibit 1.

Exhibit 1: Summary Schedule

Security	Rating	Nominal Spread (bp)
GG Auto Loans	AA	124
KK Auto Loans	AA	118
CC Credit Card Receivables	AA	136
HH Home Equity Loans	AA	168
LL Home Equity Loans	AA	174

The second file included the following schedule of information relating to a specific CMO that Williams had been considering. Exhibit 2 reflects the results of a Monte Carlo simulation based on 15% volatility of interest rates. This security is still available, and Pierce needs to evaluate the investment merit of any or all of the listed tranches.

Exhibit 2: Monte Carlo Simulation Based on 15% Interest Rate Volatility

Tranche	Par Amount ($ million)	OAS (bp)	Z-Spread (bp)	Effective Duration (years)
PAC A	75.0	40	40	1.5
PAC B	40.0	43	95	4.2
PAC C	25.0	65	117	5.0
PAC D	50.0	72	140	7.9
Support S	100.0	51	142	11.8

A third file contained notes Williams had taken at a seminar a couple of months ago on valuing various types of asset-backed and mortgage-backed securities. These notes included the following comments that Pierce found interesting:

"Cash flow yield (CFY) is one method of valuing mortgage-backed securities. An advantage of the CFY is that it does not rely on any specific prepayment assumptions. An important weakness of CFY is the assumption that interim cash flows will be reinvested at the CFY. This is rarely true for mortgage-backed securities."

"Cash flow duration is similar to effective duration, but its weakness is that it fails to fully account for changes in prepayment rates as cash flow yields change. Empirical duration suffers two disadvantages as a measure of interest rate exposure: reliance on theoretical formulas and reliance on historical pricing data that may not exist for many mortgage-backed securities."

"The recent increase in the default rate for subprime adjustable rate mortgages can be traced to the structure of these loans. The negative amortization feature of these loans basically gave the borrower an at-the-money call option on their property. Once the property decreased in value, this call option was worthless, and the borrower had no incentive to make any additional payments."

103. Based on Williams's summary information on asset-backed securities, Pierce has decided to purchase the securities based on the LL Home Equity Loans because these securities offered the highest nominal spread and, therefore, the best return. Williams believes the risk of the ABS securities is similar based on their credit ratings. Pierce's purchase decision is:
    A. incorrect, because the nominal spread does not account for the higher prepayment risk of the LL securities.
    B. incorrect, because the nominal spread does not account for the longer term of home equity loans relative to auto loans.
    C. correct, because the LL securities do indeed offer the best return of the securities listed.

104. Pierce is analyzing the data related to the CMO tranches. Based only on the information in Exhibit 2, the option cost (in bp) of the PAC C tranche is:
    A. greater than the option cost of the PAC D tranche.
    B. greater than the option cost of the Support S tranche.
    C. equal to the option cost of the PAC B tranche.

105. Pierce realizes that she will need to do a more in-depth analysis, but based only on the information in Williams's CMO table, she can conclude that:
    A. there is no prepayment risk in the PAC A tranche.
    B. the high OAS of the PAC D tranche indicates it is most likely to be overvalued.
    C. the Support S tranche is undervalued because its OAS is below that of both the PAC C and PAC D tranches.

106. Evaluate the validity of Williams's comments regarding cash flow yield. She was correct:
    A. regarding the advantage of the CFY but incorrect about the weakness of the CFY.
    B. regarding the weakness of the CFY but incorrect about the advantage of the CFY.
    C. regarding both the advantage of the CFY and the weakness of the CFY.

107. Evaluate the validity of Williams's comments regarding different duration measures. Her comments as to the weaknesses of each duration measure were:
    A. correct only with regard to cash flow duration.
    B. correct only with regard to empirical duration.
    C. correct with regard to both duration measures.

108. The OAS in Exhibit 2 *most likely* reflect:
    A. simple spreads over the Treasury yield curve.
    B. average spreads over the Treasury yield curve.
    C. average spreads over the Treasury spot rate curve.

Use the following information to answer Questions 109 through 114.

Michelle Norris, CFA, manages assets for individual investors in the United States as well as in other countries. Norris limits the scope of her practice to equity securities traded on U.S. stock exchanges. Her partner, John Witkowski, handles any requests for international securities. Recently, one of Norris's wealthiest clients suffered a substantial decline in the value of his international portfolio. Worried that his U.S. allocation might suffer the same fate, he has asked Norris to implement a hedge on his portfolio. Norris has agreed to her client's request and is currently in the process of evaluating several futures contracts. Her primary interest is in a futures contract on a broad equity index that will expire 240 days from today. The closing price as of yesterday, January 17, for the equity index was 1,050. The expected dividends from the index yield 2% (continuously compounded annual rate). The effective annual risk-free rate is 4.0811%, and the term structure is flat. Norris decides that this equity index futures contract is the appropriate hedge for her client's portfolio and enters into the contract.

Upon entering into the contract, Norris makes the following comment to her client:

> "You should note that since we have taken a short position in the futures contract, the price we will receive for selling the equity index in 240 days will be reduced by the cash flows associated with having a long position in the underlying asset. This is known as the convenience yield. If there were no cash flows associated with the underlying asset, the price would be higher. Additionally, you should note that if we had entered into a forward contract with the same terms, the contract price would most likely have been lower but we would have increased the credit risk exposure of the portfolio."

Sixty days after entering into the futures contract, the equity index reached a level of 1,015. The futures contract that Norris purchased is now trading on the Chicago Mercantile Exchange for a price of 1,035. Interest rates have not changed. After performing some calculations, Norris calls her client to let him know of an arbitrage opportunity related to his futures position. Over the phone, Norris makes the following comments to her client:

> "We have an excellent opportunity to earn a riskless profit by engaging in arbitrage using the equity index, risk-free assets, and futures contracts. My recommended strategy is as follows: We should sell the equity index short, buy the futures contract, and pay any dividends occurring over the life of the contract. By pursuing this strategy, we can generate profits for your portfolio without incurring any risk."

109. Determine the price of the futures contract on the equity index as of the inception date, January 18.
    A. 1,064.
    B. 1,071.
    C. 1,078.

110. Which of the following types of futures markets *best* characterizes the observed market for the 240-day equity index futures contract?
    A. Inverted.
    B. Backwardation.
    C. Contango.

111. Evaluate Norris's comments regarding convenience yield on the equity index futures contract and the differences between a forward and a futures contract with the same terms.
    A. Norris is only correct with respect to the convenience yield.
    B. Norris is only correct with respect to the difference between forwards and futures.
    C. Norris is incorrect with respect to both the convenience yield and the difference between forwards and futures.

112. Which of the following *best* describes the movement of the futures price on the 240-day equity index futures contract as the contract moves toward the expiration date?
    A. The futures price will move toward zero as expiration nears.
    B. The futures price will move toward the (at inception) expected spot price as expiration nears.
    C. The futures price will move toward the spot price as expiration nears.

113. Sixty days after the inception of the futures contract on the equity index, Norris has suggested an arbitrage strategy. Evaluate the appropriateness of the strategy. The strategy is:
    A. appropriate since the futures contract is underpriced.
    B. inappropriate since the futures contract is overpriced.
    C. inappropriate since the futures contract is properly priced in the market.

114. If the expected growth rate in dividends for stocks increases by 75 basis points, which of the following would benefit the most? An investor who:
    A. is short futures contracts on the equity index.
    B. is long futures contracts on the equity index.
    C. has a long position in put options on the equity index.

Use the following information to answer Questions 115 through 120.

MPT Associates (MPTA) is an investment advisory firm that makes asset allocation and stock selection recommendations for its clients. MPTA currently manages three portfolios: X, Y, and Z. Portfolio X is the mean-variance efficient market portfolio. Portfolio Y is the portfolio of risky assets with minimum variance. Portfolio Z consists exclusively of 90-day Treasury bills. The three portfolios have the following characteristics:

Expected return for Portfolio X	= 15%
Standard deviation of returns for Portfolio X	= 20%
Expected return for Portfolio Y	= 7%
Standard deviation of returns for Portfolio Y	= 5%
Expected return on Portfolio Z	= 5%

Recently, MPTA was contacted simultaneously by two clients: Danielle Burk and Derek Kitna. Burk and Kitna have known each other since college and are both currently working for the same company.

Burk currently owns a $100,000 portfolio which she is holding in her Roth IRA retirement account. Her investment strategy is a passive approach. Her retirement portfolio has the following risk-return characteristics:

Expected return on Burk's portfolio	= 10%
Standard deviation of returns on Burk's portfolio	= 12%

Kitna requests advice from MPTA on the proper valuation of two stocks that he is considering. Kitna is interested in determining the fair value of shares of Long Drives, Inc. (LDI), a manufacturer of state-of-the-art golf clubs, and of Cell Chip Technologies (CCT), a manufacturer of cell phone chip processors. MPTA maintains a database of analyst forecasts and finds that the 1-year consensus analyst forecast return for the CCT stock equals 15% and the LDI stock equals 13%.

After lengthy conversations with both Burk and Kitna, MPTA decides to advise both of them to use the capital market line, security market line, and capital asset pricing model as their primary analytical tools.

MPTA's senior executives are analyzing trends in asset pricing over the past several decades. They conclude that in the period 1998–1999, there was a bubble in stock prices. Stock prices subsequently corrected, however, from 2000–2001. They believe that the downward trend in stock prices from 2002–2003 was an overcorrection; that is, prices fell significantly below fundamental values.

MPTA executives have been discussing the use of the Treynor-Black model with the investment consultants, Benesh Associates. The advisors at Benesh recommend that each investor be allocated a combination of a passive portfolio and an actively managed portfolio, depending on the investor's risk and return preferences. In his presentation on the Treynor-Black model, David Benesh, the principal at Benesh Associates, makes the following statements:

Statement 1: With respect to the actively managed portfolio, the Treynor-Black model will allocate more funds to securities with large alphas and low systematic risk.

Statement 2: The capital asset pricing model assumes that short selling of securities is unrestricted and that unlimited borrowing at the risk-free rate is allowed. Unlike the theoretical capital asset pricing model, the Treynor-Black model avoids this problem because it does not consider short positions in securities.

In further discussion, Benesh recommends that MPTA consider subscribing to the investment newsletters of two independent equity analysts: Jack Nast and Elizabeth Tackacs. Their alphas, residual risk, and correlation between forecasted and realized alphas are provided in the table below.

	Nast	*Tackacs*
Alpha	4%	7%
Residual risk (σ_ε^2)	0.30	0.40
Correlation between forecasted and realized alphas	0.85	0.60

A regression of forecast alphas on realized alphas, $\alpha^f = a_0 + a_1 \alpha^r + \varepsilon$, indicated that Nast's and Tackacs's forecasts were not biased (i.e., could not reject that $a_0 = 0$ and $a_1 = 1$).

115. MPTA plans to invest Burk's $100,000 in a combination of portfolios X and Z that will have the same standard deviation as her original portfolio. Relative to Burk's original portfolio, the change in her expected portfolio value over one year, resulting from following MPTA's recommendation rather than keeping her current portfolio, is:
    A. an increase of $1,000.
    B. an increase of $2,000.
    C. a decrease of $3,000.

116. Kitna has hired MPTA to evaluate the CCT stock and to make a valuation recommendation. In order to determine if the CCT stock is undervalued, overvalued, or properly valued, MPTA must first determine the appropriate value for the CCT beta. Given a CCT beta of 1.5, what is the conclusion that MPTA should make about the value of CCT based on the consensus analyst forecast of CCT returns?
    A. Undervalued.
    B. Overvalued.
    C. Properly valued.

117. MPTA uses the capital market line (CML) as one of its primary analytical tools. To construct the CML, MPTA is aware that the appropriate risk measure is the standard deviation but is unsure of the slope for the CML. The slope that MPTA should use when constructing the CML is:
    A. 0.10.
    B. 0.50.
    C. 0.75.

118. Assume that the MPTA executives are correct in their characterization of capital market valuation. According to the theory of active portfolio management, in which period(s) of time did large numbers of investors turn their attention to actively managed funds?
    A. The period 1998–1999 only.
    B. The period 2000–2001 only.
    C. The periods 1998–1999 and 2002–2003.

119. Regarding the statements made by Benesh on the Treynor-Black model, are both statements correct?
    A. Yes.
    B. No, both statements are incorrect.
    C. No, one statement is correct but the other statement is incorrect.

120. Assume that there are two stocks in the active portfolio, one recommended by Nast and the other by Tackacs. Using the Treynor-Black model and alphas adjusted for each analyst's forecast accuracy, what is the optimal allocation of the stock recommended by Nast to the active portfolio?
    A. 43%.
    B. 57%.
    C. 60%.

End of Afternoon Session

Exam 1
Morning Session Answers

To get valuable feedback on how your score compares to those of other Level II candidates, use your Username and Password to gain Online Access at schweser.com and choose the left-hand menu item "Practice Exams Vol. 2."

1. B	21. C	41. A
2. A	22. C	42. C
3. A	23. C	43. B
4. C	24. B	44. A
5. C	25. C	45. C
6. C	26. C	46. A
7. C	27. C	47. C
8. A	28. C	48. B
9. A	29. A	49. B
10. B	30. B	50. C
11. C	31. C	51. A
12. B	32. A	52. C
13. C	33. C	53. C
14. C	34. B	54. C
15. A	35. B	55. B
16. A	36. A	56. A
17. B	37. B	57. A
18. A	38. B	58. B
19. B	39. A	59. A
20. A	40. A	60. C

Exam 1
Morning Session Answers

1. **B** **Standard I(B).** Attending the conference would be appropriate, but Gillis must avoid any situation that would affect her independence in order to properly comply with Standard I(B) Professionalism – Independence and Objectivity. Since Gingeria is remotely located, it is reasonable for the government to pay her travel expenses. However, the gift of emeralds must be refused. The fact that the host is a sovereign government does not matter—the obvious objective is to give the analysts a favorable bias toward the currency and the proposed reforms. (Study Session 1, LOS 2.a)

2. **A** **Standard V(C).** Gillis's reports may not be specific investment recommendations, but because they are client communications, she should keep either electronic or hard copy records of her conversations with the government officials and copies of the research reports she used in developing her weekly summary reports, in order to comply with Standard V(C) Investment Analysis, Recommendations, and Actions – Record Retention. (Study Session 1, LOS 2.a)

3. **A** **Standard VI(B).** Gillis is attempting to trade ahead of her employer and her clients in violation of the Standards. She was wrong to take the long position in anticipation of a positive recommendation and wrong to sell the position before issuing her negative recommendation. These trades were wrong regardless of whether they were disclosed. In accordance with Standard VI(B) Conflicts of Interest – Priority of Transactions, client interests must take precedence over personal interests. (Study Session 1, LOS 2.a)

4. **C** **Standard I(A).** Warning Gillis and/or reporting the violation up Trout's management structure are inadequate solutions. Limiting the trading activity and increased monitoring to prevent future violations are more appropriate initial responses, in accordance with Standard I(A) Professionalism – Knowledge of the Law. (Study Session 1, LOS 2.a)

5. **C** **Standard VI(B).** The main problem in this case appears to be that there is no system to identify potential front-running violations before they occur. Standard VI(B) Conflicts of Interest – Priority of Transactions recommends both preclearance of trades and duplicate trade confirmations as procedures for compliance. (Study Session 1, LOS 2.a)

6. **C** **Standards II(B) and V(B).** The strategy based on interest rate parity would provide riskless profits until the prices moved into equilibrium and the forward rates accurately reflected the interest rate differentials. Trout's guarantee is therefore accurate. The low transaction costs available to Trout are a competitive advantage that can be exploited without violating Standard II(B). (Study Session 1, LOS 2.a)

7. **C** A foreign currency dealer buys currency at a low (bid) price and resells it at a high (ask) price in order to make a profit. The easiest way to interpret a currency quote is to put the currency in which you want to transact in the denominator. The quotes are $0.008852-56/¥ and $0.02874-6/NT$. So the dealer will buy yen for $0.008852 and resell it at $0.008856. The dealer will buy NT$ for $0.02874 and resell it at $0.02876.

Carr will be selling yen at the dealer's bid and buying NT$ at the dealer's ask. To determine the yen cost of buying the NT$, we set up the currency quotes so U.S.$ and NT$ cancel and we are left with ¥.

NT$ 10,000,000 × $0.02876/NT$ × ¥/$0.008852 = ¥32,489,833. (Study Session 4, LOS 14.b)

8. **A** Surratt is correct. Market conditions affect currency spreads such that the bid-ask spread on foreign currency quotations increases as exchange rate volatility (uncertainty) increases. In this example, an economic crisis in the Asian markets would create uncertainty, thereby impacting the $/¥ and $/NT$ exchange rates and increasing the bid-ask spread.

   Castillo is incorrect. Bank and other currency dealer positions are not considered to directly impact the size of foreign currency spreads.

   In this example, it is true that the dealer would likely reduce her yen ask (selling price) if she wanted to unload an excess inventory of yen. However, the dealer would also probably reduce her bid (buying price) so that she did not buy any additional yen. The result would be that the spread would remain relatively unchanged. (Study Session 4, LOS 14.a)

9. **A** Surratt is correct. Restrictive monetary policy reduces the growth rate of the money supply and will lead to appreciation of a country's currency. Restrictive monetary policy will increase the real interest rate and, consequently, the demand for domestic physical and financial assets. This increase in financial inflows (increase in the financial account) increases the demand for the domestic currency for investment purposes leading to its appreciation. Choice C is incorrect because we are given in the vignette that the foreign interest rates remain constant. (Study Session 4, LOS 14.l)

10. **B** Castillo is incorrect with respect to the impact of unanticipated restrictive fiscal policies on the value of the dollar.

    A reduction in the budget deficit means that government borrowing will decline, which reduces real interest rates and causes investment funds to flow out of the country. As a result, the value of the dollar tends to decline. (Study Session 4, LOS 14.l)

11. **C** The relevant information here is the spot rate, the forward rate, and the interest rates in the two countries. The first step in covered interest arbitrage is to determine in which currency funds will be borrowed and in which currency funds will be invested. The 3-month interest rate in the United States is 18% / 4 = 4.5% and 12% / 4 = 3% in Switzerland.

    In covered interest rate parity, the hedged foreign return (combining the foreign interest rate (SF) with the forward-spot rate differential) should be equal to the domestic (USD) return:

$$1+r_D = \frac{(1+r_F)(\text{forward rate})}{\text{spot rate}}$$

    If we insert the data from the example into this relationship, we get the following:

$$1.045 \neq 1.03\left(\frac{0.80}{0.85}\right) = 0.9694$$

Because the effective rate is lower in Switzerland, Ponder will borrow in Switzerland and invest in the United States. Assuming that Ponder will utilize $1,000,000, we convert this amount to SF at the spot rate to determine the amount of the Swiss franc loan:

$1,000,000 × SF/$0.85 = SF1,176,470.59.

The amount of the Swiss franc loan to be paid back in three months uses the Swiss interest rate of 3%:

SF1,176,470.59 × 1.03 = SF1,211,764.71.

At inception of the arbitrage, Ponder will have entered into a forward contract where he buys Swiss franc and sells U.S. dollars. Using this forward contract and rate, the cost of the loan in U.S. dollars is:

SF1,211,764.71 × $0.80/SF = $969,411.76.

In the United States, Ponder will have invested the $1,000,000 at 4.5% and will have in three months:

$1,000,000 × 1.045 = $1,045,000.

The covered interest arbitrage profit is thus:

$1,045,000 − $969,411.76 = $75,588.24.

> *Professor's Note: If you are asked to calculate a covered interest arbitrage profit on the exam, the quickest way to arrive at your answer would be to multiply the return differentials calculated at the beginning of this problem by the $1,000,000:*
>
>
>
> *$1,000,000 × (1.045 − 0.9694) = $75,600.*
>
> *Using six decimal places for the Swiss return to get 0.969412 (or carrying the calculation in your calculator's memory) will give you the more precise $75,588.*
>
> *Also note that the expected spot rate and inflation rates are not necessary in this problem. Do not confuse covered interest rate parity with purchasing power parity.*

(Study Session 4, LOS 14.e)

12. **B**   Only Surratt is correct. Castillo is incorrect—FX carry trade risk management is often structured such that whenever the *investment* currency becomes overvalued, the trade is closed or reversed. (Study Session 4, LOS 14.i)

13. **C**   Statement 1: McDonnell is correct. Private firms are usually smaller than public firms and, thus, thought to be riskier. Accordingly, private firms are usually assigned higher risk premiums and required returns than public firms. The lack of access to liquid public equity markets can also limit a private firm's growth.

Statement 2: McDonnell is correct that small private firms may not be able to attract as many qualified applicants for top positions as public firms. This may reduce the depth of management, slow growth, and increase risk at private firms. She is, however, incorrect that private firm managers and investors have a shorter-term view. Public firm shareholders often focus on short-term measures such as quarterly earnings and the consistency of such. Public management may therefore take a shorter-term view than they otherwise would. So it is private firms that should be able to take a longer-term view.

Furthermore, in most private firms, management has substantial equity ownership. In this case, external shareholders cannot exert as much control, and the firm may be able to take a longer-term perspective. (Study Session 12, LOS 37.a)

14. **C** McDonnell and Lutge will use the investment value of Albion Biotechnology to determine what the firm is worth to Thorngate. Investment value is the value to a specific buyer and may be different for each investor due to different cash flow estimates, perceived firm risk, discount rates, financing costs, and synergies that lead to decreased costs.

   Market value is frequently used in real estate and other real asset appraisals where the purchase will be levered. Intrinsic value is the value that should be the market value once other investors arrive at this "true" value.

   McDonnell and Lutge are determining the firm's value to Thorngate. The firm is not publicly traded so there is no market for its shares at the present time.

   Furthermore, combining Albion with Thorngate's current pharmaceutical firm would result in advances that no pharmaceutical competitor could match. The synergies appear to be unavailable to other potential buyers (i.e., the value that McDonnell and Lutge will determine is specific to Thorngate and is not a value determined in a market of many buyers and sellers). (Study Session 12, LOS 37.c)

15. **A** In a strategic transaction, a firm is acquired based in part on the synergies it brings to the acquirer. A financial transaction occurs when there are no synergies. The previous suitor of Balanced, a competitor in the same industry, was a strategic buyer and could realize the synergistic cost savings of $1,200,000.

   Thorngate currently does not own a manufacturing firm, so it would be a financial buyer. Thorngate will not be able to realize any synergistic cost savings, so these are not included in the free cash flow to the firm (FCFF) estimates in the following tables.

   The calculations are as follows.

Pro forma Income Statement	
Revenues	$23,540,000
Cost of goods sold	$17,655,000
Gross profit	$5,885,000
SG&A expenses	$5,400,000
Pro forma EBITDA	$485,000
Depreciation and amortization	$235,400
Pro forma EBIT	$249,600
Pro forma taxes on EBIT	$74,880
Operating income after tax	$174,720

Adjustments to Obtain FCFF	
Plus: Depreciation and amortization	$235,400
Minus: Capital expenditures	$297,000
Minus: Increase in working capital	$231,000
FCFF	–$117,880

The following provides a line by line explanation for the above calculations.

Pro forma Income Statement	Explanation
Revenues	Current revenues times the growth rate: $22,000,000 × (1.07)
Cost of goods sold	Revenues times one minus the gross profit margin: $23,540,000 × (1 − 0.25)
Gross profit	Revenues times the gross profit margin: $23,540,000 × 0.25
SG&A expenses	Given in the question
Pro forma EBITDA	Gross profit minus SG&A expenses: $5,885,000 − $5,400,000
Depreciation and amortization	Revenues times the given depreciation expense: $23,540,000 × 0.01
Pro forma EBIT	EBITDA minus depreciation and amortization: $485,000 − $235,400
Pro forma taxes on EBIT	EBIT times tax rate: $249,600 × 0.30
Operating income after tax	EBIT minus taxes: $249,600 − $74,880
Adjustments to Obtain FCFF	
Plus: Depreciation and amortization	Add back noncash charges from above
Minus: Capital expenditures	Expenditures cover depreciation and increase with revenues: $235,400 + 0.04 × ($23,540,000 − $22,000,000)
Minus: Increase in working capital	The working capital will increase as revenues increase 0.15 × ($23,540,000 − $22,000,000)
FCFF	Operating income net of the adjustments above

(Study Session 12, LOS 37.e)

16. **A**   The free cash flow method can accommodate multiple stage growth assumptions and is the most appropriate. The firm's growth is expected to slow considerably in the years ahead, so the constant growth assumption of the capitalized cash flow method would be inappropriate. The capitalized cash flow method is a single-stage model.

The excess earnings method is useful when there are intangible assets to value, but that does not appear to be a concern in the valuation of Balanced. The firm's assets appear to be largely tangible (consisting of equipment and the factory). (Study Session 12, LOS 37.f)

17. **B** Lutge is using the guideline transactions method (GTM) because his database uses the price multiples from the sale of entire public and private companies. The interest in Jensen is a noncontrolling equity interest, so a discount for lack of control (DLOC) will be applied to its valuation. A discount for lack of marketability (DLOM) will also be applied because the Jensen interest cannot be easily sold.

The DLOC is backed out of the control premium.

$$DLOC = 1 - \left[\frac{1}{1 + \text{Control Premium}} \right]$$

$$DLOC = 1 - \left[\frac{1}{1 + 0.187} \right] = 15.75\%$$

The total discount includes the discount for lack of marketability (DLOM).

Total discount = 1 − [(1 − DLOC)(1 − DLOM)]

Total discount = 1 − [(1 − 0.1575)(1 − 0.24)] = 36.0%

(Study Session 12, LOS 37.i,k)

18. **A** Statement 1: McDonnell is correct. Using data from the smallest cap segment of public equity to get the size premium may include a distress premium that is not applicable to a healthy private firm such as Jensen. If so, the estimated size premium will be too large, resulting in a discount rate that is too high and an undervaluation of the Jensen equity interest.

Statement 2: McDonnell is correct. Using the CAPM and estimating beta from public firm data may not be appropriate for private firms that have little probability of going public or being acquired by a public firm. In the build-up method, an industry risk premium is added to the risk-free rate along with an equity risk premium, the small stock premium, and a company-specific risk premium.

(Study Session 12, LOS 37.g,h)

19. **B** Funded status equals fair value of plan assets minus PBO (395 − 635 = −240). Because the funded status is negative, Iron Parts would report a liability of $240 million. (Study Session 6, LOS 20.b)

20. **A** The discount rate increased from 5.5% to 6.0%. An increase in the discount rate will result in lower service cost. Lower service cost will result in a *lower* PBO. A lower PBO will result in a higher funded status (more funded). Lower service cost will result in lower pension expense and *higher* retained earnings. The impact on interest cost cannot be determined without more information. (Study Session 6, LOS 20.d)

21. **C** $327 beginning balance plan assets + $37 actual return + contributions − $22 benefits paid = $395 ending balance plan assets. Solving for the contributions, we get $53. (Study Session 6, LOS 20.b)

22. **C** The higher expected return reduces pension expense. Lower pension expense results in higher net income. Higher net income results in higher retained earnings. Neither the PBO nor the funded status is affected by the expected return on plan assets. (Study Session 6, LOS 20.d)

23. **C**   Amount reported under IFRS:

Service cost	$37
Interest cost[1]	$10.4
Past service cost	$80
Pension cost on P&L	$127.4 million

[1]Interest cost = discount rate × beginning funded status = 0.06 × (500 − 327)

(Study Session 6, LOS 20.c)

24. **B**   Total periodic pension cost can be calculated by summing the changes in the PBO for the period (excluding benefits paid) and then subtracting the actual return on assets. The change in the PBO (excluding benefits) is $157 (635 reported 20X8 PBO + 22 benefits paid − 500 reported 20X7 PBO). Subtract the actual return to get economic pension expense of $120 (157 change in PBO excluding benefits paid − 37 actual return).

Alternatively, total periodic pension cost is equal to contributions minus change in funded status. 20X8 funded status was −240 (395 plan assets − 635 PBO) and the funded status for 20X7 was −173 (327 plan assets − 500 PBO). Contributions were $53 (calculated in Question 21). Thus, total periodic pension cost is $120 [53 − (−67)]. (Study Session 6, LOS 20.c)

25. **C**   The target payout ratio approach to estimating a company's expected dividend uses the following formula:

increase in dividends = increase in earnings × target payout ratio × adjustment factor

Rearranging the formula to solve for the target payout ratio, we obtain:

$$\text{target payout ratio} = \frac{\text{increase in dividends}}{(\text{increase in earnings} \times \text{adjustment factor})}$$

Managers at MavsHD want to move toward the target payout ratio over a period of 8 years, which makes the adjustment factor equal to: 1 / 8 = 0.125. The expected dividend increase is given as $250,000, and the increase in earnings can be computed as the difference between expected earnings and earnings from the prior year: 153,000,000 − 145,000,000 = $8,000,000. Plugging each of these figures into the previous formula, the target payout ratio is calculated as:

$$\text{target payout ratio} = \frac{250,000}{(8,000,000 \times 0.125)} = 0.25 = 25\%$$

(Study Session 8, LOS 27.f)

26. **C**   Paying a premium price for the shares (i.e., a price higher than the current market price of the stock) will reduce the value of the remaining shareholders' shares. However, this value reduction is actually transferred to the selling shareholders since they receive more than the market value per share for selling their shares. (Study Session 8, LOS 27.g)

27. **C** $\Delta p = D(1 - T_D) / (1 - T_{CG}) = 2.25(1 - 0.15) / (1 - 0.396) = 3.17$

(Study Session 8, LOS 27.c)

28. **C** Investors do not like instability in the dividends paid by a company. Any volatility in dividends is seen as a negative sign by investors, and the company's stock price would be punished as a result of varying dividends. According to the bird-in-the-hand theory, investors prefer the assurance of receiving a higher dividend today rather than waiting for returns in the form of capital appreciation. Because of the uncertainty associated with capital appreciation and the relative certainty of dividends, the bird-in-the-hand theory predicts that investors will reward dividend paying companies with a lower cost of equity and, thus, a higher equity value. A repurchase does not provide the same type of assurance since it is an unpredictable and possibly one-time event. (Study Session 8, LOS 27.a,b,f)

29. **A** If the company plans on spending $160 million on net investments, then only 60% of the funds need to come from retained earnings. Therefore, MavsHD needs 0.6 × 160 = $96 million in retained earnings. Net income is projected to be $153 million, leaving $57 million (153 − 96) available to pay dividends. Thus, the dividend payout ratio would equal 57 / 153 = 37.3%. (Study Session 8, LOS 27.f)

30. **B** Under a residual dividend policy, a firm determines the optimal capital budget and then uses retained earnings to fund the optimal capital budget, paying out what is left over to shareholders. Because the amount of distributable earnings is not known in advance and is determined as a function of the capital budget, the dollar dividend paid to shareholders will fluctuate widely from year to year. However, the firm will be able to use internally generated funds to a greater extent when deciding how to fund the optimal capital budget. It is not true, however, that the residual dividend policy will reduce the firm's cost of capital. Investors do not like unpredictable dividends and will penalize the company in the form of a higher required return on equity to compensate for the additional uncertainty related to dividend payments. (Study Session 8, LOS 27.f)

31. **C** BMC is a mature company. The most appropriate model for valuation is the single-stage Gordon growth model.

	In $ millions
EBIT (operating income)	3,290.0
Interest expense	600.0
Earnings before tax	2,690.0
Tax at 30%	807.0
Earnings	1,883.0
Dividends at 72%	1,355.8
Dividend per share	1.36

Cost of Equity:	
CAPM beta	0.90
Risk-free rate	4.0%
Market risk premium	5.0%
Discount rate	(0.90)(5.0%) + 4.0% = 8.5%

LT growth rate = 3.4% (given)

$$\frac{1.36 \times (1.034)}{(0.085 - 0.034)} = \$27.57$$

(Study Session 10, LOS 31.c; Study Session 11, LOS 33.c)

32. **A**   MSC is best valued using a two-stage growth model. For the first three years, dividends grow at 25.0%; after Year 3, dividends grow at 3.4%. Calculate the Year 4 dividend and use this to find the terminal value, which is treated as additional cash flow in Year 3.

Value of Dividend	In $ millions
Year 0	278.0
Year 1	347.50
Year 2	434.38
Year 3	542.97
Terminal value (Year 3 cash flow)	(542.97 × 1.034) / (0.094 – 0.034) = 9357.18

Cost of Equity:	
CAPM beta	1.12
Adjusted beta	1.12(2/3) + 1.00 (1/3) = 1.08
Market risk premium	5.0%
Discount rate	(1.08)(5.0%)+ 4.0% = 9.4%

Using a financial calculator, CF0 = 0; CF1 = 347.50; CF2 = 434.38; CF3 = 542.97 + 9357.18 = 9,900.15; I/Y = 9.4; solve for NPV = $8,241.77 million.

Divide $8,241.77 million by 250 million shares results in $32.97 per share.

(Study Session 10, LOS 31.d; Study Session 11, LOS 33.l)

33. **C**   SGC is a growing company that has no dividend history, so the dividend discount model would be inappropriate. Residual income is appropriate for companies with high quality earnings. The value of SGC stock is best estimated using free cash flow model, as we are told that earnings are erratic but cash flows are stable. (Study Session 11, LOS 33.a)

34. **B**   Using the Pastor-Stambaugh model to calculate SCG's cost of equity:

0.04 + (1.20 × 0.05) + (0.50 × 0.02) + (–0.20 × 0.04) + (0.20 × 0.045) =11.10%

$$\$28.45 = \frac{\$1.60(1.30)}{0.111} + PVGO$$

$28.48 = $18.74 + PVGO
PVGO = $9.71
PVGO/Price = $9.71 / $28.45
           = 34.13%

(Study Session 10, LOS 31.c; Study Session 11, LOS 33.e)

35. **B**   If the justified fundamental leading P/E ratio is 14.1X, then the justified fundamental trailing P/E ratio is (14.1) × (1.034) = 14.6X.

	In $ millions
EBIT (operating income)	3,290.0
Interest expense	600.0
Earnings before tax	2,690.0
Tax at 30%	807.0
Earnings	1,883.0
Shares outstanding	1000.0
EPS	$1.883

Based on the current market price, the trailing price-to-earnings is $26.50 / $1.883 = 14.1X. This means that the fundamental value is greater than the market price; the stock is undervalued. (Study Session 11, LOS 33.f)

36. **A**   Using the H-model, valuation of SGC is:

$$V_0 \ = \ \frac{D_0 \times (1 + g_L)}{r - g_L} + \frac{D_0 \times H \times (g_S - g_L)}{r - g_L}$$

$$= \frac{\$0.80 \times (1.034)}{0.12 - 0.034} + \frac{\$0.80 \times 8/2 \times (0.30 - 0.034)}{0.12 - 0.034}$$

$$= \$19.55$$

(Study Session 11, LOS 33.p)

37. **B**   Normalizing EPS using the method of average EPS is accomplished by averaging the EPS over the six-year period from 2002–2007:

EPS(normalized) = (1.90 + 1.65 + 0.99 + 1.35 + 0.77 + 1.04) / 6 = 1.283. The P/E ratio based on this normalized EPS is 26.5 / 1.283 = 20.649. (Study Session 12, LOS 35.e)

38. **B**   Normalizing EPS using the method of average return on equity is accomplished by (1) averaging the ROE over the six-year period from 2002-2007, and then (2) multiplying the average ROE times the 2008 BVPS. ROE(average) = (0.178 + 0.178 + 0.122 + 0.177 + 0.114 + 0.160) / 6 = 0.155. EPS(normalized) = 0.155(9.11) = 1.412. The P/E ratio based on this normalized EPS is 26.5 / 1.412 = 18.77. (Study Session 12, LOS 35.e)

39. **A**   Book values are more likely to be positive than EPS. Thus, the P/B ratio suffers less often from the problem where P/E ratios are not meaningful because of a negative EPS. The other two advantages given are actually disadvantages associated with using P/B ratios. (Study Session 12, LOS 35.c,d)

40. **A**   Aims is correct about both ratios. For example, let's take the trailing P/E ratio, which is P_0/E_0. Multiplying by the net profit margin results in $P_0/E_0 \times E_0/S_0 = P_0/S_0$. If the justified P/E is (1 − b)(1 + g) / (r − g), the justified P/S is (E_0/S_0) (1 − b)(1 + g) / (r − g). Multiplying the leading P/E ratio by the ROE results in $P_0/E_1 \times E_1/B_0 = P_0/B_0$. If the justified P/E is (1 − b) / (r − g), the justified P/B is ROE(1 − b) / (r − g). This becomes (ROE − b × ROE) / (r − g). Since b × ROE = g (from sustainable growth equation), the equation becomes (ROE − g) / (r − g). (Study Session 12, LOS 35.h)

41. **A**   Both criteria are poorly applied by the associate. Generally, a lower PEG ratio is considered desirable, not a higher one. The difference in the trailing and leading P/E ratios could be due to transitory elements in the current year's income in the denominator of the trailing P/E. In a constant growth model (admittedly a strong assumption), the leading P/E will naturally be smaller than the trailing P/E because earnings are growing by g. (Study Session 12, LOS 35.e,r)

42. **C**   Comment 1 about EBITDA ratios is incorrect. EBITDA is a pre-interest variable, so it is a flow available to all suppliers of capital, not just common shareholders. The comment about dividend yields is reasonable. (Study Session 12, LOS 35.m,n)

43. **B**   Ordon is not correct with regard to auto loan ABS collateral. The collateral structure for ABS backed by amortizing assets (such as auto loans) generally does not change once the security is issued. The collateral simply gets smaller as the loans are paid off by the borrower. In contrast, the collateral structure for ABS backed by nonamortizing assets (such as credit card receivables) changes during the lockout period. During the lockout period, principal payments on the collateral are used to purchase additional collateral assets. This is known as a revolving structure. As part of the structure, a call provision, which causes cash flows to be directed at principal reduction rather than purchasing new collateral assets, is usually included. One such call provision is a cleanup call, which is triggered by a decline in the value of the collateral. Thus, Ordon is correct with regard to credit card receivable ABS collateral. (Study Session 15, LOS 46.c)

44. **A**   The credit enhancement described for the auto loan ABS is an internal credit enhancement known as an excess servicing spread. Under the excess servicing spread, the ABS issuer pays a coupon to investors that is less than the coupon earned on the collateral. The excess of cash inflows over cash outflows is used to fund credit losses in the collateral. The credit enhancement described for the credit card receivable ABS is an external credit enhancement known as a letter of credit. A letter of credit is a third-party guarantee, usually a bank, against collateral losses up to a certain point. Defaults on the collateral are thus mitigated to a certain extent. Third-party guarantees are subject to the weak-link philosophy, and any credit downgrades associated with the third party will negatively affect the rating of the ABS. (Study Session 15, LOS 46.d)

45. **C**   Ordon has correctly described the prepayment risk of the auto loan ABS. Because auto loans are short-term loans and the underlying asset (the automobile) has a tendency to rapidly depreciate in the early years, there is little incentive for borrowers to prepay the loan even if interest rates decline. Borrowers who take out an auto loan generally do not refinance their vehicles as interest rates decline. Weil is forecasting an increase in interest rates, which is unlikely to have a significant effect on the prepayment rate of the auto loan ABS. Ordon has not correctly described the prepayment risk of the credit card receivable ABS. During the lockout period, any principal payments (and prepayments) are used to purchase additional collateral for the ABS. Thus, any changes in prepayment rates induced by interest rate changes would be offset by additional purchases of collateral. A contraction, or extension, would be unlikely to occur. (Study Session 15, LOS 46.e)

46. **A** The home equity loan ABS has an internal credit enhancement known as over-collateralization. The principal of the collateral equals $475 million. The principal of the tranches, however, totals only $450 million (180 + 112.5 + 67.5 + 36 + 54). The over-collateralization feature is included in ABS to protect the tranches from collateral defaults. Thus $25 million of the $30 million default stated in the question would first be absorbed by the extra collateral. This leaves a $5 million default that must be absorbed by one of the tranches. Tranche E has been subordinated to Tranches A – D, a structure known as credit tranching. Losses resulting from defaults (a credit event) are absorbed by Tranche E first until the principal backing the tranche is exhausted. The remaining $5 million default gets absorbed by Tranche E, reducing the principal to $49 million (54 – 5). (Study Session 15, LOS 46.b,e)

47. **C** If the prepayment speed has been a constant 200 PPC (or 200% of the prospectus payment curve), then Tranches A, B, and C have been receiving principal payments as scheduled. This occurs since the prepayment speed falls within the PAC collar. Tranche D is a designated support tranche for the PAC tranches and will absorb excess prepayments in order to maintain the scheduled prepayments for the PAC tranches. This type of structure is known as prepayment tranching (i.e., one or more tranches absorbs faster or slower prepayments to decrease the prepayment risk of other tranches). The PAC II tranche (Tranche C) could potentially absorb a greater amount of prepayments since PAC II tranches also support the PAC I tranches. Since prepayments have been within the initial collar up to this point, however, it is less likely that excess prepayments would be large enough to wipe out Tranche D, thereby forcing Tranche C to absorb excess prepayments. Tranche D will have the greatest contraction since it has no prepayment protection mechanisms in place. (Study Session 15, LOS 46.b,e)

48. **B** Weil has stated several objectives for the MBS investment. He desires low interest rate sensitivity and a large option adjusted spread (OAS) for a cheap price. In order to have low interest rate sensitivity, a tranche with a low effective duration should be chosen. A cheap price means that Weil wants the option cost of the purchased tranche to be low while the OAS is high. Option cost is defined as the z-spread minus the OAS and reflects the cost of the embedded prepayment option. Since the term structure of interest rates is flat, the z-spread and nominal spread are effectively the same. Thus, we can create the following table of OAS, option cost, and effective duration for the three choices given.

	Nominal Spread	OAS	Option Cost	Effective Duration	OAS/Option Cost
PAC Tranches					
PT5	62 bp	47 bp	15 bp	7.9	3.1
Support Tranches					
ST1	**60 bp**	**36 bp**	**24 bp**	**1.3**	**1.5**
ST2	69 bp	35 bp	34 bp	1.7	1.0

PT5 has the best OAS per unit of option cost but has the highest effective duration. Of the tranches with a low effective duration, ST1 has the highest ratio of OAS to option cost, indicating that it is the cheapest tranche in the duration range that Weil finds acceptable. (Study Session 15, LOS 47.e,h)

49. **B** Jacobs needs to offset the returns on the S&P 500 Index. She is currently receiving the returns on the index (which means if there is a negative return on the Index, Jacobs must make a payment), so she will need to enter into a swap in which she pays the index and receives a fixed rate. (Study Session 17, LOS 51.e)

50. **C** Calculate the contract rate on a fixed-rate receiver equity swap using the following formula:

$$C_N = \frac{1-Z_N}{\left(Z_1 + Z_2 + ... + Z_N\right)}$$

Note that this is the same formula for determining the fixed interest rate on an interest rate swap. The discount (Z) factors are given in Exhibit 1. Therefore, the contract rate is:

$$C_N = \frac{1-0.8251}{\left(0.9690 + 0.9242 + 0.8718 + 0.8251\right)} = 4.9\%$$

(Study Session 17, LOS 51.e)

51. **A** A floating-rate equity swap will have zero value on the reset date. The value of the floating-rate side is par or $10 million. The value of a $10 million exposure to the index is also $10 million. Intuitively, this position could be established by borrowing for three years at a floating rate of 1-year LIBOR and investing the proceeds in the index, a zero value portfolio. (Study Session 17, LOS 51.e)

52. **C** The swap spread represents the general level of credit risk in the marketplace. The fixed rate on any particular swap is the same for any interested party regardless of their credit quality. Therefore, the swap spread (the difference between the fixed rate and the reference rate) is a general measure of credit quality in the global economy. (Study Session 17, LOS 51.j)

53. **C** Credit risk in a swap is generally highest in the middle of the swap. At the end of the swap, there are few potential payments left, and the probability of either party defaulting on their commitment is relatively low. Therefore, Widby's first comment is incorrect. If Jacobs wants to delay establishing a swap position, a swaption would potentially be an appropriate investment. However, Jacobs should buy a receiver swaption, not a payer swaption. In a payer swaption, Jacobs would pay the fixed rate and receive the equity index return. The swap underlying a payer swaption would not offset Jacobs's current position. (Study Session 17, LOS 51.f,i)

54. **C** The credit risk underlying the equity swap is associated with the swap counterparty, not the companies in the equity index. This credit risk arises from the possibility that the counterparty to the swap will be unable or unwilling to make payments to Jacobs if the equity return is less than the fixed rate on the swap (i.e., the counterparty owes a payment to Jacobs). (Study Session 17, LOS 53.a)

55. **B** Hedge funds differ from mutual funds in that they may extensively use multiple asset classes in their strategies. Hedge fund fee structures are usually asymmetric, while U.S. regulations require mutual fund fee structures to be symmetric; if fees are levied on gains, mutual fund managers have to share in losses as well. Compared to mutual funds, hedge funds generally require a high minimum investment. (Study Session 13, LOS 41.a)

56. **A** Merger arbitrage strategies attempt to profit by taking a long position in a target's stock and a short position in the acquirer's stock. The mispricings associated with merger arbitrage are typically small, so leverage is often used to magnify these discrepancies. A risk arbitrage strategy is often compared to *writing* (selling) insurance against the failure of a merger; the strategy pays off if the merger is completed, but incurs a large loss if the merger fails. (Study Session 13, LOS 41.b)

57. **A** Merger arbitrage funds take a long position in the target stock and a corresponding short position in the acquirer's stock. If the merger is successful, the position pays off, resulting in positive returns for the fund. However, if the merger fails, a large loss for the fund is likely to result. This leads to a negative skewness and excess kurtosis (kurtosis > 3) in the fund's returns. (Study Session 13, LOS 41.e)

58. **B** Hedge fund strategies such as market neutral or arbitrage funds exhibit relatively low exposures to traditional market factors; factor models will explain only a small portion of the returns of such funds. For distressed and long/short equity funds, however, studies have shown that traditional risk factors explain 50–80% of the returns of these strategies, indicating that hedge funds using these strategies take a substantial amount of market risk. (Study Session 13, LOS 41.d)

59. **A** One advantage that funds of funds provide to investors is higher liquidity than that of single manager funds. Funds of funds tend to have return performance similar to that of the average single manager hedge fund; generally, funds of funds add value by reducing risk rather than by increasing return. (Study Session 13, LOS 41.h)

60. **C** Statement 1 is incorrect. While FFO is indeed a better indicator of future earnings than is reported net income, FFO does not exclude straight-line rent from accounting income. Statement 2 is correct. (Study Session 13, LOS 38.c, 39.f)

Exam 1
Afternoon Session Answers

To get valuable feedback on how your score compares to those of other Level II candidates, use your Username and Password to gain Online Access at schweser.com and choose the left-hand menu item "Practice Exams Vol. 2."

61. C	81. B	101. A
62. B	82. B	102. C
63. B	83. B	103. C
64. C	84. A	104. B
65. C	85. C	105. C
66. A	86. B	106. B
67. B	87. B	107. C
68. A	88. A	108. A
69. A	89. C	109. A
70. C	90. C	110. A
71. C	91. A	111. B
72. B	92. C	112. A
73. B	93. C	113. A
74. A	94. C	114. C
75. A	95. B	115. B
76. C	96. A	116. A
77. C	97. C	117. B
78. A	98. C	118. C
79. B	99. B	119. A
80. A	100. B	120. A

Exam 1
Afternoon Session Answers

61. **C** **Standards III(A), III(B), and III(C).** Under CFA Institute Standards of Professional Conduct, Lee must adopt a trade allocation procedure that allocates assets in an equitable manner. By allocating the Tasty IPO to only employee benefit accounts, Lee is discriminating against other accounts that could also benefit from participating in the IPO. Lee has violated Standard III(B) Duties to Clients – Fair Dealing, which states that members must deal fairly and objectively with all clients. Purchasing Tasty Doughnuts for Ultra Airlines's underfunded pension fund without their knowledge and consent is a clear violation of Standard III(A) Duties to Clients – Loyalty, Prudence, and Care. Lee placed his own interest in potentially increasing his bonus ahead of his client's interests. Lee is required to comply with Ultra Airlines's investment constraint of not investing in IPOs. Lee should have also considered Standard III(C) – Duties to Clients – Suitability, which requires CFA Institute members to ensure that an investment is suitable, and consistent with the client's written objectives, mandates and constraints prior to taking such investment action. By violating this express prohibition from investing in IPOs in the Ultra Airlines pension account, Lee has violated Standard III(C). (Study Session 1, LOS 2.a)

62. **B** **Standard III(B).** Standard III(B) – Duties to Clients – Fair Dealing requires that all clients be dealt with fairly and objectively. Note that Standard III(B) does not state "equally." In this case, Mason had a reasonable basis to include and exclude clients based on their perceived risk level. Lower-risk clients were excluded and higher-risk clients were included. Further, Mason has a reasonable basis of allocating the stock he receives (i.e., assets under management). Since both measures seem objective and reasonable, it appears that Mason dealt fairly with his clients. (Study Session 1, LOS 2.a)

63. **B** **Standard VI(A).** There is no violation inherent in tying a manager's compensation to the performance of his accounts. There is, of course, a risk is that managers will take inappropriate actions in an attempt to boost their performance, as Lee has in this case. But, there is no violation of Standard VI(A) Conflicts of Interest – Disclosure of Conflicts. Whether Ultra owned a stock at the end of any particular day is not relevant so long as they did own the stock at some time. Thus, Lee has violated Standard III (C) Duties to Clients – Suitability. Mason did not have a reasonable basis to buy into the IPO solely because Lee had placed an order. Thus, Mason has violated Standard V(A) Investment Analysis, Recommendations, and Action – Diligence and Reasonable Basis. (Study Session 1, LOS 2.a)

64. **C** **Standard III(C).** The prospectus requires that he hold stocks that are greater than $2.5 billion in market cap and have paid a dividend for two quarters. Parsons has remained in compliance with the market cap requirement. Parson's decision to include non-dividend paying stocks is a clear violation of the FIF mandate. The fact that four of the five stocks initiated dividends, and that these stocks apparently outperformed, is irrelevant. This is a violation of Standard III(C) Duties to Clients – Suitability. (Study Session 1, LOS 2.a)

65. **C** **Standard IV(A).** By soliciting potential clients while still being an employee of FIMCO, Ryan has violated Standard IV(A) Duties to Employers – Loyalty, which states that in matters related to their employment, members and candidates must act for the benefit of their employer and not deprive their employer of the advantage of their skills and abilities, divulge confidential information, or otherwise cause harm to their employer. The standard applies regardless of whether Ryan is on her own time. Even though FIMCO does not have a risk arbitrage product and FIMCO had actually decided against going into the risk arbitrage business, Ryan is offering a service (asset management) that is in competition with her employer's business and will direct funds away from FIMCO. (Study Session 1, LOS 2.a)

66. **A** **Standard IV(A).** Ryan violated Standard IV(A) Duties to Employers – Loyalty by misappropriating employer property. Ryan should not have taken the SelectStock software or manuals off the firm's property, as they are owned by the firm until disposed of by the firm. It does not matter if the SelectStock software and manuals are out of date or even just about to be thrown away, they are not Ryan's property. Ryan should have asked for written permission to take the software and manuals. (Study Session 1, LOS 2.a)

67. **B** The p-value is the probability that the null hypothesis, H_o: slope = zero, is true. The decision rule is to reject the null hypothesis if the p-value is less than the significance level (i.e., there is only a very small chance that the null hypothesis is correct). The p-value for the R_M slope is less than the significance level, and the p-value for the VMG slope is greater than the significance level. Therefore, the R_M slope is statistically significant (reject the null hypothesis that the R_M slope equals zero) and the VMG slope is not statistically significant (cannot reject the null hypothesis that the VMG slope equals zero). (Study Session 3, LOS 12.a)

68. **A** The equation for the R^2 equals the regression sum of squares divided by the total sum of squares. The total sum of squares equals the regression sum of squares plus the error sum of squares. Therefore, the R^2 equals:

$$R^2 = \frac{\text{regression sum of squares}}{\text{regression sum of squares} + \text{error sum of squares}}$$

The problem states that the R^2 equals 0.80. Because the R^2 exceeds 50%, the regression sum of squares must exceed the error sum of squares. (Study Session 3, LOS 12.e)

69. **A** Conditional heteroskedasticity refers to regression errors whose variance is not constant. If there is conditional heteroskedasticity, the variance changes as function of the independent variables. The squared residual (i.e., residual is the estimated error) is used to proxy the error variance. A low R^2 in equation (2) indicates that the slopes in equation (2) are very close to zero, indicating that the error variance is unaffected by the independent variables. For instance, if all the slopes in equation (2) equal zero, then the error variance equals the intercept (a_0, which is constant over time). (Study Session 3, LOS 12.i)

70. **C** According to Recommendation 1 provided by Lockhart, the inflation change variable is highly correlated with the Wilshire index returns (one of the independent variables). If Sawyer includes the inflation change variable along with the Wilshire index returns, the regression will be plagued by multicollinearity (the inclusion of correlated independent variables). Multicollinearity causes the standard errors for the regression parameter estimates to be biased upward, which, in turn, causes the t-statistics to be biased downward (deflated). (Study Session 3, LOS 12.j)

71. **C**   According to Recommendation 2, the data should not be pooled across all 36 months. The sample clearly is split into two parts: pre-Reg FD and post-Reg FD. Sawyer should run separate regressions for each subperiod, or should employ dummy variables to control for the structural shift related to the passage of Reg FD. In either case, by pooling across the two very different sample periods, Sawyer's regression is an example of a misspecified functional form. (Study Session 3, LOS 12.k)

72. **B**   Sawyer is incorrect with respect to Claim 1 and is correct with respect to Claim 2. If the omitted variables are correlated with the included variables, then the omitted variable regression parameter estimates [i.e., from equation (1)] will be biased and inconsistent. Desirable properties, on the other hand, are unbiasedness and consistency. An estimator is unbiased if the expected value of the estimate equals the true population value. An estimator is consistent if the estimate approaches the true population value as the sample size increases. The existence of omitted variables (that are correlated with the included variables) destroys both of these desirable properties. (Study Session 3, LOS 12.k)

73. **B**   Statement 2 is correct. Under defined benefit plans, the employer promises the employee a specific income stream upon retirement. Employee age and turnover determine the liquidity needs and time horizon for a defined benefit pension plan.

   Statement 1 is incorrect. Even though the decisions of individual security selection add value to the portfolio, the real foundation of returns comes from the original asset allocation policy decisions (determining allowable asset classes and weighting these classes). (Study Session 18, LOS 56.e)

74. **A**   Instability in the minimum-variance frontier means that the results of optimization are very sensitive to input assumptions. The result of this high sensitivity to small changes in inputs is that too-frequent portfolio rebalancing may be recommended, which can be costly. Overfitting refers to the situation where optimization is greatly impacted by small differences in the data that are not meaningful. Time instability refers to the changing of input forecasts over time. (Study Session 18, LOS 54.i)

75. **A**   The information ratio is excess return relative to a benchmark, per unit of excess risk relative to a benchmark. It is a relative Sharpe ratio in that the manager is being measured on excess return per unit of risk relative to a benchmark rather than relative to the risk-free rate. An active manager can have a lower information ratio than a passive manager; this is likely to occur when the active manager has negative relative returns. The information ratio is itself a measure of the risk-adjusted return. (Study Session 18, LOS 54.m)

76. **C**   Both of the statements are important implications of the CAPM. If the CAPM holds, all investors can satisfy their investment needs by combining the market portfolio (that includes all risky assets) with the risk-free asset. Furthermore, the tangency portfolio is the market portfolio of all risky assets; no risky asset is excluded from this portfolio. (Study Session 18, LOS 54.e)

77. **C** To construct an arbitrage portfolio, the factor sensitivity of long and short positions should be the same. The factor sensitivity of the long position (stock C) is 0.55. Let x denote the weight of stock A and $(1 - x)$ denote the weight of stock B.

$$1.00x + 0.50(1 - x) = 0.55 \rightarrow x = 0.10$$

In the short portfolio, the weight of stock A is 0.1 and weight of stock B is 0.9.

The expected percentage return on the arbitrage portfolio is the weighted average return on the portfolio:

$$1(0.09) - (0.1)(0.12) - (0.9)(0.08) = 0.006$$

Thus the expected DKK return on this portfolio = $(0.006)(1,000,000)$ = DKK 6,000.

(Study Session 18, LOS 54.l)

78. **A** Let w denote the percentage allocation to stock X and $(1 - w)$ denote the allocation to stock Y. To hedge oil price risk:

$$1.2(w) + 0.9(1 - w) = 0 \rightarrow w = -3 \text{ or } -300\%.$$

Weight of stock Y = $(1 - w) = 1 - (-3) = 4$ or 400%.

This result tells us that the investor should fund an investment in stock Y of 4 times investable assets, with a short position in stock X of 3 times investable assets. (Study Session 18, LOS 54.k)

79. **B** Historically, two accounting methods have been used for business combinations: (1) the purchase method and (2) the pooling-of-interests method. However, over the last few years, the pooling method has been eliminated from U.S. GAAP and IFRS. Now, the acquisition method is required.

The pooling-of-interests method, also known as uniting-of-interests method under IFRS, combined the ownership interests of the two firms and viewed the participants as equals—neither firm acquired the other. The assets and liabilities of the two firms were simply combined. Key attributes of the pooling method include the following:
- The two firms are combined using historical book values.
- Operating results for prior periods are restated as though the two firms were always combined.
- Ownership interests continue, and former accounting bases are maintained.

Note that fair values played no role in accounting for a business combination using the pooling method—the actual price paid was suppressed from the balance sheet and income statement. (Study Session 6, LOS 19.c)

80. **A** If the target of a merger has unused tax losses accumulated, the merged company can use the tax losses to immediately lower its tax liability, thus increasing its net income (Correct). The Internet operation of The Daily is insignificant compared to the overall merger value. Any improvement in the cost structure of the Internet operation will not have a significant impact on overall earnings. In addition, the high-growth characteristics of the Internet segment would not warrant a cost restructuring of the operations. (Incorrect) (Study Session 9, LOS 29.b)

81. **B** First, we must separate the synergistic value from the combined value of the firm as follows:

$$V_{AT} = V_A + V_T + S - C$$

where:
V_{AT} = the combined value of the firm
V_A = the value of the acquirer before the merger
V_T = the value of the target before the merger
S = the synergistic value from the merger
C = the cash paid to the target

Rearranging the formula, the synergistic value can be isolated as follows:

$$S = V_{AT} - V_A - V_T + C$$
$$= 17,500 - (68 \times 117.6) - (35 \times 213.1) + (45 \times 213.1)$$
$$= 17,500 - 7,996.8 - 7,458.5 + 9,589.5$$
$$= \$11,634.2 \text{ million}$$

Next, calculate the acquirer's gain as follows:

$$\text{acquirer's gain} = S - (P_T - V_T)$$

where:
S = the synergistic value from the merger
P_T = the price paid for the target
V_T = the value of the target before the merger

$$\text{acquirer's gain} = 11,634.2 - [(45 \times 213.1) - (35 \times 213.1)]$$
$$= 11,634.2 - (9,589.5 - 7,458.5)$$
$$= \$9,503.2 \text{ million}$$

(Study Session 9, LOS 29.k)

82. **B** total shares = 63.0 + 117.6 = 180.6 million

$$V_{AT} = 7,996.8 + 7,458.5 + 11,634.2 - 0 = 27,089.5$$

new share price = 27,089.5 / 180.6 = 150.0 (Study Session 9, LOS 29.k,l)

83. **B** The legal action based on antitrust is the only choice given that is a post-offer defense. Staggered boards, restricted voting rights, and poison puts are all pre-offer defenses that would not be possible after the tender offer has been made. (Study Session 9, LOS 29.f)

84. **A** A hostile merger occurs when the management of a merger target is opposed to the proposed merger. In such a situation, the acquiring company may initiate a bear hug in which the merger proposal is delivered directly to the board of directors of the target company. Voyager has initiated a bear hug in the hopes of gaining board support for the proposed merger before management can react to the proposal. If the bear hug is unsuccessful, the acquirer may appeal directly to the target's shareholders through a tender offer in which the acquirer offers to buy shares directly from shareholders or through a proxy fight in which a proxy solicitation is used to convince shareholders to elect a board of directors chosen by the acquirer. The board of directors would then replace the target's management and allow the merger to move forward. A white knight is a takeover defense, not a type of merger. (Study Session 9, LOS 29.e)

85. **C** Because YTC operates independently and makes its own financing decisions, the local currency (AUD) should be the functional currency. When the local currency is the functional currency, the subsidiary's financial statements are consolidated with the parent's financial statements using the current rate method. Under the current rate method, all of the income statement items are translated using the average rate for the year. To calculate the percent change in net income, we must translate these items for 2008 and 2007 and then calculate the rate of change.

    2007 translated net income = 25 / 1.30 = 19.23

    2008 translated net income = 12 / 1.45 = 8.28

    growth in net income = (8.28 / 19.23) − 1 = −56.94% (Study Session 6, LOS 21.c)

86. **B** Under the temporal method, the nonmonetary assets and liabilities are remeasured at historical rates. Thus, only the monetary assets and liabilities are exposed to changing exchange rates. Therefore, under the temporal method, exposure is defined as the subsidiary's net monetary asset or net monetary liability position. A firm has net monetary assets if its monetary assets exceed its monetary liabilities. If the monetary liabilities exceed the monetary assets, the firm has a net monetary liability exposure.

    Since very few assets are considered to be monetary (mainly cash and receivables), most firms have net monetary liability exposures. If the parent has a net monetary liability exposure when the foreign currency (AUD) is appreciating, the result is a loss. Conversely, a net monetary liability exposure coupled with a depreciating currency will result in a gain. (Study Session 6, LOS 21.c)

87. **B** total asset turnover = revenue / total assets

    Note that no calculations are necessary to answer this question. Revenues are translated using the same average exchange rate in the temporal and current rate methods. The only difference in the total asset turnover ratio must therefore be in the denominator (i.e., total assets). Under the current rate method, assets are translated using the current rate. Under the temporal method, monetary assets are translated using the current rate, and nonmonetary assets are translated using the historical rate. Because the historical rate is lower than the current rate, the nonmonetary assets (and therefore total assets) will have a higher value under the temporal method. A higher asset value means a lower total asset turnover ratio under the temporal method. The calculation of the total asset turnover ratio using both methods is provided for reference below:

	Temporal		*Current Rate*	
Cash	20 / 1.50 =	13.33	20 / 1.50 =	13.33
Accounts receivable	460 / 1.50 =	306.67	460 / 1.50 =	306.67
Inventories	30 / 1.20 =	25.00	30 / 1.50 =	20.00
Prepaid expenses	25 / 1.20 =	20.83	25 / 1.50 =	16.67
Fixed assets	400 / 1.20 =	333.33	400 / 1.50 =	266.67
Total assets		699.16		623.34
Revenues	870 / 1.45 =	600.00	870 / 1.45 =	600.00
Total asset turnover	600.00 / 699.16 =	0.86	600.00 / 623.34 =	0.96

(Study Session 6, LOS 21.c)

88. **A** The appropriate translation method for the Ukrainian subsidiary is the temporal method since the functional currency is the U.S. dollar (the parent's currency). Under the temporal method, realized gains or losses on nonmonetary assets are recognized in operating profits through depreciation and cost of goods sold. Unrealized gains or losses in nonmonetary assets are not recognized under the temporal method. (Study Session 6, LOS 21.c)

89. **C** Under both the current rate and temporal methods, the revenues for the Ukrainian subsidiary would be translated using the average rate. Cost of goods sold (COGS) would be translated using the historical rate for the temporal method and the average rate for the current rate method. Note that because local currency prices are expected to be constant in the Ukraine, there will be no difference between LIFO and FIFO since all beginning, purchased, sold, and ending inventory will have the same cost. When a currency is depreciating, the COGS based on historical cost (temporal method) will be higher than COGS translated at the average rate (current rate method) since the average rate will incorporate the historical exchange rate and the most recent (depreciated) exchange rate, decreasing the COGS. For instance, if COGS in the local currency is 10 and the historical and average exchange rates are 1 and 1.5 (local currency per reporting currency), then COGS under the temporal method will be 10 and under the current rate method will be 6.67. Since translated sales are the same under both methods, gross profit and the gross profit margin will be higher under the current rate method. (Study Session 6, LOS 21.e)

90. **C** U.S. accounting standards define a hyperinflationary economy as one in which the 3-year cumulative inflation rate exceeds 100%. The Indian economy can be characterized as hyperinflationary. The inflation rate over the past three years can be calculated as follows:

year 1 inflation = [(1 + 0.3464) / (1 + 0.020)] − 1 = 32%

year 2 inflation = [(1 + 0.2915) / (1 + 0.025)] − 1 = 26%

year 3 inflation = [(1 + 0.2566) / (1 + 0.030)] − 1 = 22%

cumulative 3-year inflation = (1.32)(1.26)(1.22) − 1 = 103%

U.S. accounting standards allow the use of the temporal method, with the functional currency being the parent's reporting currency, when a foreign subsidiary is operating in a hyperinflationary environment. IFRS accounting standards allow the parent to translate an inflation-adjusted value of the nonmonetary assets and liabilities of the foreign subsidiary at the current inflation rate, removing most of the effects of high inflation on the value of the nonmonetary assets and liabilities in the reporting currency. In a hyperinflationary environment, the parent company can reduce translation losses by reducing its net monetary assets or increasing its net monetary liabilities. In order to do this, the parent should issue debt denominated in the subsidiary's local currency and invest the proceeds in fixed assets for the subsidiary to use in its operations. (Study Session 6, LOS 21.f)

91. **A** The required rate of return for Aussie Shipping is:

$$r = R_F + \beta_i[E(R_M) - R_F] = 5.2\% + 1.20(4.5\%) = 10.6\%$$

The estimated intrinsic value using the Gordon growth model is:

$$V_0 = \frac{D_0(1+g)}{r-g} = \frac{2.20 \times (1.05)}{0.106 - 0.05} = \frac{2.31}{0.056} = \text{AUD } 41.25$$

The intrinsic value exceeds the market price of AUD 33.50, so the firm should buy.

(Study Session 11, LOS 33.c)

92. **C** The values of the next three dividends are:

$$D_1 = 4.00(1.40) = 5.60$$

$$D_2 = 4.00(1.40)^2 = 7.84$$

$$D_3 = 4.00(1.40)^2(1.06) = 8.3104$$

The terminal value of the stock (at the beginning of the final constant growth phase) is:

$$V_2 = \frac{D_3}{r-g} = \frac{8.3104}{0.12 - 0.06} = 138.507$$

The present value of the first two dividends plus the terminal value of the stock is:

$$V_0 = \frac{5.60}{1.12} + \frac{7.84}{1.12^2} + \frac{138.507}{1.12^2}$$

$$V_0 = 5.00 + 6.25 + 110.42 = \text{£}121.67$$

(Study Session 11, LOS 33.l)

93. **C** The first three dividends remain at:

$$D_1 = 4.00(1.40) = 5.60$$

$$D_2 = 4.00(1.40)^2 = 7.84$$

$$D_3 = 4.00(1.40)^2(1.06) = 8.3104$$

You need to find a rate of return that gives a value closest to £90. Trial and error is a sound approach to finding the answer, and the test wise candidate should use the values given as multiple-choice answers. Basically substitute 12%, 13%, or 14% into the valuation equation:

$$V_0 = \frac{5.60}{1+r} + \frac{7.84}{(1+r)^2} + \frac{8.3104/(r-0.06)}{(1+r)^2}$$

For r = 12%, V_0 = £121.67

For r = 13%, V_0 = £104.11

For r = 14%, V_0 = £90.96

The answer, to three decimal places, is 14.085%. (Study Session 11, LOS 33.l,m)

94. **C** PVGO is the part of a stock's total value that comes from future growth opportunities. It is estimated as $V_0 = E_1/r + PVGO$, where E_1/r is the no-growth value per share. Note that earnings are divided by r, not dividends. The reason for this is that a no-growth firm should distribute all of its earnings as dividends. (Study Session 11, LOS 33.e)

95. **B** Sustainable growth is growth that can be achieved by retaining some earnings and keeping the capital structure (debt to equity) constant. (Study Session 11, LOS 33.o)

96. **A** Given the assumptions of a constant growth model, the justified forward P/E is smaller than the justified trailing P/E. The equations for the two concepts are:

forward P/E:
$$\frac{P_0}{E_1} = \frac{D_1/E_1}{r-g} = \frac{1-b}{r-g}$$

trailing P/E:
$$\frac{P_0}{E_0} = \frac{D_0(1+g)/E_1}{r-g} = \frac{(1-b)(1+g)}{r-g}$$

The trailing P/E will equal the forward P/E times $(1+g)$.

The other two phrases from the investment banker are correct. (Study Session 11, LOS 33.f)

97. **C** A decrease in the value of available-for-sale securities that bypasses the income statement would artificially increase net income and, consequently, ROE. Book value is unaffected as the decrease is accounted for in the OCI section of shareholders' equity. (Study Session 12, LOS 36.k)

98. **C**
$$WACC = \left(\frac{MVD}{MVD+MVCE}\right) \times \left[r_d(1-\text{tax rate})\right] + \left(\frac{MVCE}{MVD+MVCE}\right)r$$

r_d = debt coupon given as 7.0%

tax rate = 40% (given in Exhibit 1)

r = equity cost = 0.15 (given in Exhibit 2)

MVD = market value of debt = book value of debt for YD = 12

MVCE = market value of common equity = $15.50 \times 18.6 = \$288.3$

$$WACC = \left(\frac{12}{12+288.3}\right) \times \left[0.07(1-0.40)\right] + \left(\frac{288.3}{12+288.3}\right) \times 0.15 = 0.146$$

(Study Sessions 7 and 10, LOS 24.a and 31.g)

99. **B** $WACC = WACC \times capital = 0.12 \times 200 = 24$

EVA = NOPAT − $WACC = 42 − 24 = 18

(Study Session 12, LOS 36.a)

100. **B** $V_0 = B_0 + [(ROE - r) \times B_0] / (r - g)$

book value = equity / total shares

book value = 131 / 18.6 = 7.04 (from Exhibit 1)

r = cost of equity = 0.15 (given in Exhibit 2)

ROE = 0.17 (given in Exhibit 2)

g = 0.10 (given in Exhibit 2)

$V_0 = 7.04 + [(0.17 - 0.15) \times 7.04] / (0.15 - 0.10) = 9.86$

(Study Session 12, LOS 36.f)

101. **A**   It is difficult for a company to maintain a high ROE because of competition. The persistence factor will be lower for those companies. A company that has a low dividend payout has greater growth opportunities than a company with a high dividend payout. The greater growth opportunities should support a higher persistence factor. (Study Session 12, LOS 36.h)

102. **C**   Statement 1 is correct. The multistage residual income model uses continuing residual income to denote the long-run residual income. Based on reversion to the mean, and increasing competition for YD, continuing residual income would be expected to decline to zero over time. Statement 2 is correct. Based on the residual income model formula, $V_0 = B_0 + (ROE - r) \times B_0 / (r - g)$. If ROE = r, then $V_0 = B_0$. (Study Session 12, LOS 36.d,j)

103. **C**   Differences among CCRs of the same issuer is called notching. Notching is more prevalent among low-rated issuers (not issuers with investment grade ratings) due to differences in seniority. Sometimes corporate credit ratings on different issues by the same issuer can vary significantly. (Study Session 14, LOS 42.c)

104. **B**   Notching is primarily due to differences in the seniority rankings of different issues and the corresponding differences in recovery rates. Restricted vs. non-restricted status would only be relevant to bonds issued by different subsidiaries (or the parent) in a holding company structure. Cross default provisions apply when default of one issue triggers default on other issues of the same issuer and is not a relevant explanation for differences in ratings between multiple issues by the same issuer. (Study Session 14, LOS 42.c)

105. **C**   Reese's first statement is correct. High-yield issuers generally depend heavily on short-term bank debt because it is difficult for those issuers to obtain long-term financing. Because of the short-term nature of bank debt and its priority of claim to assets over existing bondholders, a careful examination of the issuer's debt structure is necessary. Reese's second statement is also correct. High-yield issuers usually have a holding company structure requiring cash flows from its subsidiaries to pay the interest and principal on its debt issues. If the subsidiaries have their own debt obligations to service and if the cash flow between subsidiaries and the parent company is restricted, it will be difficult for the parent issuer to obtain funds to pay interest and principal when due. (Study Session 14, LOS 42.j)

106. **B**   The first statement regarding general obligation securities is incorrect. General obligation (GO) municipal bonds are serviced using the general taxing authority of the municipality. They do not have a claim to the revenue generated from public works projects. Therefore, analyzing a GO bond's claim to revenue from public works projects is not necessary. The second statement, regarding revenue securities, is correct. Of particular concern for the analysis of municipal revenue bonds is the sufficiency of revenues in excess of expenses to cover debt service. (Study Session 14, LOS 42.j)

107. **C** Both statements are correct. Implied volatility can be estimated using observed prices for interest rate derivatives and options. Implied volatility is criticized because it is based on the assumptions that the option pricing model is correct and that volatility is constant. Yield volatility has been observed to follow patterns over time that can be modeled and used to forecast volatility using autoregressive statistical models. (Study Session 14, LOS 43.g)

108. **A** Market participants typically prefer to use the swap-rate curve as a benchmark (rather than a government bond yield curve) for the following reasons:
   - The availability of swaps and the equilibrium pricing are driven only by the interaction of supply and demand. It is not affected by technical market factors that can affect government bond yields.
   - The swap market is not regulated by any government, which makes swap rates across different countries more comparable.
   - Swap curves across countries are also more comparable than sovereign bond yield curves because swap curves reflect similar levels of credit risk, while sovereign bond yield curves also reflect credit risk unique to each country's government bonds.
   - The swap curve typically has yield quotes at 11 maturities between 2 and 30 years. The U.S. government bond yield curve typically only has on-the-run issues trading at four maturities between 2 and 30 years.

   (Study Session 14, LOS 43.d)

109. **A** First, calculate the conversion ratio: $\text{conversion ratio} = \dfrac{\text{par value}}{\text{conversion price}} = \dfrac{1{,}000}{55.56} = 18$

   Now, calculate market conversion price:

   $\text{market conversion price} = \dfrac{\text{market bond price}}{\text{conversion ratio}} = \dfrac{947}{18} = 52.61$

   Finally, calculate the market conversion premium per share as the difference between the market conversion price and the market price of the stock:

   $\text{market conversion premium} = 52.61 - 50.00 = 2.61$

   (Study Session 14, LOS 44.j)

110. **A** $\text{premium payback period} = \dfrac{\text{market conversion premium per share}}{\text{favorable income differential per share}}$

   We calculated the market premium per share in the previous question, so we must now calculate the favorable income differential per share as follows:

   $\dfrac{\text{coupon interest} - (\text{conversion ratio} \times \text{dividends per share})}{\text{conversion ratio}}$

   $\text{favorable income differential} = \dfrac{72.50 - (18 \times 1.80)}{18} = 2.23$

   $\text{premium payback period} = \dfrac{2.61}{2.23} = 1.17$

   (Study Session 14, LOS 44.j)

111. **B** A bond with an embedded soft put is redeemable through the issuance of cash, subordinated notes, common stock, or any combination of these three securities. In contrast, a bond with a hard put is only redeemable using cash. (Study Session 14, LOS 44.e,j)

112. **A** If interest rates are not expected to change then the straight value of the bond will not change (ignoring the change in value resulting from the passage of time). If the straight value does not change, then downside risk is indeed limited to the difference between the price paid for the bond and the straight value. If, however, interest rates rise as the price of the common stock falls, the conversion value will fall and the straight value will fall, exposing the holder of the convertible bond to more downside risk. (Study Session 14, LOS 44.j)

113. **A** A stock split would affect the market price of the common stock and the conversion ratio of a convertible bond. Since the split is a one-for-two split, the number of shares outstanding in the marketplace will be reduced by one half. Therefore, the stock price will double, keeping the total market value of the stock the same. Just as the total market value of the common stock should not change because of a split, so too should the conversion value of a convertible bond stay the same before and after a stock split. Since conversion value equals the price of common stock times the conversion ratio, and the market price is now double, the conversion ratio must be cut in half. (Study Session 14, LOS 44.j)

114. **C** Decreasing volatility of common stock prices would devalue any options related to the stock. The convertible bond contains an embedded call option on the stock, which would experience a decrease in value. Increasing interest rate volatility would increase the value of options related to interest rates. MediSoft's convertible bond is also callable and the value of the call on the bond would increase. The total value of the convertible bond is as follows: convertible bond value = straight value + call on stock – call on bond. The combined effect of the changes in the values of the options is a decrease in the value of the convertible bond. Thus the statement regarding the volatility effects on MediSoft's convertible bonds is incorrect. The value of the putable bond can be summarized as follows: putable bond value = option-free value + put on bond. The increase in put option value resulting from the increase in interest rate volatility would increase the value of the putable bond. Therefore, the statement regarding the volatility effects on MediSoft's putable bonds is also incorrect. (Study Session 14, LOS 44.j)

115. **B** Walker is entering into a 6 × 8 forward rate agreement (FRA), which represents a 2-month (60-day) loan that will begin six months (180 days) from now. The relevant LIBOR rates for this contract are 180-day and 240-day LIBOR. To calculate the contract rate on the 6 × 8 FRA, first un-annualize the 180- and 240-day rates as follows:

$$R_{180} = 0.0452 \left(\frac{180}{360} \right) = 0.0226 \qquad R_{240} = 0.0511 \left(\frac{240}{360} \right) = 0.0341$$

Next, calculate the rate on the 6 × 8 FRA as follows (note we are using the 180-day and 240-day LIBOR rates to find the 60-day rate that lies between them):

$$FRA_{6 \times 8} = \left(\frac{1 + R_{240}}{1 + R_{180}} \right) - 1 = \left(\frac{1.0341}{1.0226} \right) - 1 = 0.0112$$

The 0.0112 or 1.12% rate represents a 60-day rate. Annualizing the rate will yield the following:

$$FRA_{6 \times 8} = 0.0112 \left(\frac{360}{60} \right) = 0.0675 = 6.75\% \approx 6.8\%$$

(Study Session 16, LOS 48.c)

116. **A** For this question, we must find the value of the FRA three months (90 days) after the inception of the contract. First find the contract rate on a new FRA. Since we are 90 days past the inception of the original contract an equivalent new contract would be a 3 × 5 FRA, which would represent a 2-month (60-day) loan that would begin three months (90 days) from now. Thus, the relevant LIBOR rates are going to be 90-day and 150-day LIBOR. Calculate the FRA rate the same way as in the previous question:

$$R_{90} = 0.0512\left(\frac{90}{360}\right) = 0.012800 \qquad R_{150} = 0.0596\left(\frac{150}{360}\right) = 0.024833$$

$$FRA_{3\times5} = \left(\frac{1+R_{150}}{1+R_{90}}\right) - 1 = \left(\frac{1.024833}{1.012800}\right) - 1 = 0.011881$$

$$FRA_{3\times5} = 0.011881\left(\frac{360}{60}\right) = 0.07129 = 7.129\%$$

Now take the difference between the new FRA rate and the original rate (given as 6.0% in the question) on an un-annualized basis and multiply by the notional principal (i.e., the amount that will be borrowed).

$$\left[(0.07129 - 0.06)\left(\frac{60}{360}\right)\right] \times \$1,275,000 = \$2,399$$

Finally, discount this difference to the present using the 150-day LIBOR rate.

$$\frac{\$2,399}{\left[1 + \left(0.0596 \times \frac{150}{360}\right)\right]} = \$2,340$$

(Study Session 16, LOS 48.c)

117. **B** In forward markets, there is no clearinghouse. Forward contracts are between two private entities, and as such, the credit risk is borne by the party with a positive contract position. In Walker's case, since the contract has positive value three months after inception, he is exposed to the risk that the short position will be unable to make the required payment at the contract expiration. This problem could be alleviated through periodically marking the contract to market. Mark-to-market features are not common to all forward contracts but can be included if so desired by the parties entering into the contract. (Study Session 16, LOS 48.d)

118. **C** The company will need to sell silver in eight months. Thus, if the price of silver is expected to fall over that time frame, Walker should be short a forward contract on the price of silver to lock in a higher selling price now. Walker will also need to convert Australian dollars to U.S. dollars after the extracted Australian silver is sold. Thus, he is effectively long Australian dollars and will need either a short currency forward contract on Australian dollars or equivalently a long currency forward contract on U.S. dollars if he expects the Australian dollar to depreciate. (Study Session 16, LOS 48.a)

119. **A** The customizable nature of forward contracts makes them less equipped for offsetting transactions. In order to create an offsetting transaction, a counterparty must be found that is willing to accept the exact terms of the existing forward contract. This is an unlikely occurrence. Futures, on the other hand, are standardized and creating an offsetting transaction is simple since the clearinghouse is the counterparty to all transactions and is continually making a market for all futures contracts.
(Study Session 16, LOS 49.c)

120. **A**   In answering this question, you must first compute the contract rate for a zero value (arbitrage free) 7 × 10 FRA (i.e., the FRA expires in 210 days and the underlying loan expires in 300 days). The contract rate for the 7 × 10 FRA is computed as follows:

$$R_{210} = 0.0603\left(\frac{210}{360}\right) = 0.0352 \qquad\qquad R_{300} = 0.0641\left(\frac{300}{360}\right) = 0.0534$$

$$FRA_{7\times10} = \left(\frac{1+R_{300}}{1+R_{210}}\right) - 1 = \left(\frac{1.0534}{1.0352}\right) - 1 = 0.0176$$

$$FRA_{7\times10} = 0.0176\left(\frac{360}{90}\right) = 0.0704 = 7.04\%$$

Since the contract rate on an arbitrage free is higher than the desired rate of 6.95%, Walker must establish a position in an off-market FRA. He will need a long position because he will be borrowing at the contract rate, not lending. Since having a contract rate that is lower than the market rate (6.95% < 7.04%) is valuable to the long, Walker will have to make a payment to the short position at the contract inception. (Study Session 16, LOS 48.a)

Exam 2
Morning Session Answers

To get valuable feedback on how your score compares to those of other Level II candidates, use your Username and Password to gain Online Access at schweser.com and choose the left-hand menu item "Practice Exams Vol. 2."

1. C	21. A	41. A
2. A	22. B	42. C
3. C	23. C	43. C
4. C	24. A	44. B
5. B	25. B	45. C
6. A	26. B	46. A
7. B	27. B	47. B
8. C	28. B	48. B
9. C	29. C	49. C
10. A	30. B	50. A
11. B	31. C	51. A
12. B	32. C	52. B
13. B	33. A	53. A
14. C	34. B	54. C
15. A	35. C	55. A
16. B	36. B	56. A
17. C	37. B	57. B
18. B	38. C	58. A
19. C	39. A	59. C
20. B	40. A	60. C

Exam 2
Morning Session Answers

1. **C** There is no violation of the Standards in Transaction A. Connor is basically hedging any potential loss from a decline in the price of Stock A prior to the completion of his sale transaction. There is no apparent attempt to manipulate the market in this transaction. (Study Session 1, LOS 2.a,b)

2. **A** A critical factor in assessing any violation of Standard II(B) Integrity of Capital Markets – Market Manipulation is the intent of the parties involved. In this case, Connor is hoping that his options transaction drives up the price of Stock B, which would improve the reported performance of the Biogene Fund. This type of manipulation would be a violation of the Standard. (Study Session 1, LOS 2.a,b)

3. **C** Transactions meant to minimize tax liabilities are not prohibited by the Standards. If the Biogene Fund benefits, the investors in the fund will presumably benefit also. (Study Session 1, LOS 2.a,b)

4. **C** Connor was not pressured to take the IPO, and he believed it was a good investment. Connor received no confidential information. The IPO had been made available to all Apple clients prior to Biogene. There is no evidence of a violation of either of these Standards. (Study Session 1, LOS 2.a,b)

5. **B** By suggesting that Biogene might need to acquire more shares to support the price in the future, Arnold is suggesting that Apple would be willing to manipulate the market by creating false trading volume. This is transaction-based manipulation in violation of Standard II(B) Integrity of Capital Markets – Market Manipulation. (Study Session 1, LOS 2.a,b)

6. **A** By changing his previous decision and accepting the 2% based on Arnold's e-mail, Connor has violated the Standards related to material nonpublic information. He has acted based upon the receipt of inside information. Arnold has violated the Standards related to both material nonpublic information and preservation of confidentiality. Arnold violated Standard III(E) – Duties to Clients – Preservation of Confidentiality by revealing information he received based upon a special relationship with Stock D. By passing that information to another area of Apple, Arnold has violated Standard II(A) Integrity of Capital Markets – Material Nonpublic Information as well. (Study Session 1, LOS 2.a,b)

7. **B** Krosse is a developing nation with the highest α (share of capital in GDP) among all the countries. A high value of α indicates that the next unit of capital added will increase output almost as much as the previous unit of capital. Developing nations with a high α are more likely to benefit from capital deepening, which should result in an increase in productivity (at least in the short term). (Study Session 4, LOS 15.d)

8. **C** Krosse's labor growth rate is greater than that of Procken's. Labor growth can be accomplished by an increase in the labor force participation rate, an increase in average hours worked, additional supply of labor by immigration, or a higher population growth rate. We are told that the population growth rate is equal for the two countries. The only choice that allows for higher labor growth rate is then higher average hours worked. (Study Session 4, LOS 15.g)

9. **C** Growth rate in potential GDP = long-term growth rate of technology + α × (long-term growth rate of capital) + $(1 - \alpha)$ × (long-term growth rate of labor).

    The growth rate in potential GDP using a calculator: PV = –$4,800; FV = +$5,778; N = 5; solve for I/Y. I/Y = 3.78%.

    Rearrange the equation to solve for long-term growth rate of technology.
    3.78% = LTGRT + (0.225) × 3.8% + (0.775) × 0.8%
    LTGRT = 3.78% – 0.86% – 0.62%
    LTGRT = 2.30%
    (Study Session 4, LOS 15.e)

10. **A** If the neoclassical theory holds then the sustainable growth rate of output of G* is the same as the long-term growth rate of capital.

    The growth rate in potential GDP using a calculator:
    Procken (Past = 4.0%): PV = –$250; FV = +$306; N = 5; solve for I/Y = 4.12%.
    Krosse (Past = 4.7%): PV = –$250; FV = +$315; N = 5; solve for I/Y = 4.73%.
    Weira (Past = 4.5%): PV = –$4,500; FV = +$5,262; N = 5; solve for I/Y = 3.18%.
    Toban (Past = 3.8%): PV = –$4,800; FV = +$5,778; N = 5; solve for I/Y = 3.78%.

    Weira's stock market appreciation rate of 4.5% exceeds the potential growth rate of GDP of 3.2% significantly. The difference between potential GDP growth rate and past stock market appreciation for the other three countries differences is relatively smaller. (Study Session 4, LOS 15.b,i)

11. **B** It is stated in the vignette that Weira has reached steady-state. In steady state (i.e., in equilibrium), the marginal product of capital (MPK = αY/K) and marginal cost of capital (i.e., the *rental price of capital*, r) are equal; hence: αY/K = r.

    r = (0.25)(4,500) / (18,750) = 0.06 or 6%

    (Study Session 4, LOS 15.d)

12. **B** Based on the data in the vignette, Krosse and Procken are developing countries. The GDP per capita for Krosse is $250 billion divided by 20.0 million people, which is equal to $12,500. The GDP per capita for Procken is $250 billion divided by 20.4 million people, which is equal to $12,255. Krosse is more likely to achieve convergence because Krosse is showing more willingness towards opening up the economy to trade and financial flows than is Procken; Krosse's international trade as a proportion of GDP is higher than Proken's, and comments by Krosse's representative indicate that inflow of foreign capital would be welcome. Finally, comments by Procken's representative indicate an inward-oriented policy, which could hinder convergence. (Study Session 4, LOS 15.j)

13. **B** The increase in Jefferson's revenues relative to cash collections along with the large increase in accounts receivable indicates declining cash collections in 2008 compared to its experience in 2007 and relative to Adams's, which showed consistency in both years. (Study Session 7, LOS 23.f)

14. **C** Jefferson's revenue and inventory levels may be distorted by revenue recognition for new business from the special offer. Although the customers agreed to delay delivery of the products, recognition of these sales prior to customer delivery lowers the quality of these sales and understates inventory. Inventory is understated if the sale is not totally complete. (Study Session 7, LOS 23.f)

15. **A** The more favorable trends in Jefferson's expenses may reflect more aggressive depreciation accounting and controls imposed on discretionary expenses to offset declining gross profit margins. (Study Session 7, LOS 23.f)

16. **B** The lower the ratio, the higher will be the earnings quality. Jefferson's ratio rose sharply in 2008 compared to the previous years and was substantially above Adams's. Thus, Jefferson's earnings quality is lower. (Study Session 7, LOS 23.f)

17. **C** The lower the ratio, the higher will be the earnings quality. Jefferson's ratio rose sharply in 2008 and exceeded Adams's ratio for the first time in the three years. Thus, Jefferson's earnings quality is lower. (Study Session 7, LOS 23.d,f)

18. **B** According to the simple measures of earnings quality, balance sheet, and cash flow accruals ratios, Jefferson's earnings quality in 2008 was lower than its 2007 levels and relative to Adams's. The more aggressive accounting treatment for the overseas special offer lowered the quality of revenues and may have understated inventories if some of these customers did not take delivery of the shipments. Jefferson also instituted a more liberal policy toward depreciable lives versus Adams, another indicator of lower earnings quality. (Study Session 7, LOS 23.d,f)

19. **C** Assuming International Oilfield is an integrated sales division and Continental Supply makes virtually all of the decisions, the functional currency is likely the presentation currency. Thus, the temporal method is used. Under the temporal method, remeasurement gains and losses are reported in the income statement. (Study Session 6, LOS 21.c)

20. **B** International Oilfield is carrying 867 (i.e., 975 − 108) LCU original cost of equipment purchased in 2006 on their books. The 2007 losses due to fire and related insurance settlement do not affect depreciation in 2008 (other than depreciating fewer assets). The new equipment purchased during the year would be depreciated for a half year in 2008. Depreciation will be translated at the historical exchange rate under the temporal method.

Equipment	Calculation	LCU Depreciation	Historical Exchange Rate	USD Depreciation
Originally purchased in 2006	867 / 10	86.7	1	$ 86.70
Purchased in 2008 (1/2 year)	1/2 × (225 /10)	11.25	1.25	$ 9.00
Total				$ 95.70

(Study Session 6, LOS 21.c)

21. **A**   Under the current rate method, gains and losses that occur as a result of the translation process do not show up on the income statement but are instead accumulated in a balance sheet account called the cumulative translation adjustment account (CTA). The translation gain or loss in each year is calculated and added to the account, acting like a running total of translation gains and losses. The CTA is simply an equity account on the balance sheet.

   To compute the CTA for Continental's balance sheet, force the accounting equation (A = L + E) to balance with the CTA; [(120 million cash and receivables + 631.3 million inventory + 820.7 million equipment – 600 million liabilities) / 1.50] – $350 million capital stock – $525 retained earnings = –$227 million. The LCU 350 capital stock was issued at the end of 2005 at an exchange rate of LCU 1 = $1. The $525 retained earnings figure was given in the text. (Study Session 6, LOS 21.c)

22. **B**   Compared to the temporal method, the current rate method will result in a higher gross profit margin percentage (higher numerator) when the local currency is depreciating as is the case in this scenario (the exchange rate has risen from LCU 1 per $1 to LCU 1.25 per $1; thus, it costs more LCUs to buy $1 which is the result of a depreciating LCU). Under the temporal method, COGS is remeasured at the historic rate; thus, COGS is not impacted by the depreciating currency. Under the current rate method, COGS is translated at the average rate; thus, COGS is lower because of the depreciating currency. Lower COGS results in a higher gross profit margin percentage. (Study Session 6, LOS 21.d)

23. **C**   Both the numerator (cash + receivables) and denominator (current liabilities) of the quick ratio are remeasured at the current exchange rate under the temporal method. Inventories are ignored in the quick ratio. Since the same rate is used to remeasure both the numerator and denominator, the ratio does not change when stated in the presentation currency. (Study Session 6, LOS 21.d)

24. **A**   The temporal method is required if the foreign subsidiary is operating in a highly inflationary environment, defined as cumulative inflation of more than 100% in a 3-year period. Compounded inflation of 30% annually for three years is approximately 120% ($1.30^3 - 1$). Under the temporal method, remeasurement gains and losses are recognized in the income statement. In this case, International Oilfield has a net monetary liability position (monetary liabilities of 600 million > monetary assets of 120 million). Holding net monetary liabilities denominated in a currency that is depreciating will result in a gain. (Study Session 6, LOS 21.f)

25. **B**   Because 80% of Sampson's business is with one customer (the U.S. government), we can expect a great deal of bargaining power from that customer. The government will likely use competitive bidding to encourage strong price competition. There is no indication that suppliers have great bargaining power. The threat of new entrants is likely low because of barriers to entry, including high capital expenditures required to enter the industry and perhaps proprietary knowledge about production and company-owned patents. (Study Session 11, LOS 32.a)

26. **B**   Sampson's strategy is based around offering unique products and services, and their acquisition strategy also supports this. This is a strategy of differentiation and is apparently successful, since Sampson has increasing market share as well as high profit margins relative to the rest of the industry. Focus refers to a strategy based on capturing one particular segment of the market, and cost leadership refers to a strategy of producing undifferentiated products at the lowest production cost in the industry. (Study Session 11, LOS 32.a)

27. **B** Sampson intends to make a purchase offer for controlling equity interests in the target companies. Cash flow models are more appropriate because a controlling interest allows Sampson to set the target company's financing, investment, and distribution policies. (Study Session 10, LOS 30.h)

28. **B** NavTech recently has decided to capitalize much of its research and development expense, thereby deferring much of its R&D expense (rather than immediately recognizing R&D as expense on the income statement). This is an example of aggressive accounting, especially if revenues cannot be matched directly with R&D expense. By reducing the investment return assumption on its pension investments, Sampson is moving to a more conservative approach. By capitalizing its leases (treating as finance leases rather than operating leases), Aerospace Communications more clearly reports its liabilities and assets. (Study Session 10, LOS 30.e)

29. **C** If the company's business model is not sustainable, the liquidation value is more appropriate than its value as a going concern (which could be negative). Balance sheet value is an accounting concept, not a valuation concept. (Study Session 10, LOS 30.b)

30. **B** Defining P_0 as the current stock price, D_1 as the expected year-end dividend, r as the required cost of equity, and g as the dividend growth rate, the present value formula for constant growth dividends is:

$$P_0 = \$21.40 = \frac{D_1}{r-g} = \frac{\$1.07}{0.12-g}$$

$$0.12 - g = \frac{\$1.07}{\$21.40}$$

$$g = 0.12 - \frac{\$1.07}{\$21.40} = 0.07 = 7\%$$

(Study Sessions 10 and 11, LOS 30.d and 33.d)

31. **C** The hospice industry's cost structure indicates a preponderance of variable costs and hence a lower need for economies of scale. Industries with such cost structures have low entry barriers and a low degree of rivalry among existing competitors. Bargaining power of suppliers would be affected by the cost structure of the supplier industry. Threat of substitutes would not be affected by industry's cost structure. (Study Session 11, LOS 32.a)

32. **C** Medicare represents 85% of the hospice industry's revenues. If Medicare reduces the benefit package covering hospice services, patients are more likely to seek alternative care options. In this instance, the 3rd party payer (Medicare) essentially represents the bargaining power of buyers. Increasing competition could be a concern; however, entry barriers in the form of state certification as well as robust revenue growth of the industry makes it an unlikely choice. The importance of Medicare reimbursements makes C the best answer. (Study Session 11, LOS 32.a)

33. **A** The existence of several for-profit firms, none of which appear to have dominant market shares, suggests a high probability of rivalry among existing competitors. The existing competitive structure, in itself, does not offer much insight into the power of suppliers or the threat of substitutes. (Study Session 11, LOS 32.a)

34. **B** Change in technology is considered a fleeting factor (or transient factor), which should be evaluated in the context of its influence on the five forces. There is no indication that the patient monitoring system would affect threat of new entrants or bargaining power of suppliers. (Study Session 12, LOS 32.b)

35. **C** CEO compensation is consistent with market estimates and no adjustment is necessary. Long-term leases on facilities are legally binding; hence, no adjustment is necessary until the lease comes up for renewal. Elimination of excessive perks is a valid adjustment. (Study Session 12, LOS 37.e)

36. **B**

Normalized EBITDA	32
(−) Depreciation	11
(=) EBIT	21
Taxes @ 25%	5.25
Operating income after tax	15.75
(+) Depreciation	11
(−) Capex	6
(−) WCInv	5
(=) FCFF	15.75

(Study Session 12, LOS 37.e)

37. **B** An analyst must review the cash flows from a company's operating, investing, and financing activities to generate a useful free cash flow, while dividends are simply set by the board of directors. Analysts use free cash flow whenever an investor takes a control perspective, such as in the event of an acquisition. The P/E model is considered weak because accounting issues can impact earnings. Companies that do not generate free cash flow in the long run are in financial trouble. (Study Session 12, LOS 34.a)

38. **C** Free cash flow to the firm (FCFF) can be calculated in many ways but in this question, you are given enough information to calculate the measure in the following way:

FCFF = net income + non-cash charges + interest $(1 − t)$ − fixed capital investment − working capital investment

$FCFF_0 = 20,000,000 + 1,250,000 + 0 − 8,450,000 − (9,985,000 − 7,460,000) = 10,275,000$

The next step is to forecast the future FCFFs and the terminal value:

$FCFF_1 = 10,275,000(1.25) = 12,843,750$

$FCFF_2 = 12,843,750(1.25) = 16,054,688$

terminal value = $16,054,688(1.12) / (0.15 − 0.12) = 599,375,000$

Next, calculate the present value of the FCFFs and the terminal value:

$$PV_{FCFs} = \frac{12,843,750}{1.15} + \frac{(16,054,688 + 599,375,000)}{(1.15)^2} = 476,521,739$$

If a firm has non-operating assets (e.g., land held for investment) on its balance sheet, the value of these assets must be added to the value of the operating assets (determined using the present value of the FCFFs and terminal value) to find the total firm value.

total firm value = value of operating assets + value of non-operating assets

total firm value = 476,521,739 + 875,000 = 477,396,739

(Study Session 12, LOS 34.j)

39. **A** If BioTLab established a dividend there would no impact on either FCFF or FCFE. Changing the company capital structure by increasing debt will not impact FCFF, although it will initially increase FCFE by the amount of debt issued and then reduce FCFE thereafter by the after-tax interest expense. (Study Session 12, LOS 34.g)

40. **A** The FCFF model is better than the FCFE model in valuing debt laden, cyclical companies, and companies with a changing capital structure. Since Groh Group does not pay a dividend, the DDM model would be the least appropriate model to value the company. (Study Session 12, LOS 34.a,g)

41. **A**
$$\text{firm value} = \frac{\text{FCFF}_0(1+g)}{\text{WACC}-g}$$

$$1,308,000,000 = \frac{24,000,000(1+g)}{0.11-g}$$

$$g = 0.09$$

The growth rate using the FCFE model would be:

$$\text{equity value} = \frac{\text{FCFE}_0(1+g)}{r-g}$$

$$1,110,000,000 = \frac{20,000,000(1+g)}{0.13-g}$$

$$g = 0.11$$

The growth rate in the FCFE is greater than the growth rate in the FCFF because of the leverage effect. (Study Session 12, LOS 34.j)

42. **C** FCFF can be inflated by decreasing capital expenditures relative to depreciation. All other statements are true. (Study Session 12, LOS 34.e,g)

43. **C** *Interest rate tree*: Discount maturity value back one year at different 1-year forward rates, then take the equally weighted average of those values discounted back to today at today's 1-year rate:

V = 0.5 × [(108 / 1.08530) + 8] / 1.0725 + 0.5 × [(108 / 1.06983) + 8] / 1.0725

V = 0.5 × (99.512 + 8) / 1.0725 + 0.5 × (100.951 + 8) / 1.0725

V = 50.122 + 50.793 = 100.915

Today	Year 1	Year 2
		108
	107.512	
100.915		108
	108.951	
		108

(Study Session 14, LOS 44.c,d)

44. **B**   Use the same formula as in the previous problem, but remember that if the value at one node exceeds the call price, then the call price should be used for that node. In this case, the value at the lower node would be 108 / 1.06983 = 100.951. The assumption is that the bond would be called at the call price one year from now, or 100.

V = 0.5 × (99.512 + 8) / 1.0725 + 0.5 × (100 + 8) / 1.0725

V = 50.122 + 50.350 = 100.472

(Study Session 14, LOS 44.d)

45. **C**   Statement 1 is correct. The value of the option would be the difference between the value calculated with no call feature (the Bratton bonds) and the value calculated assuming the bond is callable (the Hardin bonds). Recall that the vignette stated the Bratton and Hardin bonds were identical except for the call feature in the Hardin bonds. The option value would therefore be: 100.915 − 100.472 = 0.443. Statement 2 is also correct. Increased volatility would increase the value of the option, thus lowering the value of the callable bond. (Study Session 14, LOS 44.e,f)

46. **A**   The OAS removes the yield difference due to the features of the embedded option, and leaves a spread that reflects the difference in credit risk and liquidity risk. Since in this case the credit risk of the bonds is similar, the OAS could prove helpful in evaluating the relative liquidity risk. OAS will be affected by different assumptions regarding the volatility of interest rates. (Study Session 14, LOS 44.g)

47. **B**   By using on-the-run rates of the issuing company, there will be no difference in credit risk captured in the spread. The only risk left will be liquidity risk. Answer A is incorrect because using U.S. Treasury rates would not isolate the credit risk since liquidity risk would also be included. Answer C would not help differentiate the Hardin bonds from the Bratton bonds. (Study Session 14, LOS 44.g)

48. **B**   The duration formula given will calculate the percentage change in price for a 100 basis point change in yield, regardless of the actual change in rates used to derive BV_- and BV_+. Using the binomial model, the derived values of BV_- and BV_+ will take into account any potential change in cash flows due to embedded options. (Study Session 14, LOS 44.h)

49. **C**   An option that is deep in-the-money will have the largest delta. Call options that are deep in-the-money will have a delta close to one, while put options that are deep in-the-money will have a delta close to −1. Options that are out-of-the-money will have deltas close to zero. Put F is the option that is deepest in-the-money, and therefore has the largest delta (even though it is negative, the change in the price of Put F given a change in the price of BIC stock will be larger than any of the other options). Call C is the deepest out-of-the-money option, and thus has the smallest delta. (Study Session 17, LOS 50.e)

50. **A**   An option's gamma measures the change in the delta for a change in the price of the underlying asset. The gamma of an option is highest when an option is at-the-money since the probability of moving in or out of the money is high. Put E is close to being at-the-money and because it has a gamma of greater than zero, the sensitivity of Put E's price to changes in BIC's stock price (i.e., the delta) is likely to change. The higher the gamma, the greater the change in delta given a change in stock price. (Study Session 17, LOS 50.f)

51. **A**   As the option moves further into the money and as the expiration date approaches, the delta of a put option moves closer to −1. (Study Session 17, LOS 50.e)

52. **B** The premium on Put D has risen from $2.31 to $3.18 and there is still time left until expiration. Therefore, the increase in value must have come from either a decrease in stock price, an increase in volatility, or both of these events. Choice A would be correct if the option was at expiration and the $3.18 represented only intrinsic value. Since we are not yet at the expiration date, the stock price must be above $26.82. A negative earnings surprise would most likely cause a drop in the market price of the stock. Since there is no indication of the exact amount of the drop in price, the premium observed is a possibility. A decrease in BIC volatility would reduce the put premium, not increase it. (Study Session 17, LOS 50.d)

53. **A** To protect a portfolio against an expected decrease in the value of a long equity position, put options can be purchased (i.e., a protective put strategy). The number of puts to purchase depends on the hedge ratio, which depends on the option's delta. Because the delta of the put options is negative, as the option delta moves closer to −1, the number of options necessary to maintain the hedge falls. (Study Session 17, LOS 50.e)

54. **C** Grimell is incorrect in both of his statements. Using put-call parity, Mabry could create a position in which he would earn the risk-free rate of return but he would need to sell calls and buy puts with the same strike price, not the same premium. As the vega (volatility relative to price) of an option increases, it would become more sensitive to changes in the volatility of the underlying asset. Therefore, the price would likely rise, not fall. (Study Session 17, LOS 50.a)

55. **A** The models in equations 1 through 4 employ factors derived from macroeconomic variables. (Study Session 18, LOS 54.j)

56. **A** The intercept in a macroeconomic factor model equals the expected return for the portfolio examined in the model (assuming no surprises in the macroeconomic variables). The factors in the multifactor equations, F_{IS} and F_{BC}, are factor "surprises," which by definition are expected to equal zero (i.e., by definition, zero "surprise" is "expected"). So, by assumption, F_{IS} and F_{BC} are expected to equal zero. Therefore, the expected return for Portfolio A equals its intercept (17.5%). (Study Session 18, LOS 54.j)

57. **B** The multifactor equation for Portfolio A is used to answer this question. Simply insert the factor surprises for F_{IS} and F_{BC}. From Exhibit 1, $F_{IS} = 0.01 − 0.02 = −0.01$ and $F_{BC} = 0.02 − 0.03 = −0.01$. Therefore, both factor surprises equal −1%. Substituting into the multifactor equation for Portfolio A: $0.1750 + 2(−0.01) + 1.5(−0.01) = 14\%$. (Study Session 18, LOS 54.j)

58. **A** A portfolio that has a sensitivity of 1.0 to one of the macroeconomic factors, and zero sensitivity to the remaining macroeconomic factors is called a factor portfolio. Portfolios D and E are factor portfolios. A portfolio that has factor sensitivities that equal the sensitivities of the benchmark is called a tracking portfolio. Portfolio Z has factor sensitivities that exactly match those of the S&P 500. (Study Session 18, LOS 54.m)

59. **C** According to the Arbitrage Pricing Model, the expected return equals risk-free rate + $b_1RP_1 + b_2RP_2$, where RP_i is the risk premium for factor i. Portfolio D is designed to have sensitivity equal to one to the investor sentiment risk factor and sensitivity equal to zero to the business cycle risk factor. Similarly, Portfolio E is a portfolio designed to have sensitivity equal to zero to the investor sentiment risk factor and sensitivity equal to one to the business cycle risk factor. Portfolios that have a sensitivity equal to 1.0 to one factor and zero sensitivity to the remaining factors are called *factor portfolios*. Therefore, Portfolio D is the investor sentiment factor portfolio, and Portfolio E is the business cycle factor portfolio. According to the multifactor equations, the expected return for the investor sentiment factor portfolio (D) equals 9% and for the business cycle factor portfolio (E) equals 8%. Risk premiums are defined as the difference between the expected return on the appropriate factor portfolio and the risk-free rate. The risk-free rate is 5% (the long-term government bond yield). Therefore, the investor sentiment risk premium equals $0.09 - 0.05 = 0.04$. Similarly, the business cycle risk premium equals $0.08 - 0.05 = 0.03$. Therefore, the expected return for Portfolio P equals $0.05 + 1.25(0.04) + 1.1(0.03) = 13.3\%$. (Study Session 18, LOS 54.l)

60. **C** Active factor risk is caused by deviations of a portfolio's factor sensitivities from the benchmark factor sensitivities. Deviations are quite large for both Portfolios D and E, but Portfolio Z's factor sensitivities match those of the S&P 500 benchmark (1.5 and 1.25). (Study Session 18, LOS 54.m)

Exam 2
Afternoon Session Answers

To get valuable feedback on how your score compares to those of other Level II candidates, use your Username and Password to gain Online Access at schweser.com and choose the left-hand menu item "Practice Exams Vol. 2."

61. A	81. C	101. C
62. C	82. A	102. B
63. C	83. B	103. B
64. A	84. C	104. B
65. C	85. B	105. C
66. A	86. C	106. A
67. A	87. A	107. B
68. A	88. B	108. B
69. C	89. C	109. B
70. B	90. B	110. B
71. C	91. C	111. B
72. B	92. B	112. C
73. C	93. C	113. B
74. B	94. C	114. B
75. C	95. B	115. B
76. A	96. C	116. A
77. B	97. B	117. B
78. A	98. A	118. B
79. C	99. B	119. B
80. C	100. C	120. C

Exam 2
Afternoon Session Answers

61. **A** CFA Institute Research Objectivity Standards recommend that rating systems include the following three elements: (1) the recommendation or rating category, (2) time horizon categories, and (3) risk categories. Holly's report on BlueNote provides all three elements (strong buy, 6- to 12-month time horizon, average level of risk) and also includes the recommended disclosure on how investors can obtain a complete description of the firm's rating system. (Study Session 1, LOS 4.a,b)

62. **C** Standard II(A). Holly has utilized public information to conduct an intensive analysis of BlueNote and has also utilized information obtained from a supplier that, while nonpublic, is not by itself material. When combined with his knowledge of BlueNote's material public information, however, the information from the supplier allows Holly to make a significant and material conclusion that would not be known to the public in general. This situation falls under the Mosaic Theory. Holly is free to make recommendations based on her material nonpublic conclusion on BlueNote since the conclusion was formed using material public information combined with *nonmaterial* nonpublic information. Thus, the BlueNote report did not violate Standard II(A) Integrity of Capital Markets – Material Nonpublic Information, and since there appears to be a reasonable and adequate basis, does not appear to violate any other Standards either. Holly's report on BigTime, however, is based in part on a conversation that he overheard between executives at BigTime. The information he overheard related to the sale of one of BigTime's business units was both material and nonpublic. The fact that several other analysts overheard the conversation as well does not make the information public. Because Holly is in possession of material nonpublic information, he is prohibited by Standard II(A) from acting or causing others to act on the information. Therefore, his report on BigTime violates the Standard. (Study Session 1, LOS 2.a,b)

63. **C** CFA Institute Research Objectivity Standards (ROS) require disclosures of conflicts of interest such as beneficial ownership of securities of a covered firm. The ROS recommend that such disclosure be made either in the supporting documents or on the firm's Web site. It is further recommended that the disclosure, or a page reference to the disclosure, be made in the report itself. Holly owns shares of BigTime that may potentially benefit from his recommendation. His best course of action would be to disclose the conflict on both the firm's Web site and in the report. (Study Session 1, LOS 4.a,b)

64. **A** Standard II(B) – Market Manipulation. Holly has issued a buy recommendation on BigTime stock. The analysis is based on a very optimistic analysis of the company's fundamentals. Yet, three days after issuing the report, Holly decides to sell all of his clients' holdings as well as his own holdings of BigTime stock after observing a rise in the price of the stock. Holly's report, which caused an increase in the price of BigTime stock, was intended to deceive market participants into believing the company was a good investment when, as indicated by his subsequent sale of the shares, Holly believed otherwise. The combination of actions indicates that Holly is likely attempting to manipulate the price of the stock for his clients', and his own, benefit. Thus, he has likely violated Standard II(B) – Integrity of Capital Markets – Market Manipulation. (Study Session 1, LOS 2.a,b)

65. **C** Standard I(B) – Professionalism: Independence and Objectivity. Members and candidates are prohibited from accepting any gift that could reasonably be expected to interfere with their independence and objectivity. The desk pen is a token item with little material value and can be accepted without violating the Standard. However, the concert tickets are likely to have a very substantial amount of material value since the concert is sold out and involves a popular musical act. Best practice dictates that Holly should not accept the concert tickets since they could reasonably be expected to compromise Holly's independence and objectivity. (Study Session 1, LOS 2.a,b)

66. **A** Standard V(B) – Communication With Clients and Prospective Clients. Standard V(B) requires members and candidates to promptly disclose any changes that materially affect investment processes. Holly has provided a detailed description of the new valuation model that will be used to generate investment recommendations and has disclosed the new limitations on the investment universe (i.e., no alcohol or tobacco stocks). Therefore, it does not appear that he has violated Standard V(B). Holly also has not violated any other standards. It is acceptable for him to e-mail those clients with e-mail addresses and send his letter by regular mail to those who do not. Standard III(B) – Fair Dealing does not require that all clients receive investment recommendations or other communications at exactly the same time, only that the system treats clients fairly. (Study Session 1, LOS 2.a,b)

67. **A** The standard error can be determined by knowing the formula for the *t*-statistic:

t-statistic = (slope estimate – hypothesized value) / standard error

Therefore, the standard error equals:

standard error = (slope estimate – hypothesized value) / *t*-statistic

The null hypothesis associated with each of the *t*-statistics reported for the slope estimates in Table 1 is: H_o: slope = zero. So, the standard error equals the slope estimate divided by its *t*-statistic: 0.2000 / 2.85 = 0.07.

The confidence interval equals: slope estimate ± (t_{crit} × standard error), where t_{crit} is the critical *t*-statistic associated with the desired confidence interval (as stated in the question, the desired confidence interval equals 99%). Exhibit 3 provides critical values for a portion of the Student *t*-distribution. The appropriate critical value is found by using the correct significance level and degrees of freedom. The significance level equals 1 minus the confidence level = 1 – 0.99 = 0.01. The degrees of freedom equal N – k – 1, where *k* is the number of independent variables: 30 – 3 – 1 = 26 degrees of freedom. Note that the table provides critical values for one-tail tests of hypothesis (area in upper tail). Therefore, the appropriate critical value for the 99% confidence interval is found under the column labeled "0.005," indicating that the upper tail comprises 0.5% of the *t*-distribution, and the lower tail comprises an equivalent 0.5% of the distribution. Therefore, the two tails, combined, take up 1% of the distribution. The correct critical *t*-statistic for the 0.01 significance level equals 2.779. Therefore, the 99% confidence interval for the FORECAST slope coefficient is:

0.2000 ± 2.779(0.07) = (0.0055, 0.3945)

The lower bound equals 0.0055 and the upper bound equals 0.3945. (Study Session 3, LOS 11.f and 12.c)

68. **A** The *F*-statistic is used to test the overall significance of the regression, which is formulated with the null hypothesis that all three slopes simultaneously equal zero. Note that this null hypothesis is identical to a test that the *R*-square equals zero. (Study Session 3, LOS 12.e)

69. **C** Pilchard should test the following null hypothesis: H_o: $b_2 \geq 0$. The alternative hypothesis is: H_A: $b_2 < 0$ (a negative estimate for b_2 supports the small firm effect). The test is a one-tail hypothesis test. The critical value at the 0.01 value for a one-tail test equals –2.479 (area in lower tail equals 0.01; degrees of freedom equal 26). Exhibit 1 indicates that the *t*-statistic for the b_2 estimate equals –2.50, which exceeds the critical value. Therefore, the null hypothesis that small firms do not outperform large firms, after controlling for COVERAGE and FORECAST should be rejected in favor of the alternative hypothesis that small firms outperform large firms (after controlling for COVERAGE and FORECAST). (Study Session 3, LOS 11.g and 12.c)

70. **B** The slope on the dummy variable (COVERAGE), which is 0.05 or 5%, equals the change in average returns between neglected and non-neglected firms after controlling for SIZE and FORECAST. (Study Session 3, LOS 12.h)

71. **C** The ANOVA (Analysis of Variance) Table provides data on the sources of variation in the dependent variable (stock returns). The degrees of freedom for the regression sum of squares (a.k.a., the explained sum of squares) equals *k*, the number of independent variables: k = 3 in Pilchard's regression. The total sum of squares equals the numerator of the sample variance formula for the dependent variable. Recall from Level I Quantitative Methods that the denominator of a sample variance equals N – 1. The denominator in the sample variance equals the degrees of freedom for the numerator (the total sum of squares). Therefore, the degrees of freedom for the total sum of squares in Pilchard's regression equals 30 – 1 = 29. (Study Session 3, LOS 11.i and 12.e)

72. **B** The estimated regression equation equals:

    return = 0.06 + 0.05Coverage – 0.003LN(SIZE) + 0.20Forecast

    where:
    coverage equals zero if number of analysts exceeds 3

    Therefore, the predicted return for Eggmann Enterprises equals:

    return = 0.06 + 0 – 0.003LN(500) + 0.20(0.50)

    return = 14.14%

    (Study Session 3, LOS 11.h and 12.c)

73. **C** Angle uses the uncovered interest rate parity relationship to forecast future spot rates. If the Canadian dollar is expected to depreciate relative to the U.S. dollar and the Mexican peso, then nominal interest rates in Canada must be higher than those in the United States and Mexico. The 13% nominal interest rate in Mexico is higher than the nominal interest rate in the U.S., so the nominal interest rate in Canada must be greater than 13%. (Study Session 4, LOS 14.e)

74. **B** Hohlman is incorrect regarding the implications of an expansionary monetary policy in the U.S. under the Mundell-Fleming model, which predicts a depreciation of the dollar. The asset market approach focuses on fiscal policy—not monetary policy. (Study Session 4, LOS 14.l)

75. **C**   If relative purchasing power parity holds, then inflation differentials drive future exchange rates. If the international Fisher relationship holds, then inflation differentials will be equal to interest rate differentials. Hence, when both relative purchasing power parity and the international Fisher relationship hold, uncovered interest rate parity should also hold. Covered interest rate parity always holds (by arbitrage) and is not a necessary additional condition. Real interest rate parity links the Fisher effect to the international Fisher relationship. (Study Session 4, LOS 14.f)

76. **A**   When the expected future spot rate is equal to the forward rate (and covered interest parity holds—by arbitrage), uncovered interest rate parity should hold as well. The international Fisher relationship links relative purchasing power parity to uncovered interest rate parity. Real interest rate parity links the Fisher effect to the international Fisher relationship. (Study Session 4, LOS 14.f)

77. **B**   Angle assumes the forward rate is an accurate predictor of the expected future spot rate, so we will use ¥200/£ as the future spot rate.

   She also assumes that relative purchasing power parity holds, which states that the future spot rate is a function of the current spot rate and relative inflation rates. We will use relative purchasing power parity to obtain the current spot rate.

   To obtain the expected inflation rates in each country, we back them out using the domestic Fisher relation:

   $$1 + \text{nominal interest rate} = (1 + \text{real interest rate})(1 + \text{expected inflation rate})$$

   $$\Rightarrow \text{expected inflation rate} = \left[\frac{(1 + \text{nominal interest rate})}{(1 + \text{real interest rate})} \right] - 1$$

   In Great Britain, the expected inflation rate is:

   $$\text{expected inflation rate} = \left[\frac{(1.097)}{(1.032)} \right] - 1 = 6.30\%$$

   In Japan, the expected inflation rate is:

   $$\text{expected inflation rate} = \left[\frac{(1.064)}{(1.019)} \right] - 1 = 4.42\%$$

   Note that unlike the *international* Fisher relation, we did not assume that real interest rates were equivalent throughout the world when we used the domestic Fisher relation.

   We now back out the current spot rate, using relative purchasing power parity:

   $$\frac{E(S_t)}{S_0} = \frac{(1 + \text{expected inflation rate}_b)^t}{(1 + \text{expected inflation rate}_a)^t}$$

   $$\Rightarrow S_0 = E(S_t) \div \left[\frac{(1 + \text{expected inflation rate}_b)^t}{(1 + \text{expected inflation rate}_a)^t} \right]$$

   Note: Because the Japanese currency is in the numerator in the exchange rate, we will put the Japanese inflation rate on top in the relative purchasing power parity calculation.

So, if Japan is country b and Great Britain is country a, then we have:

$$S_0 = 200 \div \left[\frac{(1+0.0442)^4}{(1+0.0630)^4} \right] = 214.80 \approx 215$$

Notice that the exchange rate will move from ¥215/£ to ¥200/£. So it takes less yen to buy one pound (i.e., the yen has strengthened), which relative purchasing power parity predicts because Japanese inflation is lower. (Study Session 4, LOS 14.e,f)

78. **A** Statement 3: Hohlman is correct regarding absolute purchasing power parity. It is based on the law of one price, which states that the price of goods should not differ internationally. Absolute purchasing power parity is not used to predict exchange rates.

Statement 4: Hohlman is correct regarding relative purchasing power parity. It does not hold in the short-run and therefore is not useful for predicting short-run currency values. It does tend to hold in the long run, however, and is therefore useful for long-run exchange rate forecasts. (Study Session 4, LOS 14.e)

The following financial statements are provided for informational purposes only. The numbers in the proportionate column are derived as EPI + (0.5)(EP/BM LLC), except for the equity items which are not included under proportionate consolidation.

In Millions, Year End 2008	EPI	EP/BM LLC	Proportionate
Revenue	$3,115	$421	$3,326
Cost of goods sold	$2,580	$295	$2,728
SG&A	$316	$50	$341
EBIT	$219	$76	$257
Interest expense	$47	$8	$51
Equity in earnings of EP/BM	$22		
Pretax income	$194	$68	$206
Income tax	$60	$24	$72
Net income	$134	$44	$134

In Millions, December 31, 2008	EPI	EP/BM LLC	Proportionate
Assets			
Cash	$118	$13	$125
Accounts receivable	$390	$50	$415
Inventory	$314	$41	$335
Property	$1,007	$131	$1,073
Investment	$38		
Total	$1,867	$235	$1,948
Liabilities and Equity			
Accounts payable	$274	$35	$292
Long-term debt	$719	$125	$782
Equity	$874	$75	$874
Total	$1,867	$235	$1,948

79. **C** Revenues and expenses are higher under proportionate consolidation. None of the joint venture's revenues and expenses are reported under the equity method. Rather, the pro-rata share of the joint venture's earnings are reported under the equity method. Net income is the same under both methods. Under proportionate consolidation, total assets and total liabilities include the pro-rata ownership of the separate assets and liabilities of the joint venture. Thus, total assets and total liabilities are *higher* under proportionate consolidation. Note: The investment in EP/BM LLC is not included as an asset under proportionate consolidation. (Study Session 6, LOS 19.a)

80. **C** current ratio = current assets / current liabilities; (125 + 415 + 335) / 292 = 3.0. (Study Session 6, LOS 19.c)

81. **C** interest coverage = EBIT / interest expense; 257 / 51 = 5.0. (Study Session 6, LOS 19.c)

82. **A** Long-term debt is higher under the proportionate consolidation method since the pro-rata share of the joint venture's debt is reported by EPI. Under the equity method, none of the joint venture's debt is reported by EPI. Equity is the same under both methods. Thus, long-term debt-to-equity is higher under proportionate consolidation (higher numerator). (Study Session 6, LOS 19.a)

83. **B** Accounting for an equity investment depends on the investor's ability to significantly influence or control the investee. The acquisition method is used to account for a business combination, usually defined as an ownership interest of over 50%. However, the degree of ownership is used only as a practical guideline. (Study Session 6, LOS 19.a)

84. **C** Divestitures should be a rare event. A divestiture usually sends a negative signal. It is unlikely that investors want management to sell profitable assets. The other statements are all accurate. (Study Session 9, LOS 29.n,o)

85. **B** The final period cash flow will include the project cash flows, the return of net working capital, and the after-tax sale of fixed capital used in the project. Because Tera is a replacement project, the incremental cash flows must be calculated. In other words, we are concerned with the additional sales and costs derived from the new equipment.

    incremental sales = 708,000 − 523,000 = $185,000

    incremental cash expenses = 440,000 − 352,000 = $88,000

    incremental depreciation = 110,667 − 40,000 = $70,667

    incremental project cash flows = (185,000 − 88,000 − 70,667) × (1 − 0.40) + 70,667 = $86,467

    return of incremental net working capital = $110,000

    In the final year, the book value of the old machine (if not replaced) = 120,000 − 3 × 40,000 = 0. Similarly, the book value of the new machine (if replaced) = 332,000 − 3 × 110,667 = 0.

    incremental cash flow from after-tax sale of equipment = (113,000 − 90,000) − 0.40[(113,000 − 90,000) − (0 − 0)] = $13,800

    total cash flow in final period = 86,467 + 110,000 + 13,800 = $210,267

    (Study Session 8, LOS 25.a)

86. **C** In scenario analysis, the analyst simultaneously changes several key variables to generate several different scenarios. Generally, three scenarios are created: (1) worst case, (2) most likely, and (3) optimistic. For the worst case scenario, for example, the analyst will use the slowest growth in sales, highest growth in expenses, and highest discount rate to derive an NPV under the worst of all possible situations. A similar approach is used to generate the optimistic scenario, but the best possible growth in each of the variables is used. The most likely is simply what the analyst thinks are the most reasonable assumptions for the discounted cash flow forecast under normal conditions. Using the different cases, the analyst can assess the risk of the project. (Study Session 8, LOS 25.d)

87. **A** Once the Tera Project is begun, the project will be necessary for continuing operations. This is likely a result of the replacement nature of the project. If the equipment necessary for GigaTech's operations is replaced with newer equipment, abandoning the project is not really an option. Management does have the option of scaling up the project after initiation, which is known as an expansion option. Management can also wait up to nine months to make a decision on the Tera Project, giving them a timing option (note that this is not one of the answer choices). Finally, the equipment used in the Tera Project can support additional shifts if demand for GigaTech's products temporarily exceeds supply, giving them a flexibility option (specifically a production-flexibility option). (Study Session 8, LOS 25.f)

88. **B** The least common multiple of lives approach requires estimating the least common denominator between two mutually exclusive projects with unequal lives. Since the Zeta and Sigma projects have lives of 3 and 2, the least common multiple is 6. The cash flows must be stated over a 6-year period, repeating the cash flow pattern as often as necessary (two times for Zeta and three times for Sigma). The cash flows are then discounted to find the net present value (NPV). The project with the highest NPV is selected. The cash flows are as follows:

	Year						
	0	**1**	**2**	**3**	**4**	**5**	**6**
Zeta Project	−360,000	250,000	220,000	190,000			
				−360,000	250,000	220,000	190,000
Total	−360,000	250,000	220,000	−170,000	250,000	220,000	190,000
Sigma Project	−470,000	330,000	390,000				
			−470,000	330,000	390,000		
					−470,000	330,000	390,000
Total	−470,000	330,000	-80,000	330,000	−80,000	330,000	390,000

Before calculating the NPV of each project, the cost of capital must be restated in nominal terms since the cash flow projections are stated in nominal terms. The nominal cost of capital is equal to 15.0% = (1 + 0.1058)(1 + 0.04). The NPV of each project is calculated as follows:

$$NPV_{Zeta} = -360,000 + \frac{250,000}{1.15} + \frac{220,000}{1.15^2} + \frac{-170,000}{1.15^3} + \frac{250,000}{1.15^4} + \frac{220,000}{1.15^5} + \frac{190,000}{1.15^6}$$
$$= 246,425$$

$$NPV_{Sigma} = -470,000 + \frac{330,000}{1.15} + \frac{-80,000}{1.15^2} + \frac{330,000}{1.15^3} + \frac{-80,000}{1.15^4} + \frac{330,000}{1.15^5} + \frac{390,000}{1.15^6}$$
$$= 260,381$$

Since its NPV is greater, GigaTech should select the Sigma project. (Study Session 8, LOS 25.c)

89. **C**   The comments in the memo from GigaTech's board of directors are both incorrect. Earnings per share (EPS) is not a suitable criteria to evaluate capital budgeting projects. Under capital rationing, a firm selects the projects that increase the value of the firm by the greatest amount (i.e., have the highest NPV) subject to the capital constraints of the firm's budget. It is perfectly possible that projects that increase EPS will not get selected. For example, if a project has an NPV of $80 and increases EPS by $0.50 and a second project has an NPV of $200 but will initially reduce EPS by $0.20, the firm should select the second project (if its capital budget will allow it) since it adds more value. The capital budgeting process should not consider sunk costs (i.e., past costs that do not affect the cash flows of the project) such as costs to find investment projects. The cash flow projections should consider the economic impact from increased competition resulting from highly profitable investment projects. (Study Session 8, LOS 25.c)

90. **B**   When evaluating potential capital investment projects, the discount rate should be adjusted for the risk of the project under consideration. This is frequently accomplished by determining a project beta and using this beta in the CAPM security market line equation: $r_i = R_F + \beta_i[E(R_M) - R_F]$. Project betas can be determined in a number of ways including using proxy firms with operations similar to the project under consideration, estimating an accounting beta, or through cross-sectional regression analysis. Whatever method used to determine the discount rate, it should be clear that the weighted average cost of capital (WACC) is only appropriate for projects with risk similar to the overall firm. If a project is more (less) risky than the overall firm, the discount rate used to evaluate the project should be greater (less) than the firm's WACC. (Study Session 8, LOS 25.e)

91. **C**   Foster's risk tolerance consists of two components: (1) her ability to take risk and (2) her willingness to take risk. Her willingness is high, as she will accept the risk necessary to meet her financial goals. Her ability is also high due to a long time horizon and large portfolio size relative to spending needs. She needs $150,000 per year for her living expenses. This translates to a pre-tax return of 150,000 / (1 − 0.35) = $230,769 or a yield of 230,769 / $4,500,000 = 5.1% on her portfolio. In the absence of specific information about her desires for leaving an estate, she could also deplete her portfolio (spend from principal). (Study Session 18, LOS 56.e)

$$R = N + \varepsilon_T$$

92. **B** Foster's time horizon is long-term and multi-stage. The first stage is the five years until her retirement. During this time, there are no income needs for the portfolio, and higher allocations can be made to assets offering superior capital appreciation potential. This strategy might even allow the portfolio to grow beyond Foster's estimate of $4.5 million, which implies roughly 7.0% growth compounded annually from her current balance of $3.2 million. The second stage begins when Foster retires, at which time the portfolio will need to provide her $150,000 annual income after taxes. (Study Session 18, LOS 56.f)

93. **C** The Sharpe ratio of reward to variability is calculated as:

$$S = \frac{E(r_p) - r_f}{\sigma_p}$$

Fund A = (8.0 − 3.0) / 6.0 = 0.833

Fund B = (10.0 − 3.0) / 8.0 = 0.875

Fund C = (12.0 − 3.0) / 10.0 = 0.900, this is the highest value for the Sharpe ratio so Foster should select Fund C. (Study Session 18, LOS 55.a)

94. **C** The TB model calls for identifying positive (or negative) alpha securities, which are bought (sold short) in an active portfolio. This active portfolio is combined with a passive portfolio, to achieve diversification while adding incremental return. The active portfolio does not become the market portfolio, nor does the addition of the active portfolio move the investor along the capital market line. The benefit occurs because the active portfolio is less than perfectly correlated with the passive market portfolio. (Study Session 18, LOS 55.b)

95. **B** The asset weights given are relative to the active portfolio only. Typically in a TB framework, these weights will fall dramatically as the active portfolio is combined with the market portfolio. The weights relative to the overall portfolio should be reasonable. The portfolio beta of the active portfolio is a weighted average of betas of all securities in the portfolio. The combination of long (positive weights) and short (negative weights) positions in the active portfolio would most likely reduce the aggregate portfolio beta. (Study Session 18, LOS 55.b)

96. **C** Securities with negative alphas should be shorted in the active portfolio, to take advantage of their negative expected returns, however Welch is considering banning short sales. The cost of banning short sales is:

alpha with short sales: (0.5 × 0.06) + (−0.25 × -0.06) + (0.5 × 0.08) + (0.5 × 0.07) + (−0.25 × −0.04) = 0.13

alpha without short sales: (0.33333 × 0.06) + (0.33333 × 0.08) + (0.33333 × 0.07) = 0.07

lost performance = 0.13 − 0.07 = 0.06

(Study Session 18, LOS 55.b,c)

97. **B** The risk that the private equity portion of the IS University's Endowment Fund would most likely suffer from is illiquidity. It can be difficult to trade the private equity investments because they are usually not listed on secondary securities markets. The private equity investments are diversified in terms of vintage and strategies. The IS endowment fund is exempt from taxation on capital gains or dividends. (Study Session 13, LOS 40.f; Study Session 18, LOS 56.e)

98. **A** Percentage management fee = management fee / paid-in capital

   paid-in capital = Σ called-down

   2008 % management fee = 1.95 / (75 + 25 + 30) = 0.015

   (Study Session 13, LOS 40.h,i)

99. **B** $195 million Alpha Fund (all data in millions)

Year	Called-down	Mgmt. Fees	Operating Results	NAV before Distributions	Carried Interest	Distributions	NAV after Distributions
2006	30	0.45	–10	19.55		0	
2007	25	0.83	55	98.72		0	
2008	75	1.95	75	246.77	10.35	0	236.42

   2006 NAV before distributions = 30 – 0.45 + (–10) = 19.55

   2007 NAV before distributions = 19.55 + 25 – 0.83 + 55 = 98.72

   2008 NAV before distributions = 98.72 + 75 – 1.95 + 75 = 246.77

   When NAV before distribution exceeds committed capital, the 20% carried interest is applied. (246.77 – 195) × 0.2 = 51.77 × 0.2 = 10.35

   In years 2009 and beyond, the 20% carried interest is applied to the change in NAV before distributions. For example, if the 2009 NAV before distributions was 296.77, then the carried interest would equal (296.77 – 246.77) × 0.2 = 50 × 0.2 = 10.

   The NAV after distributions subtracts carried interest and distributions from NAV before distributions.

   (Study Session 13, LOS 40.i)

100. **C** Venture capital investments require considerable capital to develop and grow. Companies that require venture capital usually have significant cash burn as they develop new products. Venture capital investments are primarily funded through equity and utilize little or no debt. Risk measurement of venture capital investments is difficult because of their short operating history, and the required development of new markets and technologies. (Study Session 13, LOS 40.c)

101. **C** post-money valuation = $V / (1 + r)^t$

   V = $300 million; r = 40%; t = 5 years

   post-money valuation = 300 million / $(1 + 0.4)^5$ = 55.78 million

   Note that the adjusted discount rate incorporating the probability of failure is directly given in the question as 40%. (Study Session 13, LOS 40.j)

102. **B** The ownership proportion of the venture capital (VC) investor is f = INV / POST = $9,000,000 / 90,000,000 = 0.10 or 10%.

shares$_{VC}$ = shares$_{Founders}$ $(f / 1 - f)$ = 2,500,000 × (0.10 / 0.90) = 277,778

price = INV / shares$_{VC}$ = $9,000,000 / 277,778 = $32.33 per share

(Study Session 13, LOS 40.j)

103. **B** $$\beta_u \approx \left[\frac{1}{1+\left(D/E\right)}\right]\beta_E = \left[\frac{1}{1+\left(40/60\right)}\right]0.90 = 0.54$$

The calculation is not required if you understand the steps involved. Since Midwest News has no debt and Freedom's beta must be unlevered, the beta to be used must be less than 0.90 (Freedom's beta). (Study Session 10, LOS 31.d)

104. **B** $$\text{required return estimate} = \frac{\text{year-ahead dividend}}{\text{market price}} + \text{expected dividend growth rate}$$

$$\text{required return estimate} = \frac{\left(\$3.00 \times 0.40\right)}{\left(\$15,000 \text{ million}/375 \text{ million}\right)} + 0.06 = 0.09$$

Since Freedom Corporation has a dividend policy of paying 40% of earnings, dividend growth equals earnings growth.

The assumption is that Freedom's stock is correctly valued.

(Study Session 10, LOS 31.a)

105. **C** The Gordon growth model calculates the equity risk premium by starting with the dividend yield on the market index, adding the consensus long-term earnings growth rate and subtracting the current long-term government bond yield. The expected growth in the market index's P/E ratio is an input used in the macroeconomic model. (Study Session 10, LOS 31.b)

106. **A** r_i = risk-free rate + equity risk premium + size premium$_i$ + specific-company premium$_i$

r_i = 3.5% + 4.0% + 3.5% + 2.0% = 13.0%

(Study Session 10, LOS 31.b)

107. **B** $\quad V_0 = B_0 + \dfrac{(ROE-r)(B_0)}{r-g}$

$B_0 = \dfrac{\$79.5 \text{ million}}{1.5 \text{ million}} = \$53 \text{ per share}$

ROE = \$19.5 million / \$79.5 million = 0.245

r = 0.15 (given in problem)

g = 0.03 (given in Exhibit 2)

$V_0 = 53 + \dfrac{0.245-0.15}{0.15-0.03}(53) = \$94.96 \text{ per share}$

(Study Session 11, LOS 36.d)

108. **B** An issue not described in Exhibit 2 is control premium. Any control premium adjustment is normally added directly to a company's value estimate. Statement 1 is not correct. Since Midwest News does not pay a dividend, the free cash flow model would be better suited to compute the company's equity value rather than the dividend discount model. Statement 2 is correct. (Study Sessions 10 and 12, LOS 31.c and 34.f)

109. **B** First find the appropriate CPR by using the following formula: $6\% \times \left(\dfrac{t}{30}\right) \times PSA$. In this problem, t will equal 20 since this is the month of interest.

The CPRs using 200 PSA is: $6\% \times \left(\dfrac{20}{30}\right) \times 2.00 = 8.0\%$.

Then, use the following equation to find the SMM: $SMM = 1 - (1-CPR)^{\frac{1}{12}}$.

The SMM for 200 PSA is: and $SMM_{200PSA} = 1 - (1-0.08)^{\frac{1}{12}} = 0.0069$.

(Study Session 15, LOS 45.d)

110. **B** For 125 PSA, CPR = (1.25) × (0.002 × 20) = 0.05

$SMM_{125PSA} = 1 - (1-0.05)^{\frac{1}{12}} = 0.0043$

Then use the following equation to find the prepayment amount for the current month:

prepayment$_t$ = SSM$_t$ × (beginning mortgage balance$_t$ – scheduled principal payment$_t$)

0.0043 × (\$183 – \$0.42) = \$0.785 million

(Study Session 15, LOS 45.c)

111. **B** MBS-X has the highest OAS relative to the cost of the option embedded in the MBS. Therefore, it is the most attractive of the four alternatives. (Study Session 15, LOS 47.e)

112. **C** Commercial mortgage-backed securities are collateralized using non-recourse loans on commercial (i.e., income-producing) properties. Non-recourse means that the only cash flow support provided from the loan comes from the ability of the property to generate income and from the value of the property itself. The lender cannot seize personal assets of the borrower to satisfy any portion of the unpaid obligation. (Study Session 15, LOS 45.m)

113. **B** Increased economic growth increases incomes and worker migration. In turn, higher incomes will lead some households to purchase more expensive houses. Workers who migrate to a new location because of increased job opportunities will also repay mortgages when they sell their homes. If the Fed increases reserve requirements, interest rates will increase as a result of the restrictive monetary policy and prepayments will decrease. If interest rates hit a low point a second time, prepayments will occur but at a significantly lower rate than when the first interest rate low occurred. (Study Session 15, LOS 45.f)

114. **B** Robinson's statement regarding the cash flows of the MBS is incorrect. Cash flows from an MBS will, in general, vary inversely with interest rates. As interest rates fall, prepayments will increase, causing cash flows to be realized earlier than expected. The opposite is true in a rising interest rate environment when refinancing becomes less attractive and prepayments decrease, delaying expected cash flows. If the endowment fund has cash flow needs that vary directly with interest rates, it will need a source of funds that varies in the same way. Robinson is correct about the planned amortization class CMOs. The structure gives these securities a relatively predictable life. (Study Session 15, LOS 45.f,h)

115. **B** To calculate the fixed payment in pesos, first use the Mexican term structure to derive the present value factors:

$Z_{360} = 1 / [1 + 0.050(360 / 360)] = 0.9524$

$Z_{720} = 1 / [1 + 0.052(720 / 360)] = 0.9058$

The annual fixed payment per peso of notional principal would then be:

$FS(0,2,360) = (1 - 0.9058) / (0.9524 + 0.9058) = 0.0507$

The annual fixed payment would be: $0.0507 \times \$100M / 0.0893 = 56.8$ million pesos. (Study Session 17, LOS 51.d)

116. **A** The swap spread is derived from the term structure of interest rates used to price the cash flows of the swap. These rates do not reflect the credit risk of the counterparties. They reflect the credit risk in the overall global economy because they reflect the credit spread of the reference rate used to calculate the fixed-rate and expected floating-rate payments. (Study Session 17, LOS 51.j)

117. **B** The assumption is that the credit risk is low at the beginning of the swap because each counterparty accepted the creditworthiness of the other in order to initiate the transaction. By the middle of the swap's life, payments are coming due and credit risk increases. In interest rate swaps, the credit risk would then decline as the remaining payments were made towards the end of the swap's life. For currency swaps, however, with the exchange of notional principal, the final payment keeps credit risk high through the end of the swap life, causing it to peak between the middle and the end of the swap's life. (Study Session 17, LOS 51.i)

118. **B** Torrey is only correct regarding mark-to-market agreements. Using mark-to-market agreements for interest rate swaps will reduce credit risk by periodically computing the value of the swap and then requiring payment of that amount by one of the counterparties. At some predetermined time, the swap is revalued according to the new term structure of interest rates, and one party pays the other party any amount due. The swap is then repriced, essentially creating a new swap with no credit risk. Netting payments is also an effective way to reduce credit risk in interest rate and equity swaps. However, currency swap payments are generally not netted. Torrey has incorrectly stated that netting is almost always used in currency swaps. Using off-market swaps is not generally a method to reduce credit risk. If IRI enters into an off-market swap in which they do not owe a payment, then a payment is owed to IRI by the counterparty. This would actually increase credit risk since the counterparty could potentially default on the initial payment. (Study Session 17, LOS 51.i)

119. **B** The fixed dollar payment under the swap using the original yield curve is computed as:

$$Z_{360} = 1 / [1 + 0.040(360 / 360)] = 0.9615$$

$$Z_{720} = 1 / [1 + 0.045(720 / 360)] = 0.9174$$

The annual fixed payment per dollar of notional principal would then be:

$$FS(0,2,360) = (1 - 0.9174) / (0.9615 + 0.9174) = 0.044$$

The annual fixed payment would be:

$$0.044 \times \$100M = \$4.4 \text{ million}$$

Using the new U.S. term structure to derive the present value factors:

$$Z_{180}(360) = 1 / [1 + 0.042(180 / 360)] = 0.9794$$

$$Z_{180}(720) = 1 / [1 + 0.048(540 / 360)] = 0.9328$$

The present value of the fixed payments plus the $100M principal is:

$$\$4.4M \times (0.9794 + 0.9328) + \$100M \times 0.9328 = \$101.69 \text{ million}$$

(Study Session 17, LOS 51.d)

120. **C** Use the new Mexican term structure to derive the present value factors:

$$Z_{180}(360) = 1 / [1 + 0.050(180 / 360)] = 0.9756$$

$$Z_{180}(720) = 1 / [1 + 0.052(540 / 360)] = 0.9276$$

The present value of the fixed payments plus the principal is:

$$0.0507 \times (0.9756 + 0.9276) + 0.9276 = 1.0241 \text{ per peso}$$

Apply this to notional principal and convert at current exchange rate:

$$1.0241 \times (\$100M / 0.0893) \times 0.085 = \$97.48 \text{ million}$$

The value of the swap is the difference between this value and the pay dollar fixed present value derived in the previous question:

$$\$97.48 - \$101.69M = -\$4.21 \text{ million} \text{ (Study Session 17, LOS 51.d)}$$

EXAM 3
MORNING SESSION ANSWERS

To get valuable feedback on how your score compares to those of other Level II candidates, use your Username and Password to gain Online Access at schweser.com and choose the left-hand menu item "Practice Exams Vol. 2."

1. A	21. A	41. B
2. A	22. C	42. A
3. C	23. B	43. A
4. B	24. C	44. C
5. A	25. C	45. C
6. C	26. C	46. C
7. B	27. A	47. A
8. C	28. B	48. C
9. A	29. B	49. C
10. C	30. B	50. B
11. B	31. C	51. A
12. B	32. C	52. A
13. B	33. C	53. C
14. C	34. A	54. B
15. C	35. A	55. A
16. B	36. C	56. A
17. C	37. B	57. A
18. A	38. B	58. A
19. B	39. A	59. C
20. C	40. C	60. B

Exam 3
Morning Session Answers

1. **A** **Standard I(C).** Both Sampson and Lawson have violated Standard I(C) – Professionalism – Misrepresentation. When Sampson prepared biographies with Shadow Mountain Wealth Management Team included in them, she was obviously trying to convey the image that TIM personnel are employees of the bank trust department. This does not portray the correct business relationship between Shadow Mountain and TIM. TIM is an outsourcer to Shadow Mountain and a contract investment management provider, not an employee. Sampson is attempting to create a misleading view of the service level and investment expertise that clients could rightly expect. While Lawson was not a party to preparing such misleading business cards and marketing materials, he participated in the misrepresentation by agreeing to go ahead with the client presentation. (Study Session 1, LOS 2.a)

2. **A** **Standards I(C) and III(D).** Including the BAGF performance is a violation of Standard I(C) – Professionalism – Misrepresentation and Standard III(D) – Duties to Clients – Performance Presentation. When Sampson combines the BAGF performance record with the TIM Composite Equity Composite, this gives potential clients a misleading impression of TIM's long-term equity management performance. The use of this performance data might be acceptable if full disclosure were made as to the source and nature of the data. (Study Session 1, LOS 2.a)

3. **C** **Standard III(A).** Luna has violated the CFA Institute Standards of Professional Conduct – Standard III(A) Duties to Clients – Loyalty, Prudence, and Care. Client brokerage is the property or asset of the client and not TIM. In accordance with CFA Institute Soft Dollar Standards, client brokerage should be used only for research products or services that are directly related to the investment decision-making process and not the management costs of the firm. In this case, Luna should disclose to TIM's clients that their brokerage may be used to purchase research. In addition, Luna should seek to ensure that Turn Byer is providing the best execution for TIM's clients. StockCal is clearly providing equity research products/services that aid TIM in the investment decision-making process and not the general operation or management costs of the firm. StockCal may therefore be properly paid for with client brokerage soft dollars, and this is not a violation of the Standards or Code, or the CFA Institute Soft Dollar Standards. However, Add-Invest Software provides TIM's clients with portfolio accounting and performance measurement services and is not related to the investment decision-making process. Therefore, Luna is misusing client resources when she uses client brokerage to purchase Add-Invest Software. Add-Invest is clearly a business expense of TIM and should rightly be paid for by the firm and not the clients. Per the CFA Institute Soft Dollar Standards, the product or service received must provide proper assistance to the investment manager in following through with his investment decision-making responsibilities. (Study Session 1, LOS 2.a and 3.a,b,c)

4. **B** Standard III(A). The increased commission would be a violation, but the cash referral fee would not. Doubling the commission paid to Wurtzel would be a violation of Standard III(A) Duties to Clients – Loyalty, Prudence, and Care. Client brokerage is strictly an asset of the client and must be used for the benefit of clients in research that will assist the investment manager in the investment decision-making process. Client brokerage cannot be used as a reward for bringing clients to TIM and to do so is a misappropriation of client assets. Cash referral fees are acceptable, so long as the referral arrangement is fully disclosed to the clients in advance of opening their accounts. The case mentions that this disclosure will be made. This disclosure allows the client to evaluate any potential conflict(s) of interest in the referral process. (Study Session 1, LOS 2.a)

5. **A** Standard III(A). In making a $25,000 contribution to the Hoover Study Center of Unions, Luna has violated Standard III(A) Duties to Clients – Loyalty, Prudence, and Care, which states that Members and Candidates must act for the benefit of their clients and place their clients' interest before their employers' or their own interest. In relationship with clients, Members and Candidates must determine applicable fiduciary duty and must comply with such duty to the persons and interests to whom it is owed. The contribution to the Hoover Study Center of Unions, authorized by the trustees of the union, brings into question this acting for the benefit of the client. Despite providing guidance and governance for the union, trustees are not the client of the union fund; rather, the members of the union and their beneficiaries are the clients of the fund. By making a $25,000 contribution from the client brokerage, Luna and the trustees have used funds that rightly belong to the members of the union and they have done so without direct compensation to the union members. Luna should not have authorized the pension account to make the contribution and having done so violated her duty to loyally guard the assets of her clients as a fiduciary. Luna has an obligation to follow not only the Code and Standards but also the CFA Institute Soft Dollar Standards, which stress that the client brokerage is the property of the client, not the trustee or fiduciary representing the client. (Study Session 1, LOS 2.a)

6. **C** Standard III(A). In this case, Lutz is the client and, therefore, the direct owner of the client brokerage. If Lutz's desire is to give the soft dollar client brokerage asset to the Roswell Academy, she is free to do so because it is her asset. She is sole owner of her own retirement account. Luna, by following the wishes of the client, is complying with her duty of loyalty. Thus, there is no violation of Standard III(A) Duties to Clients – Loyalty, Prudence, and Care, in the case of the $10,000 contribution to Roswell Academy. (Study Session 1, LOS 2.a)

7. **B** A logarithmic transformation of the dependent variable is the most appropriate transformation to apply when the variable grows at a constant rate over time:

    $$\ln(\text{sales}) = a^* + b^* t + e$$

    The slope of this equation equals the nominal constant rate. The effective rate equals $e^{b^*} - 1$. (Study Session 3, LOS 13.b)

8. **C** Quarter 1 of 2009 is the 61st quarter (starting with Quarter 1 of 1994): sales = 10 + 16(61) = $986 million. (Study Session 3, LOS 13.a)

9. A   The mean reverting value equals the intercept divided by 1 minus slope = 20 / (1 – 0.10) = 20 / 0.90 = $22.22 million. The last change was $50 million as shown in Exhibit 5 (1000 – 950). Therefore, the AR(1) model predicts that the series will fall anytime the current value (the last quarter in 2008) is above the mean reverting value. The change in sales for the last quarter in 2008 was $50 million, which exceeds the mean reverting value. We could also have computed the forecasted change in sales for Quarter 1, 2009 as 20 + (0.1) × 50 = 25 (which is lower than the previous change of 50). (Study Session 3, LOS 13.f)

10. C   Seasonality refers to repeating patterns each year. Using quarterly data, tests of seasonality focus on the 4th lag (i.e., "same time, last year"). The autocorrelation for the 4th lag is statistically significant. This can be observed by comparing the reported p-value (0.02), which is less than the level of significance (0.05). (Study Session 3, LOS 13.l)

11. B   Autoregressive conditional heteroskedasticity refers to an autoregressive equation in which the variance of the errors terms is heteroskedastic (i.e., error variance is not constant). The presence of ARCH is tested with the following regression:

$$e_t^2 = \beta_1 + \beta_2 e_{t-1}^2 + v_t$$

which serves as a proxy for:

$$var(e_t) = \beta_1 + \beta_2 var(e_{t-1}) + v_t$$

Exhibit 4 indicates that the slope estimate in the ARCH equation is not significant (the t-statistic for the slope estimate of the ARCH equation is not significant). Therefore, the squared error does not depend on its lagged value (i.e., if the slope equals zero, then the error variance equals the constant β_1, which indicates no conditional heteroskedasticity in the AR model). ARCH is not present. (Study Session 3, LOS 13.m)

12. B   The most recent change in sales reported in Exhibit 5 was $50 million (i.e., an increase from $950 million to $1,000 million). Therefore, the one-step-ahead forecast is 20 + 0.1(50) = $25 million and the two-step-ahead forecast is 20 + 0.1(25) = $22.5 million. (Study Session 3, LOS 13.d)

13. B   The snack foods industry, a regulated entity, has found a way to exploit the differences in regulations among the three states and is engaging in regulatory arbitrage. Regulatory competition is a result of actions taken by regulators to attract certain entities. Regulatory capture is the idea that regulatory bodies are influenced or controlled by the regulated industry. (Study Session 4, LOS 16.d)

14. C   The carbonated beverages industry is likely to be hurt by the elimination of bigger sizes of drinks. The snack industry can avoid the new manufacturing tax in East by moving manufacture of sweet snacks to the other two states. The demand for corn is expected to remain fairly high so the regulatory changes in East are unlikely to have a major impact on the Tristanyan agricultural industry. (Study Session 4, LOS 16.i)

15. C   The increase in driving miles was not the intended effect of the regulation. Unintended effects are not a component of implementation cost. Regulatory burden refers to the cost of regulation for the entity being regulated. If sunset clause provisions were included in the regulation, West's regulators would be required to revisit the cost-benefit analysis and consider the cost of unintended consequences before renewing the regulation. (Study Session 4, LOS 16.h)

16. **B** In order for developed countries to grow, technological development is critical. Proposal 2 most clearly addresses this need. Proposal 1 would be more effective if the focus was on post-secondary education, as developed nations benefit more from innovation and less from applying technology. Proposal 3 is unlikely to have a major impact on labor productivity, as developed nations have high capital-to-labor ratios, and incentives to further increase capital will have relatively little effect on labor productivity. (Study Session 4, LOS 15.h)

17. **C** Neoclassical growth theory concludes that capital accumulation affects the level of output but not the long-run growth rate. (Study Session 4, LOS 15.i)

18. **A** The objectives of regulators in financial markets include prudential supervision, financial stability, market integrity, and economic growth. Low inflation is likely to be an objective of the central bank. (Study Session 4, LOS 16.f)

19. **B** Held-to-maturity securities are reported on the balance sheet at amortized cost. At the end of 2009, the Pinto bonds have a carrying value of $9,260,000 (9,200,000 issue price + 60,000 discount amortization). The amortized discount is equal to the $60,000 difference between the interest expense of $460,000 (9,200,000 × 5%) and the $400,000 coupon payment (10,000,000 × 4%).

Trading securities are reported on the balance sheet at fair value. At the end of 2009, the fair value of the Vega bonds was $7,941,591 (N = 39, I = 2, PMT = 175,000, FV = 7,000,000, Solve for PV).

Thus, at the end of 2009, the investment portfolio is reported at $17.2 million (9,260,000 Pinto bond + 7,941,591 Vega bond). (Study Session 6, LOS 19.a)

20. **C** A $941,591 unrealized gain (7,941,591 FV – 7,000,000 BV) was included in Viper's net income because the Vega bonds were classified as trading securities. Had the Vega bonds been classified as available-for-sale, the unrealized gain would have been reported as a component of stockholders' equity. In that case, net profit margin would have been lower (lower numerator). (Study Session 6, LOS 19.a)

21. **A** Reclassifying a held-to-maturity security to available-for-sale involves stating the investment on the balance sheet at fair value and recognizing the difference in the fair value and the carrying value as other comprehensive income. (Study Session 6, LOS 19.a)

22. **C** <u>Full goodwill method (in millions)</u>
Fair value of Gremlin $1,500 (900 purchase price / 60% ownership interest)
Less: Fair value of Gremlin's
Identifiable net assets   <u>1,100</u> (700 CA + 950 NCA – 250 CL – 300 LTD)
Goodwill $400

<u>Partial goodwill method (in millions)</u>
Purchase price $900
Less: Pro-rata share of Gremlin's
Identifiable net assets at FV   <u>660</u> (700 CA + 950 NCA – 250 CL – 300 LTD) × 60%
Goodwill $240

Goodwill is not created under the pooling method. (Study Session 6, LOS 19.b)

23. **B** Viper's post-acquisition LTD is $8,000 million [7,700 million BV of Viper + 300 million fair value (FV) of Gremlin debt]. Viper's post-acquisition equity is equal to $7,300 million (5,800 million Viper pre-acquisition equity + 900 million FV of shares used to acquire Gremlin + 600 million noncontrolling interest). Under U.S. GAAP, the noncontrolling interest is based on the full goodwill method (1,500 million FV of Gremlin × 40% noncontrolling interest). Thus, the long-term debt-to-equity ratio is 1.10 (8,000 million LTD / 7,300 million equity). (Study Session 6, LOS 19.b,c)

24. **C** According to U.S. GAAP, the goodwill is not impaired because the $1,475 million fair value of Gremlin exceeds the $1,425 million carrying value. Thus, no impairment loss is recognized.

    Under IFRS, no impairment loss is recognized because the $1,430 million recoverable amount exceeds the $1,425 million carrying value. (Study Session 6, LOS 19.b)

25. **C** The institutional guidelines related to developing the specific work product is an input source in the first phase (defining the purpose and context of the analysis). Audited financial statements are an example of an input in the data collection phase. Ratio analysis is an example of the output from the data processing phase. (Study Session 7, LOS 24.a)

26. **C** If the associate reported the investment in debt securities as held-for-trading instead of designated at fair value, its reported income would be unchanged, because unrealized and realized gains and losses under both methods are reported in the income statement. Additionally, because the investment in associate is reported under equity method by Delicious, it does not report individual assets of the investee. (Study Session 6, LOS 19.b)

27. **A** Delicious's financial leverage ratio was 1.8 (54,753 average assets / 29,983 average equity) for 2009 and was 1.7 for 2008 (49,354 average assets / 28,738 average equity). Although leverage was higher, the nature of the true leverage was lower. This is because the increasing customer advances (unearned revenue) will not require an outflow of cash in the future and are, thus, less onerous than Delicious's other liabilities. (Study Session 7, LOS 24.b)

28. **B** As indicated below, the Mexico segment has the lowest EBIT margin, yet it has the highest proportional capital expenditures to proportional assets ratio. Thus, Delicious may be overallocating resources to the Mexico segment.

    Segment Analysis for 2009

	EBIT Margin	Total CapEx %	Total Assets %	CapEx % / Assets %
Europe	14.3%	35.0%	72.0%	0.5
Mexico	8.1%	65.0%	28.0%	2.3

    (Study Session 7, LOS 24.b)

29. **B**   A finance lease is reported on the balance sheet as an asset and as a liability. In the income statement, the leased asset is depreciated and interest expense is recognized on the liability. The lease adjustment involves adding the rental payment back to EBIT and then subtracting the implied depreciation expense. Next, the implied interest expense for the lease is added to reported interest.

Operating Lease Adjustment

in millions	Reported	Adjustments	Pro-Forma	
EBIT	€7,990	69[b] – 50[c]	€8,009	= 17.8
Interest expense	€420[a]	30[d]	€450	

[a] EBIT – EBT: 7,990 – 7,570 = 420
[b] Rent expense (payment)
[c] Depreciation expense: 300 / 6 years = 50
[d] Interest expense: 300 × 10% = 30

(Study Session 7, LOS 24.c)

30. **B**   Delicious's implied value without its U.S. associate is €90,736 [€97,525 Delicious market cap – €6,789 share of associate's market cap ($32,330 × 30% × €0.70 current exchange rate)].

Delicious's net income without associate is €6,147 (€6,501 net income – €354 pro-rata share of income from associate).

Implied P/E = 14.8 (€90,736 Delicious implied value without associate / €6,147 Delicious net income without associate). (Study Session 7, LOS 24.e)

31. **C**   Rogert differentiates itself by having good selection and service. Its profit margin is higher than the industry profit margin. Individual buyers are tiny relative to the size of this corporation, giving them relatively little bargaining power. A high threat of new entrants or a high threat of substitutes would reduce profitability. (Study Session 11, LOS 32.a)

32. **C**   High switching costs relate to the bargaining power of suppliers, the threat of new entrants, or the threat of substitutes. A high degree of operating or financial leverage makes it more likely that participants will engage in price competition (or respond to such competition) to defend their market share and to cover fixed costs. The shorter the shelf life, the greater the potential for price competition if the end of the shelf life is approaching. (Study Session 11, LOS 32.a)

33. **C**   The first two arguments are plausible. If Rogert had a dominant market share, such as 80%, eliminating a smaller rival would cause the benefits to accrue mostly to Rogert. But in the given case, much of the benefits would accrue to other rivals (they would be free riders). Increasing the profit margins in some markets would likely attract new rivals in the future. The cost of capital argument is weak. Acquisitions in the grocery business, an industry in which Rogert has considerable competence and success, is not especially risky. A vertical merger (into new and different industries) would be more likely to increase risks and the cost of capital. (Study Session 11, LOS 32.c)

34. **A**   Product differences/brand identity and cost and/or quality advantages relate most closely to the threat of new entrants. The threat of forward integration relates most closely to the bargaining power of suppliers. (Study Session 11, LOS 32.a)

35. **A**   Chiraq is incorrect about economies of scale. The fact that economies of scale are available for firms much smaller than Rogert would make it easier for new entrants to enter the business. (Study Session 11, LOS 32.a)

36. **C**   The method of extending the shelf life of fruits and vegetables could increase (not decrease) Rogert's profitability. Lower industry growth rates often result in greater rivalry (including price wars), a focus on differentiating products, and searching for new market niches and geographic segments. Suppliers who increase their brand awareness through national advertising could increase their bargaining position relative to Rogert's. (Study Session 11, LOS 32.d)

37. **B**   The justified price-to-book value (P/B) ratio is calculated as:

$$P/B = (ROE - g) / (r - g)$$

where:
growth rate: $g = ROE \times (1 - payout)$
Able: $g = 0.25 \times (1 - 1.00 / 2.50) = 0.15$
Baker: $g = 0.15 \times (1 - 1.60 / 4.80) = 0.10$
Charles: $g = 0.08 \times (1 - 2.50 / 4.00) = 0.03$

Justified price-to-book value (P/B):

Able: P/B = (0.25 − 0.15) / (0.20 − 0.15) = 2, implying price = 2 × 10 = $20
Baker: P/B = (0.15 − 0.10) / (0.12 − 0.10) = 2.5, implying price = 2.5 × 32 = $80
Charles: P/B = (0.08 − 0.03) / (0.10 − 0.03) = 0.71, implying price = 0.71 × 50 = $35.5

Able sells for $60, triple its value; Baker sells for $70, 12% below its value; and Charles sells for $35.5, right at its value.

(Study Session 12, LOS 35.h,j)

38. **B**   The justified price-to-sales (P/S) ratio is calculated as:

$$P/S = [\text{profit margin} \times \text{payout ratio} \times (1 + g)] / (r - g)$$

Baker: P/S = [(4.80 / 52.80) × (1.60 / 4.80) × (1 + 0.10)] / (0.12 − 0.10) = 1.67

(Study Session 12, LOS 35.h)

39. **A**   Able Corporation should sell for [(2.50 / 115) × (1.00 / 2.50) × (1 + 0.15)] / (0.20 − 0.15) = 0.20 × sales, or $23/share. The current market price of $60 is 161% overvalued. Baker trades for $70 versus a value of 1.67 × 52.8 = $88, a discount of 20%. Charles trades for $35.50 versus a value of 1.43 × 25.75 = 37, a negligible discount of 4%. (Study Session 12, LOS 35.i)

40. **C**   A high ROE does not make a company a good investment, nor does a high book value. However, Able Corporation does have the highest potential growth rate. Because the justified values for Charles Company are near the market price, there does not appear to be any problem with the valuation inputs (e.g., required return). The similarity between the justified P/B value and the market price of Charles indicates that it is fairly priced and not an especially attractive investment. (Study Session 12, LOS 35.i)

41. **B**   Based on the model presented, the predicted P/E ratios can be calculated as:

Able: $2.74 + 8.21(1.00 / 2.50) + 14.21(0.15) + 2.81(0.25) = 8.85$

Baker: $2.74 + 8.21(1.60 / 4.80) + 14.21(0.10) + 2.81(0.15) = 7.32$

Charles: $2.74 + 8.21(2.50 / 4.00) + 14.21(0.03) + 2.81(0.08) = 8.52$

(Study Session 12, LOS 35.e)

42. **A**   Swift has correctly stated that if multicollinearity is present in a model, the interpretation of the individual regression coefficients becomes problematic. The existence of multicollinearity is generally signaled by a high R-squared value and low *t*-statistics on the regression coefficients. The *t*-stat for the coefficients for *r, g,* and ROE can be calculated as $(8.21 / 6.52) = 1.26$, $(14.21 / 9.24) = 1.54$, and $(2.81 / 2.10) = 1.34$, respectively. Note that all of these *t*-stats are well below the approximate critical value of 2, indicating they are statistically insignificant. With the high R-squared of 81% and insignificant *t*-stats, it appears that multicollinearity is indeed present in this model. Swift's comment regarding predictive power is incorrect. Cross-sectional regressions have unknown predictive power outside the specific sample and time period used to generate the regression. (Study Session 12, LOS 35.i)

43. **A**   For industrial properties, the most important factor affecting economic value is retail sales growth, which is expected to be low in West Lundia. The most important factor affecting economic value for apartment REITs are job creation and population growth, which are both expected to be high. For office properties, the most important factor is job creation, which is expected to be high.(Study Session 13, LOS 39.c)

44. **C**   There are two components to this valuation. The first component is the cash flows for the first seven years. The second component is the terminal value.

PV of CFs in years 1–7:
PMT = 7.0; I/Y = 10; N = 7. The PV = WL$34.08 million.

PV of terminal value:
An appropriate terminal cap rate can be calculated using the following equation:

cap rate = discount rate – growth rate = 10% – 3.25% = 6.75%.

The terminal value is calculated using the following inputs: WL$8.5 million divided by the terminal cap rate of 6.75%. The value in Year 7 is WL$125.93 million, discounting this value to the present:
FV = WL$125.93 million; N = 7, I/Y = 10 results in a present value of WL$64.62 million.

WL$34.08 + WL$64.62 = WL$98.7 million.

(Study Session 13, LOS 38.g)

45. **C** NAVPS based on forecasted NOI:

Option #2 (REIT)	(in WL$ millions)
Recent NOI	140.0
Subtract: Non-cash rents	− 5.0
Add: Full-year adjustment for acquisition	+ 5.0
Pro forma cash NOI	140.0
Projected NOI @ 2.5% growth	143.5
Estimated value of operating real estate @ cap rate of 7.0%	2050.0
Add: Other assets	+ 50.0
Estimated gross value	2100.0
Subtract: Total liabilities	− 300.0
NAV	1800.0

NAVPS = 1800 / 15 = 120, which is lower than the current market price of WL$125.00. This REIT is selling at a premium to NAVPS. (Study Session 13, LOS 39.e)

46. **C** Option 1 represents private investment in real estate, while Options 2 and 3 entail investing through public securities. Tax advantages can be enjoyed by direct investments in real estate, as well as through public securities. Similarly, use of leverage can be pursued by all three options. Option 1 does not have the problem of structural conflicts of interest that may be present in REITs (Option 2). (Study Session 13, LOS 38.c)

47. **A** The terminal value estimate is 12.0 × WL$13.5 MM for end of year 7 or WL$162.0 MM. The discount rate is the cap rate of 7.0% plus the growth rate of 2.5%, or 9.5%. Discounting this terminal value to find the present value: FV = WL$162.0 MM; I/Y = 9.5; N = 7; PV = WL$85.83 MM. Add the present value of all dividends of WL$39.7 MM for a total of WL$125.53 MM. Divide WL$125.53 MM by 1 million shares outstanding for a value per share of WL$125.53. (Study Session 13, LOS 39.h)

48. **C** Investment in both public REOCs and public REITs enjoy high liquidity, as shares of both trade on a stock exchange. Tax advantages favor REITs as REOCs are not tax-advantaged. REOCs are more reliant on capital appreciation due to their ability to reinvest cash flows, while REITs tend to have higher current income (i.e., yield). (Study Session 13, LOS 39.a)

49. **C** Bond A is priced at par value. A negative butterfly shift would increase the humped nature of the yield curve, either through a bigger increase in intermediate rates than in short- and long-term rates or a smaller decrease in intermediate rates than in short- and long-term rates. Because Bond A has a much lower duration than Bond C, a yield curve shift would have more of a price impact on Bond C than on Bond A. Long-term investors would not be drawn to such a short-term bond unless the yield shift created significant mispricing, which is unlikely. Choice C is the only answer that accurately reflects a possible result of a negative butterfly shift. Bond A would increase in price if the shift saw short-term rates falling more than intermediate rates. The increase in price will be limited, however, by the call price, and thus the callable bond would experience price compression (usually observed at low interest rates). The interest rate decrease would be consistent with a negative butterfly shift. (Study Session 14, LOS 43.a)

50. **B** To find the overall effect on the value of the fund, multiply the key rate durations for the appropriate maturities by the change in the interest rate for that maturity.

effect of rate changes on the Nova Fund: *Nova* = [−0.40(0.50%)] + [−3.4(−0.75%)] = +2.35%

(Study Session 14, LOS 43.f)

51. **A** In a negative butterfly shift in which all interest rates decrease, the long-term and short-term interest rates will decrease by a greater amount than will the intermediate-term interest rates. The Quasar fund has a very large interest rate sensitivity (as measured by the 30-year key rate duration) to long-term interest rates. Therefore, if the interest rates at the long end decrease by a greater amount than the intermediate-term rates, the effect on the value of the Quasar Fund will be greater than the effect on the Nova Fund, which has large exposure to intermediate-term rates but much less exposure to long-term rates. Recall that a decrease in interest rates causes the value of a fixed-income security to rise. Thus, the percentage gain in the value of the Quasar Fund will be greater than that of the Nova Fund in this scenario. (Study Session 14, LOS 43.f)

52. **A** Research conducted by Litterman and Scheinkman indicated that changes in the level of interest rates had the most explanatory power for returns on Treasury securities. Because the Quasar fund is composed of Treasuries of various maturities, Litterman and Scheinkman's research would be applicable. (Study Session 14, LOS 43.b)

53. **C** Option pricing models assume a constant volatility of interest rates but not a constant level of interest rates. Walsh's first statement is incorrect. The market segmentation theory says that the term structure of interest rates is determined solely by the supply/demand for a given maturity sector. The statement is incorrect, however, because high demand from investors (who wish to lend money) would push interest rates lower, not higher, as observed in the term structure. (Study Session 14, LOS 43.e)

54. **B** Terry's justification is incorrect. There are actually more maturity points in the swap market from which a swap curve can be derived. The rest of Terry's statements are correct. (Study Session 14, LOS 43.d)

55. **A** At the initiation of GlobeCorp's fixed-rate-payer swap, the value was zero and the fixed rate was set at 2.75%. To determine the change in the value of the swap, we must determine the fixed rate on comparable swaps available today using the LIBOR curve. Because a year has passed since the initiation of the swap, a comparable swap as of today would be a 2-year swap with semiannual payments. First calculate the discount factors for the 180-, 360-, 540-, and 720-day LIBOR interest rates as follows:

$$180\text{-day} = \frac{1}{1+0.0245\left(\dfrac{180}{360}\right)} = 0.9879; \quad 360\text{-day} = \frac{1}{1+0.0375\left(\dfrac{360}{360}\right)} = 0.9639;$$

$$540\text{-day} = \frac{1}{1+0.0380\left(\dfrac{540}{360}\right)} = 0.9461; \quad 720\text{-day} = \frac{1}{1+0.0240\left(\dfrac{720}{360}\right)} = 0.9542$$

Next calculate the fixed rate currently available on 2-year semiannual pay swaps as follows:

$$\left[\frac{(1-0.9542)}{(0.9879+0.9639+0.9461+0.9542)}\right] \times \left(\frac{360}{180}\right) = 0.0119 \times 2 = 0.0238 = 2.38\%$$

GlobeCorp could enter into an equivalent swap today at an annualized fixed rate of 2.38% versus the fixed rate of 2.75% that it is currently paying on the existing swap.

Therefore, the existing swap has negative value to GlobeCorp and has thus decreased from an initial value of zero. Current credit risk is greater for NVS Bank because the negative value of the swap to GlobeCorp increases the chance that the company will default on the obligation and fail to make the required payments to NVS. (Study Session 17, LOS 51.c,i)

56. **A** A payer swap such as GlobeCorp's is obligated to pay multiple fixed-rate payments to, and receive multiple floating-rate payments from, the counterparty. The payer swap therefore gains (loses) value if interest rates rise (fall) because floating-rate payments will be greater (less) than the required fixed-rate payments. Similarly, the long position in a forward rate agreement (FRA) allows the purchaser to borrow at a specified rate (pay fixed). If interest rates rise (fall), the long FRA position gains (loses) value. Thus, we can state that a series of long off-market FRAs is equivalent to a pay fixed interest rate swap. To offset an existing pay fixed swap position, a position with opposite exposure to interest rates must be established. Therefore, Strategy 1 is appropriate because it involves a short position in a series of off-market FRA contracts. Strategy 2 will not offset GlobeCorp's existing interest rate swap position. A pay fixed interest rate swap position is equivalent to being short a fixed-rate bond and long a floating-rate bond. In order to neutralize such a position, the opposite transactions need to be established. Strategy 2 correctly states that GlobeCorp should take a short position in a floating-rate note, but this will only offset half of the swap position. GlobeCorp must also go long (purchase) a fixed-rate bond with a coupon rate equal to the fixed rate on the swap. (Study Session 17, LOS 51.b)

57. **A** NVS Bank is issuing a $100 million floating-rate note with quarterly interest rate payments and a maturity of two years to fund its operations. The interest rate risk of such a measure is that interest rates will rise dramatically, causing the interest cost on the floating-rate note to increase as well. To offset this risk, NVS Bank can take a long position in an interest rate cap. If interest rates rise, the counterparty to the cap will make a payment to NVS Bank. If interest rates fall, no payment is made. Because the cap is a set of interest rate options, NVS has the right to receive payments if the cap is in the money but will never owe any payments if the cap is out of the money. To obtain this option, NVS must pay the cap premium ($2,200,000). The most appropriate cap is the 2-year quarterly payment cap with a contract rate of 3.65%. The expected payoff after 360 days is determined by comparing the expected LIBOR rate (3.75%) to the contract rate on the cap (3.65%). Because the actual rate is expected to be above the cap rate, the cap is in the money and the payoff is calculated as follows:

$$(0.0375 - 0.0365)\left(\frac{90}{360}\right)(100,000,000) = \$25,000$$

(Study Session 17, LOS 52.a,b)

58. **A** The writer or the seller of a floor (i.e., the short position) receives the premium or fee from the buyer of the floor. This fee is the maximum gain that the seller can achieve. The seller will be forced to make a payment to the buyer if the floor expires in the money. For a floor to be in the money, the reference rate (LIBOR in this case) must be below the contract rate. The contract rate on the 2-year semiannual floor is 2.70%, which is greater than the expected LIBOR rate of 2.40% after 720 days. Therefore, the floor is in the money and the seller must make a payment to the buyer. The payment is calculated as follows:

$$(0.0240 - 0.0270)\left(\frac{180}{360}\right)(100,000,000) = -\$150,000$$

Note that the purchaser of the floor in this scenario would receive a positive $150,000 payoff. (Study Session 17, LOS 52.b)

59. **C** An interest rate collar consists of a long interest rate cap and a short interest rate floor. The long cap limits the interest rate exposure on the upside, effectively capping the maximum interest rate the purchaser of the cap will have to pay. The short floor creates exposure to interest rates on the downside, requiring payments as interest rates fall. Because NVS Bank is short a floating-rate note, its interest costs should fall with interest rates. However, the short floor limits the degree to which interest expense can fall, effectively limiting the minimum interest payment. The combination of the maximum interest rate and the minimum interest rate creates the collar within which the interest rate may fluctuate. NVS Bank is exposed to quarterly floating-rate interest payments for a period of two years. To create an appropriate collar, the bank should purchase the 2-year quarterly settlement cap and sell the 2-year quarterly settlement floor. (Study Session 17, LOS 52.a)

60. **B** NVS Bank is concerned that interest rates will rise, increasing the interest expense on its 2-year floating-rate notes. To mitigate this risk, an appropriate strategy would be to buy an interest rate cap, which would limit the exposure to rising interest rates. Other instruments can replicate the payoffs of a cap, however, if the cap itself is not desirable. An interest rate cap increases in value as interest rates rise because a payoff to the buyer of the cap becomes more probable. Put options on fixed-income instruments have a similar response to interest rates. As interest rates rise, the value of the underlying fixed-income instruments decreases. Because a put option gives the owner the right to sell a bond that has decreased in price at higher than market value, the value of the option increases as interest rates rise. With the right amount of long put options on fixed-income instruments, NVS Bank could replicate the cap payoff without actually buying the cap. Green's alternative to the cap or the floor is therefore correct. To create a collar, NVS Bank would need to purchase a cap and sell a floor. Doing so would give NVS protection from rising interest rates and would decrease the cost of gaining such protection. However, a collar would create exposure to decreasing interest rates through the short floor position. A long cap position can be replicated either through long put options on fixed-income instruments or long call options on interest rates. A short floor position can be replicated through either short call options on fixed-income instruments or short put options on interest rates. Green has correctly stated the long cap position but has incorrectly stated the short floor position. Therefore, the collar replication strategy is incorrect. (Study Session 17, LOS 52.b)

Exam 3
Afternoon Session Answers

To get valuable feedback on how your score compares to those of other Level II candidates, use your Username and Password to gain Online Access at schweser.com and choose the left-hand menu item "Practice Exams Vol. 2."

61. B	81. C	101. A
62. B	82. C	102. A
63. A	83. C	103. A
64. C	84. A	104. C
65. C	85. A	105. A
66. C	86. B	106. B
67. A	87. C	107. A
68. B	88. C	108. C
69. C	89. A	109. A
70. C	90. C	110. C
71. A	91. B	111. C
72. A	92. B	112. C
73. A	93. C	113. B
74. B	94. B	114. B
75. A	95. A	115. A
76. B	96. B	116. B
77. C	97. B	117. B
78. A	98. C	118. B
79. C	99. A	119. B
80. C	100. C	120. C

Exam 3
Afternoon Session Answers

61. **B** **Standard VI(A).** The compensation plan is acceptable under Standard VI(A) Conflicts of Interest – Disclosure of Conflicts, but Chester must disclose the plan to clients. The firm's equity strategy is described as "large cap core." The S&P 500 Index is an appropriate benchmark for such a strategy, but the incentive for portfolio managers is to invest outside the index in order to achieve excess returns. Managers may be motivated to invest in securities that would not be consistent with client objectives or risk profiles. (Study Session 1, LOS 2.a)

62. **B** **Standard VI(A).** Rogers must discuss the offer with supervisory personnel at Chester before accepting the offer. His employer then has the opportunity to evaluate the effect of the offer on Rogers's ability to continue to perform his duties for Chester. The foundation is very large, and the position appears likely to consume much of Rogers's time and effort. If compensation is involved, Rogers would have to decline the offer unless Chester consented to the arrangement. (Study Session 1, LOS 2.a)

63. **A** **Standard III(D).** Chester has violated Standard III(D) Duties to Clients – Performance Presentation. The claim in itself is acceptable. Rogers's superior performance has lasted only a short time, and the advertising does not suggest otherwise. However, the superior performance has been achieved by investing in small cap securities, which is inconsistent with the stated style of Chester's equity management. Unless Chester discloses this change in style, the performance claims do not accurately reflect the firm's performance. Chester has not violated the Standards regarding use of and reference to the CFA designation. Rogers's use of the CFA designation is acceptable, and the quote stating that a CFA charterholder is committed to high ethical standards is acceptable as well. (Study Session 1, LOS 2.a)

64. **C** **Standard IV(A).** Pierce should not have taken any employer records, and the computer model was Chester's property, regardless of Pierce's role in developing the model. Pierce has violated Standard IV(A) Duties to Employers – Loyalty by taking both items without Chester's consent. (Study Session 1, LOS 2.a)

65. **C** **Standard IV(A).** Pierce took no client records with her from Chester. It is reasonable to assume that she is using publicly available information to contact her former clients. So long as Pierce did not have a non-compete agreement, the standards do not preclude her from contacting former clients or encouraging them to move their accounts. The violation in this case was disclosing the new compensation plan. This plan should be disclosed to Chester's clients by Chester. Pierce does not have whistleblower status in this case because she stands to receive a personal gain by bringing her former clients to Cheeri. By disclosing the plan, Pierce has violated Standard IV(A) Duties to Employers – Loyalty by attempting to injure her former employer. Note that the compensation plan is not illegal; it is only a policy that should be disclosed. Had there been an illegal activity, Pierce might have had more justification as a whistleblower. (Study Session 1, LOS 2.a)

66. **C**   **Standard III (D).** The problem is that Pierce's performance over the past three quarters arose from large cap securities, not small cap securities. Excluding these results misrepresents her ability as a large cap manager. The Standards do not require compliance with GIPS, nor do they require that previous employer results be excluded. Stating results of a specific style, such as large cap, is acceptable if it is accurate. (Study Session 1, LOS 2.a)

67. **A**   2009 sales forecast = 20.1 + 0.001 × 8,000 + 1,000.6 × 0.05 + 0.1 × 97 − 3.2 × 60,000 − 40.3 × 0.055 = −$191,914 (Study Session 3, LOS 12.c)

68. **B**   Using a two-tail test at the 10% significance level, the critical value of the *t*-statistic equals 1.67 (degrees of freedom equal N − k − 1 = 76 − 5 − 1 = 70). The *t*-statistic (1.75) exceeds its critical value using a 10% significance level. (Study Session 3, LOS 12.b)

69. **C**   As a general rule, any independent variable must have a *t*-statistic of 2 or more to be statistically significant. There is no indication that sales cannot be modeled. The main weakness in this model is the lack of significance of the PC variable. (Study Session 3, LOS 12.a)

70. **C**   The *F*-value is calculated as (mean regression sum of squares) / (mean squared error) = (412,522/5) / (17,188/70) = 336. (Study Session 3, LOS 12.e)

71. **A**   Clark finds that the correlation between the regression errors across time was very close to 1, indicating the presence of significant positive serial correlation. Positive serial correlation causes the standard errors to be too small, which then causes the *t*-statistics to be too large (biased upward). (Study Session 3, LOS 12.i)

72. **A**   A regression exhibits conditional heteroskedasticity if the variance of the regression errors are not constant and are related to the regression independent variables. Clark's Finding 2 indicates that his regression exhibits conditional heteroskedasticity. (Study Session 3, LOS 12.i)

73. **A**   The accounting for an ownership interest of between 20% and 50% in an associate is handled using the equity method. Under the equity method, the initial investment is recorded at cost and reported on the balance sheet as a noncurrent asset. Because the acquisition in this case is fully funded by cash, there will be no change to total assets for Hope. (Study Session 6, LOS 19.a)

74. **B**   Hope is acquiring a 20% stake in Levitt for $185 million. The pro-rata book value of Levitt's net assets is $119.20 million (= 0.2 × [$824 million − $220 million − $8 million]). The amount of excess purchase price that should be allocated to PP&E is $28.4 million (= 0.2 × [$250 million − $108 million]). Goodwill is then computed as:

Purchase price:	$185.0 million
Less: pro-rata book value of net assets:	$119.2 million
Excess of purchase price:	$ 65.8 million
Less: excess allocated to PP&E:	$ 28.4 million
Goodwill:	$ 37.4 million

(Study Session 6, LOS 19.a)

75. **A**   Hope's proportionate share of Levitt's net income is $21.6 million (= 0.2 × $108 million). Levitt's contribution to Hope's EBT is then computed as:

Hope's proportionate share of Levitt's net income:	$21.6 million
Less: additional depreciation expenses:	$ 5.0 million
Equity income:	$16.6 million

(Study Session 6, LOS 19.a)

76. **B**   No calculations are required to solve this problem. The increase/decrease to Hope's investment balance is equal to the investment balance at the beginning of year plus equity income less dividends paid. The equity income is positive because Levitt had positive net income, and there is no additional depreciation expense to subtract. Additionally, Levitt is not expected to make any dividend payments for 2011. Based on this, Hope's investment balance will increase. (Study Session 6, LOS 19.a)

77. **C**   Under the conditions given by Gordon, the equity method, proportionate consolidation, and the acquisition method all report the same net income. ROA is higher under the equity method than under proportionate consolidation because the equity method does report lower assets than proportionate consolidation. (Study Session 6, LOS 19.c)

78. **A**   When the investment constitutes 20% to 50% of the associate, and the investor has significant influence on the associate, IFRS prescribes the equity method for accounting for the investment. (Study Session 6, LOS 19.b)

79. **C**   Management incentives are a key factor in light of Mr. Silver's desire to retire in three years and his interest in Flavoring management's capabilities to help guide the combined firm. Diversification is another key motivation because Flavoring's products are consumer based but serve a different market than Fashion's focus on consumer accessories. Because the companies have different product lines, synergies in the form of cost savings or revenue enhancement are unlikely to occur. In addition, the companies are in very different industries, making increased market power in either industry unlikely to occur as a result of the merger. (Study Session 9, LOS 29.b,d)

80. **C**   Opportunities to expand its products into different segments of the market for spices are not indicated in the vignette. Flavoring's management appears more interested in geographic expansion of its existing product line. (Study Session 9, LOS 29.b)

81. **C**   The bootstrap effect will only occur when Fashion's P/E ratio is higher than Flavoring's and Fashion's P/E post merger does not decline. At the current market price of $30.50, Fashion's P/E is 19.1, based on earnings per share of $1.60 ($80 million earnings/ 50 million shares). At its current market price of $20 and earnings per share of $1.10 ($22 million earnings/20 million shares), Flavoring's stock's P/E is 18.2x. Therefore, the combined earnings per share after the merger would be higher if Fashion issued stock at the current price and bought Flavoring at $20 or less per share. (Study Session 9, LOS 29.c)

82. **C** The following statistics show calculations of estimated takeover value using equal weighting.

Estimated Takeover Value	Flavoring	Mean Multiple	Price/Share	Equal Weight	Est. Value
Sales per share	$5.25	4.13	$21.68	0.25	$5.42
Book value per share	$3.60	5.95	$21.42	0.25	$5.36
Earnings per share	$1.10	19.78	$21.76	0.25	$5.44
Cash flow per share	$2.10	11.58	$24.32	0.25	$6.08
Total estimated value					$22.30

(Study Session 9, LOS 29.j)

83. **C** The takeover premium can be based on various statistics (mean, median, mode) of takeover premiums observed for comparable companies. In this case, the takeover premium is based on equally weighting the takeover premium for the four recently acquired companies.

	Jones Foods	Dale Inc.	Hill Brands	Lane Co.	Mean
Preacquisition price (A)	$20	$26	$35	$40	—
Acquisition price (B)	$24	$32	$40	$46	—
Takeover premium = (B − A) / A	20.0%	23.1%	14.3%	15.0%	**18.1%**

(Study Session 9, LOS 29.j)

84. **A** This is a key reason to use the comparable value method, particularly when contrasted with the use of discounted cash flow valuations. Acquisition prices are not necessarily approximations of intrinsic values. A price developed based on comparable transactions does not always indicate the potential value of the acquisition to the purchaser. (Study Session 9, LOS 29.h)

85. **A** Begin by calculating the capital structure of each plan and then multiply the percentage of debt and equity by their component costs and add the results to find the weighted average cost of capital (WACC). The plan with the lowest WACC maximizes the firm's stock price and thus reflects the optimal capital structure. In this case, Plan C meets all the criteria for optimizing X-Sport's capital structure. Plan C's debt-to-equity ratio is 1.22. Thus, there are 1.22 units of debt for every one unit of equity for a total of 2.22 units of capital. Therefore, the percentage of debt is 1.22 / 2.22 = 55%, leaving 45% equity. Thus, the WACC for Plan C is: $(0.55 \times 4.4\%) + (0.45 \times 11.2\%) = 7.46\%$.

Repeating these calculations for Plans A, B, and D, we find that the WACCs are 10.75%, 8.76%, and 7.75%, respectively. (Study Session 8, LOS 26.b)

86. **B** Kelley's report is incorrect regarding the static trade-off theory of capital structure, which states that a company should lever up to the point at which the additional increase in the costs of financial distress exceeds the additional increase in the tax shield from interest rate payments. Once this point is reached, adding more leverage to the company will decrease its value. Kelley's report is correct regarding the net agency costs of equity. Agency costs include equity holders' cost to monitor the firm's executives, management's bonding costs to assure owners that their best interests are guiding the company's actions, and residual losses that result even when sufficient monitoring and bonding exists. Adding additional debt reduces the agency costs to equity holders because less of their capital is at risk. The leverage effectively shifts some agency costs to bondholders. Additionally, managers have less cash to squander when higher leverage is employed because higher interest costs will restrict discretionary free cash flow. (Study Session 8, LOS 26.a)

87. **C** The most likely difference in the cost of debt financing between the current level of 5.0% and the 8.5% for Plan A is that there is a greater probability of bankruptcy. Using the debt-to-equity ratio, we observe that Plan A calls for 2.33 / (2.33 + 1) = 70% debt financing, which is a very large proportion of the capital structure. The chances of bankruptcy are much greater with this heavy reliance on debt financing. (Study Session 8, LOS 26.a)

88. **C** Miller and Modigliani Proposition II states that the cost of equity is a linear function of a company's debt/equity ratio. Pecking-order theory prefers internally generated equity (retained earnings) over new debt and new debt over new equity. Static trade-off theory states that the optimal level of debt is achieved when the extra cost of financial distress equals the tax benefit of debt. (Study Session 8, LOS 26.a)

89. **A** Spin-off transactions involve creating a new entity out of a company's business line or one of its subsidiaries and then granting shares in the new entity to the existing shareholders of the parent company. The shareholders are then free to sell their shares in the spin-off company in the marketplace. Spin-offs are generally viewed as a favorable sign in the market because they often result in greater efficiency for the spin-off company and the parent company. In a carve-out transaction, a new entity is created in a similar manner to the spin-off transaction. The main difference is that a minority of shares is sold to the public while the majority portion of the new shares are held by the parent company (they are not distributed to existing shareholders). (Study Session 9, LOS 29.n)

90. **C** X-Sport's board of directors suffers from a lack of independence from management. The most pressing issue is that the CEO of the company, Richard Haywood, is also the chairman of the board. Judging by his ability to convince the board of his plan to spin off GearTech, Haywood exerts an excessive degree of influence over the board. This lack of independence could negatively impact the value of X-Sport common stock because investors will demand a higher risk premium for holding the stock because there is significant risk that management will not act in the shareholders' best interest. Specifically, there is a great risk (as evidenced by their quick decision to spin off GearTech) that management will enter into future transactions (such as mergers, acquisitions, and divestitures) and assume business risks that are in management's interest but not in the shareholders' best interest. This is known as strategic policy risk, not liability risk. Note that there are two former executives of GearTech on the board who may benefit from spinning off the company. It is possible that the poor corporate governance at X-Sport may call into question the reliability of the financial disclosures of GearTech, but this risk is known as accounting risk, not asset risk. (Study Session 9, LOS 28.f,h)

91. **B**   Firm A should be valued using the one-period dividend discount model. The firm has a history of dividend payments, the dividend policy is clear and related to the earnings of the firm, and (as stated in the presentation) the perspective is that of a minority shareholder. A free cash flow model is more appropriate when examining the perspective of a controlling shareholder.

Firm B should be valued using a residual income model. The residual income approach is most appropriate for firms that do not have dividend histories, have transparent financial reporting, and have negative free cash flow for the foreseeable future (usually due to capital demands). (Study Session 11, LOS 33.a)

92. **B**   Firm C should be valued using an H dividend discount model. A firm that has little competition now, but has competition that is expected to increase, is a candidate for the H-model. Growth can be expected to decline as competitors enter the market. Growth then stabilizes as the industry matures.

Firm D should be valued using a two-stage dividend discount model. A firm that is expected to have a high rate of growth until patents expire, for example, should be modeled by the two-stage model, with one rate of growth before the patent expires and another rate thereafter. (Study Session 11, LOS 33.i)

93. **C**   The firm should be valued using an H dividend discount model given that an initially high rate of growth declines linearly over a specified period. The formula is:

$$V_0 = \frac{\left[D_0 \times (1 + g_L)\right] + \left[D_0 \times H(g_S - g_L)\right]}{r - g_L}$$

where:

$$H = \left(\frac{t}{2}\right) = \text{half-life (in years) of high-growth period}$$

where:

t = length of high-growth period
g_S = short-term growth rate
g_L = long-term growth rate
r = required return

Using the figures for Maple:

$$V_0 = \frac{\left[\$3.00 \times (1 + 0.07)\right] + \left[\$3.00 \times \left(\frac{8}{2}\right) \times (0.25 - 0.07)\right]}{0.15 - 0.07} = \$67.13$$

(Study Session 11, LOS 33.l)

94. **B**   If you grow the $5.00 dividend out for four years at 18%, the first four dividends are:

D_1	D_2	D_3	D_4
$ 5.90	$ 6.96	$ 8.22	$ 9.69

D5 is then D4 × 1.04 = $10.0816. Discounting the first four dividends at 15%, you obtain:

$PV(D_1)$	$PV(D_2)$	$PV(D_3)$	$PV(D_4)$
$ 5.13	$ 5.26	$ 5.40	$ 5.54

Discounting the dividends from the end of Year 4 to perpetuity using the dividend discount model, you obtain:

10.0816/(0.15 – 0.04) = $91.65. Discounting this figure back to the present, you have $91.65/(1.15^4) = $52.40.

Summing up the present values of all the above (5.13 + 5.26 + 5.40 + 5.54 + 52.40), you have a total price of $73.73.

Note that your answer may differ slightly from the answer above due to rounding. (Study Session 11, LOS 33.l)

95. **A**   The stock price represents the present value of the future dividends (on a no-growth basis) and the present value of the growth opportunities (PVGO):

$$\text{value} = \frac{E}{r} + PVGO$$

Thus the value of a firm's equity has two components: the value of its assets in place (E/r) and the present value of its future investment opportunities (PVGO).

We will use leading earnings because the P/E is specified as the leading P/E. Backing out the PVGO, we have:

$$90 = \frac{6}{0.15} + PVGO$$

$$PVGO = 50$$

The P/E for the firm is 90/6 = 15.00.
The P/E of the PVGO is 50/6 = 8.33.

The percentage of Wood Athletic Supplies leading P/E related to PVGO is then 8.33 / 15.00 = 56%. (Study Session 11, LOS 33.e)

96. **B**   Statement 1 is incorrect. All of Pacious's description of the initial growth phase is correct except that, in this stage, the free cash flows to equity are actually negative. This is due to the heavy capital investment. Statement 2 is correct. The terminal value in the three-stage dividend growth model can be estimated using either approach. (Study Session 11, LOS 33.j,k)

97. **B**   R&D should be capitalized and amortized rather than expensing when incurred. The other adjustments are appropriate. (Study Session 12, LOS 36.a)

98. **C** EVA = NOPAT – $WACC
NOPAT = EBIT × (1 – t) = 28.1 × (1 – 0.45) = 15.455
$WACC = WACC × invested capital = 12.5% × 110.5 = $13.81m
EVA = 15.455 – 13.81 = $1.64m

(Study Session 12, LOS 36.a)

99. **A** Residual income = accounting profit (after tax and interest) minus a charge for equity capital employed.

Net income for 20X6	12.5
Stockholders' equity 94.5	
(–)Cost of equity @ 15%	(14.2)
(=) Residual income	(1.7)

(Study Session 12, LOS 36.a)

100. **C** Market Value Added = market value of (total) capital – book value of capital
= (145 + 16) – (94.5 + 16)
= $50.5m

(Study Session 12, LOS 36.a)

101. **A** WCInv = 32.4 – 27.2 = 5.2
FCInv = (ending FA – beginning FA + depreciation) = 78.1 – 82.0 + 12 = 8.1
Net borrowing = 16-24 = –8
FCFE = NI + depreciation – WCInv – FCInv + net borrowing
= 12.5 + 12 – 5.2 – 8.1 – 8 = 3.2

(Study Session 12, LOS 34.d)

102. **A** Value of equity = book value of equity + NPV of residual income
Value as of 31 December 20X6:

Bo + (

= 94.5 + [5 ÷ (0.15 – 0.05)]
= $144.5m

(Study Session 12, LOS 36.a)

103. **A** The most likely cause of the high relative nominal spread in home equity loan-backed securities is the increased risk of prepayments in a declining interest rate environment. The other ABS securities shown would be less subject to prepayment risk, even if yields declined. (Study Session 15, LOS 46.e)

104. **C** The option cost for the PAC C tranche is the difference between the OAS and the zero volatility spread, or 117 – 65 = 52 bp. The PAC D option cost is 140 – 72 = 68 bp, Support S is 142 – 51 = 91 bp, and PAC B is 95 – 43 = 52 bp. (Study Session 15, LOS 47.d,e)

105. **A** The OAS and *Z*-spread for the PAC A tranche are identical, indicating an option value of zero. The lower OAS of the support tranche, despite its higher effective duration, suggests that this tranche might be overvalued. A high OAS would indicate that the PAC D tranche might be undervalued, not overvalued. (Study Session 15, LOS 47.e)

106. **B** The CFY is dependent on prepayment assumptions; if prepayment rates differ from the assumption, the CFY will not be realized. The reinvestment assumption of the CFY is a weakness. The CFY calculation assumes that interim cash flows are reinvested at the CFY. (Study Session 15, LOS 47.a)

107. **A** Cash flow duration assumes that one prepayment rate will apply over the life of an MBS for whatever change in interest rates is assumed. Empirical duration is reliant on historical prices that might not be easily available, but it does *not* rely on any theoretical valuation models. The values are based on historical pricing relationships. (Study Session 15, LOS 47.h)

108. **C** OAS is interpreted as the average spread over the Treasury *spot rate* curve. The *nominal spread* is measured relative to the Treasury *yield* curve. (Study Session 15, LOS 47.d)

109. **A** The futures price can be calculated by growing the spot price at the difference between the continuously compounded risk-free rate and the dividend yield as a continuously compounded rate. The continuously compounded risk-free rate is ln(1.040811) = 4%, so the futures price for a 240-day future is:

$$FP = S_0 e^{(r-d)t} = 1,050 e^{(0.04-0.02)(240/365)} = 1,064$$

(Study Session 16, LOS 49.b)

110. **C** Contango markets are characterized by futures prices that are higher than the spot price. Because the futures price calculated in the previous question is higher than the spot price, the market can be characterized as a contango market. (Study Session 16, LOS 49.e)

111. **C** Norris is incorrect regarding the convenience yield. Convenience yield refers to *non-monetary* benefits from holding an asset in short supply. A *monetary* benefit from holding the asset will also decrease the no-arbitrage futures price because the net cost of holding the asset is reduced. The comment regarding the difference between the futures and the forward contracts is also incorrect. In a flat (constant) interest rate environment (indicated in the first paragraph of the item set), there is no difference in the prices of futures or forward contracts. The part of the comment relating to credit risk is correct. Because the forward contracts are not marked to market each day, the value is not reset to zero each day and credit risk is higher because large losses are allowed to accumulate. Thus, the credit risk would increase if forwards were used instead of futures. (Study Session 16, LOS 49.c,d)

112. **C** The futures price for a given contract maturity must converge to the spot price as the contract moves toward expiration. Otherwise, arbitrage opportunities would exist. (Study Session 16, LOS 49.a)

113. **B** First, calculate the continuously compounded risk-free rate as ln(1.040811) = 4% and then calculate the theoretically correct futures price as follows:

$$FP = S_0 e^{(r-d)t} = 1,015 e^{(4.0-2.0)(180/365)} = 1,025$$

Then, compare the theoretical price to the observed market price: 1,035 − 1,025 = 10. The futures contract is overpriced. To take advantage of the arbitrage opportunity, the investor should sell the (overpriced) futures contract and buy the underlying asset (the equity index) using borrowed funds. Norris has suggested the opposite. (Study Session 16, LOS 49.f)

114. **B** An increase in the growth rate in dividends for stocks would increase the spot price of the equity index. As the spot price increases, the futures price for a given maturity also increases (holding interest rates constant). Thus, an investor who is long a futures contract already can enter into a short futures contract at the same maturity for a higher futures price than his long contract. Effectively, the investor can buy the asset in the future for a fixed price and sell the asset for a higher fixed price—a guaranteed profit. Thus, as the spot and futures prices rise, the value of a long index futures position rises as well. (Study Session 16, LOS 49.d)

115. **A** MPTA plans to invest Burk's money in a combination of the risk-free asset (Portfolio Z) and the market portfolio (Portfolio X). The risk-return values of all combinations of the risk-free asset and the market portfolio comprise the capital market line, which has the following equation:

$$E(R_p) = R_F + \left(\frac{E(R_m) - R_F}{\sigma_m} \right) \sigma_p$$

Using the portfolio standard deviation to solve for expected return, we have:

$$11\% = 0.05 + \left(\frac{0.15 - 0.05}{0.20} \right) 0.12$$

Therefore, MPTA is able to create Portfolio P, which has an expected return of 11% and a standard deviation of 12%. Burk's original portfolio had an expected return of 10% and a standard deviation of 12%. By allocating Burk's assets along the CML, MPTA is able to increase her expected return by one percentage point, while keeping her portfolio standard deviation unchanged. The expected additional gain equals 1% × $100,000 = $1,000. (Study Session 18, LOS 54.d)

116. **B** The required return for the CCT stock is determined using the CAPM:

required return = $R_F + \beta_{CCT}[E(R_M) - R_F]$

The risk-free rate equals 5% (the return on Portfolio Z). The expected return on the market portfolio equals 15% (the expected return on Portfolio X). The beta for CCT equals 1.50. Therefore, the required return for CCT equals:

required return = 0.05 + 1.50(0.15 − 0.05) = 20%

The consensus forecast return for CCT (15%) is five percentage points below the CCT required return (20%). Therefore, MPTA should determine that the CCT stock is overvalued by five percentage points. (Study Session 18, LOS 54.f)

117. **B** The CML plots the expected returns and standard deviations of all investment combinations of the risk-free asset and the market portfolio. The slope of the CML equals the Sharpe ratio for the market portfolio (MPTA Portfolio X is the market portfolio):

$$\text{Sharpe ratio} = \frac{E(R_m) - R_F}{\sigma_m} = \frac{0.15 - 0.05}{0.20} = 0.50$$

(Study Session 18, LOS 54.d)

118. **B** According to the theory of active portfolio management, one of the justifications for active management is that market equilibrium results from the activity of active managers who are seeking misvalued securities. That is, the actions of active managers result in fairly valued securities.

    MPTA executives believe that capital markets corrected from 2000 to 2001. This would result from large numbers of investors turning their attention to actively managed funds.

    The misvaluations in the periods 1998–1999 and 2002–2003 would be from not enough assets being deployed to active management. (Study Session 18, LOS 55.a)

119. **B** Statement 1: Benesh is correct that the Treynor-Black model will allocate more funds to large alpha securities. But the allocations depend on unsystematic, not systematic, risk. The model will allocate more funds to large alpha, low unsystematic risk securities.

    Statement 2: Benesh is correct that the capital asset pricing model assumes that unlimited short selling of securities and borrowing at the risk-free rate are allowed.

    However, the Treynor-Black model allows for short positions in securities. Negative alpha securities will be given negative weights in the model. (Study Session 18, LOS 54.e and LOS 55.b)

120. **C** We first must calculate the adjusted alphas for Nast (N) and Tackacs (T), given their forecasting accuracy (as measured by the correlation between forecasted and realized alphas). To do so, the unadjusted alpha is multiplied by the squared correlation:

    adjusted alpha$_N$ = $(0.85^2)(0.04)$ = 2.89%

    adjusted alpha$_T$ = $(0.60^2)(0.07)$ = 2.52%

    Notice that although Tackacs has the higher unadjusted alpha, the adjusted alpha is lower once her forecasting accuracy is accounted for. The allocation to her recommended stock will be lower as a result.

    To calculate the allocation to the stock recommended by Nast, we use the ratio of the adjusted alphas to the unsystematic (or residual) risk as follows:

$$\text{adjusted weight}_N = \frac{\dfrac{0.0289}{0.30}}{\left(\dfrac{0.0289}{0.30} + \dfrac{0.0252}{0.40}\right)} = 60\%$$

    The remaining 40% in the active portfolio is allocated to the stock recommended by Tackacs.

    Note that as the alphas are adjusted downward, not only does the allocation within the active portfolio change, but the allocation between the active portfolio and the market portfolio changes as well. The allocation to the active portfolio will decline and the allocation to the market portfolio will increase as a result of adjusting for forecast accuracy. (Study Session 18, LOS 55.c)

Notes

Notes

Notes

Notes

Notes

Notes

Notes

Notes

Notes

Notes

Notes

Notes

Notes

Swaps

oon session Exam 2 (A) (Q114-120)

chapter-4.7